a
Book
of
Wonders

Daily Reflections for Awakened Living

There are few people who consistently give us both depth and breadth—while never closing that clever and humorous edge—as Ed Hays. If a holy man is one who does not take himself too seriously, then Ed is such a man. Fortunately, he always takes God and his readers very seriously!

Richard Rohr, O.F.M.
Center for Action and Contemplation
Albuquerque, New Mexico

Although we have never met, Edward Hays has been my teacher for more than twenty years. From him, I have learned that there is no line between the sacred and the secular on this earth. All life is holy, including the parts that bend and break. With his help, I now pray as easily at the planting of a garden or the burial of a pet as I do at the blessing of a marriage or the baptism of a child. Best of all, his gifts are infectious. Those moved by the beauty of his language and the reach of his imagination will soon find their own capacities enriched.

Barbara Brown Taylor
Author of *Leaving Church: A Memoir of Faith*

The writings of Ed Hays have had a definite impact on my spiritual journey. His creative, refreshing style is always joined with depth and wisdom. Ed Hays's books have helped me find innovative ways to pray holistically and to live in a meaningful, joy-filled manner.

Joyce Rupp
Bestselling author of *Open the Door*

Fr. Ed Hays is in the vanguard of spiritual writers who remind us over and over that God is in our lives, in the midst of our messy world, that Christianity is about incarnation. The task of twenty-first-century saints, Ed Hays reminds us, will be to find God in the ten thousand things of the here and now.

Rich Heffern
National Catholic Reporter
Author of *Daybreak Within: Living in a Sacred World*

a Book of Wonders

Daily Reflections for Awakened Living

EDWARD HAYS

Forest of Peace Notre Dame, Indiana

Founded in 1865, Ave Maria Press is a ministry of the Indiana Province of Holy Cross.

www.forestofpeace.com

ISBN–10 0-939516-83-7   ISBN-13 978-0-939516-83-4

Cover and text design by Andy Wagoner.

Printed and bound in the United States of America.

Library of Congress Cataloging-in-Publication Data

Hays, Edward M.
A book of wonders: daily reflections for awakened living / Edward Hays.
    p. cm.
ISBN-13: 978-0-939516-83-4
ISBN-10: 0-939516-83-7
1. Devotional calendars--Catholic Church. I. Title.
BX2170.C56H39 2009
242'.2--dc22

                                    2008047831

◇◇◇◇◇◇◇◇◇◇◇◇◇◇◇◇◇◇◇◇◇◇◇◇ Contents

Month of

January

Introduction

Why should you read this book of daily reflections? It lacks an attention-grabbing plot, the enticing mystery of a detective novel, or the "page-turner" fascination of some thriller. Since the hustle and bustle of the work-a-day life is so dispiriting, its purpose is to inspire and nourish your spirit. Your spirit, your inner person, needs to eat just as your body does. Starvation of the soul leads to superficial living that quickly evolves into a barren drought of humanness.

The neon-glittering world prompts us daily in a million ways to feed on a diet of striving for success and acquiring more money. While both of these goals are valuable, we are body-spirit beings who also have other hungers. As humans, we hunger for wonder, to be surprised by the wonderful in our daily lives. To find the breathtaking you need not trek to India or Tibet. Like a fish in the water you already live amidst the wonderful.

A Book of Wonders is intended to tantalize your imagination to discover the wonderful in the commonplace, and by so doing to achieve that greatness of spirit for which you were created. Since another name for God is "The Astounding One," our genetic prehistoric quest for wonder is but the ageless search for the Source of all life, thought, creativity, wonderment, and mystery.

Edward Hays

January 1

Wonder Constantly Overflowing

"Wonderful things are especially wonderful the first time they happen, but their wonderfulness wanes with repetition." So says Daniel Gilbert in his book *Stumbling on Happiness*. His words should alert us to the fact that true and lasting wonder needs to be renewed regularly, even daily. Otherwise, life's inevitable formula will be: Wonderful is followed by wonder-half-full, which is followed by wonder-quarter-full, which quickly becomes wonder-less. If you want to make your capacity for awe as wide as the sky, you must take preventive action. Otherwise, you'll end up as a wonderless wanderer and life will cease to be a joyful adventure.

> *Pretend _____ isn't here any more.*
> *Imagine life void of what once was wonderful,*
> *and momentarily go blind, deaf, and suffer loss*
> *so as to generously refill your life with wonder.*

January 2

It's Never Too Late

A new year should breed dreams. Psychologist Sheelagh Manheim writes about her father who in 1938 at the age of seventy-four fell deathly ill with bronchitis. Burdened with financial problems from the Great Depression, he nevertheless went out and planted a row of redwood trees. He told his grandson that he would live to see them grow tall. Ten years later he had recovered his financial losses. He died in peace having seen his redwood trees grown tall. Regardless of your age, health, or financial status, as you read this reflection know you are not too old or sick to plant a future. Not to plant or plan is to bring the curtain down on the play of your life, since without dreams and visions, tomorrow you are either already dead or dying. Being dream-dead is like being brain-dead, it is a near-life state where the body continues its routine functions, but isn't truly alive. We humans are disposed to have visions for tomorrow as part of the natural unfolding of our latent embryonic possibilities. At every age, creation's spirit says, "You're not finished yet. Don't stop growing." Today, if you lack the space to plant a tree, then plant a dream. Plan for something that you like to do; most importantly, be.

Help me disregard my limitations,
shake off the inertia of aging,
and plant seeds of new tomorrows,
fertilizing them with enthusiasm.

January 3

Prophylactic Service

In Sicily there's a folk saying connected with the bosses of the Mafia, "To rule over others is better than making love." That folk saying about mob bosses is equally true for all those in positions of authority, either at home or at work. Be forewarned that within each of us is a sleeping tyrant who secretly longs to control the lives and behavior of others. A controller, whether a parent, spouse, or mob boss, finds security and pleasure in exercising authority over the situations of other people's lives. This need for control over others is based on the faulty belief that it protects one from being vulnerable. The Teacher of Galilee taught that humble service is the best antidote for the need to control. His prophylactic protection for the lethal disease of controlling the lives of others was, "Be a humble servant to all."

May I look up to others
as being superior to me,
attending to their needs
before turning to mine.

January 4

Contradictory Arithmetic

In Susan Montag's translation of the *Tao Te Ching*, the holy book of China, the opening lines of Chapter 39 read, "Since the beginning of time, things have added up the same way. All things = one thing." This is the math of holy madness. It declares that you are the homeless person that you see on the street, or you are the refugee in Africa dying of starvation that you see on television.

The illusion of diversity is the enemy of unity since it creates divisions, divides me from you, them from us, and humanity from creation. Ancient mystics and contemporary physicists affirm that "all things = one thing." This divine mathematics, while difficult to understand, is essential for the world. Unless we live this cosmic arithmetic we will never stop waging wars upon ourselves under the illusion we are doing so to an enemy. And the great problems of social justice, poverty, and starvation will never be resolved until we realize they are our personal problems. Today calculate your deeds, relationships with others, and responses to those in need by counting God's way: All things and persons add up to . . . One.

> *Heal me of my addiction to divide*
> *what is One into the many.*
> *Open my eyes to the Divine One*
> *what is hidden in the mirage of the multiple.*

January 5

Celebrity Spotting

The Beloved wears disguises like movie stars wear sunglasses, so as not to be recognized. The Beloved loves wearing disguises since it keeps believers guessing. One day I recognized the real identity of the wild-haired old woman dressed in a shabby, old brown coat who was pushing her rusted, rickety grocery cart crowded with her meager possessions. Overjoyed after all these years to finally come face to face with what I had sought my entire life, I suddenly become bewildered! What should I ask the Holy One?

Motivate me to ask repeatedly
in prayer life's great questions,
since by such probing questioning
I shall be led to enlightenment.

January 6

The Blessings of Excommunication

We live in a society addicted to cell phones. If someone from just a hundred years ago could observe us today, he would think that we talk perpetually.

The Cheyenne Indians believe that the Great Spirit gives each person a certain amount of words at birth. When the supply is exhausted, the person dies. Perhaps we could learn something from the Cheyenne—excessive unnecessary talking leads to an early death. Don't smile; endless talking *is* deadly! No coroner will issue a death certificate to the person with a Bluetooth device glued to his ear, but that doesn't mean he is alive! Silence is to the soul what oxygen is to the body. To be fully alive we must stop talking. The cure for addictive communicating is that most dreaded of all ecclesiastical penalties—excommunication! Be your own pope; excommunicate yourself. Turn off your phone. Escape into silence from the bedlam of noisy turmoil. London's old insane asylum was called Bedlam, so ponder today whether endlessly talking on the telephone is a form of insanity.

> *By often excommunicating myself,*
> *may I find the peace of holy communion,*
> *and so savor the taste of your quiet serenity*
> *that insures the authenticity of all my words.*

January 7

Face Value

Ralph Waldo Emerson said your face reveals what your spirit is doing. Emerson's statement is frightening since your face can and does reveal your every mood, resentment, and hidden emotion. Politicians of all stripes, as well as others eager to sway our opinion, erroneously believe they can mask the hidden activities of their spirits. A political or polite smile, however, only fools the foolish. Every genuine smile first appears on your spirit, just as an ugly and angry face springs from within you. Your face announces wordlessly and in countless ways your affection and kindness as well as your anger and envy. Thinking negative thoughts is a kind of cosmetic surgery that creates unattractive, uninviting faces. After the age of forty, we create our own faces. If you desire to have a beautiful face, regardless of your age, begin your daily facial makeup deep inside.

> *Uninvited, good and bad thoughts come.*
> *Make me vigilant of my every thought.*
> *So help me to quickly banish the dark ones*
> *as I increase the lovely ones by loving.*

January 8

A Prescription for Remaining Youthful

Dr. Mickey Mouse's personal prescription for you: "To prevent growing old, whether you're 38 or 83, include play and healthy doses of variety as an important part of your daily schedule along with your other medications." You can trust Dr. Mickey Mouse's prescription for youthfulness since as a senior citizen he knows what he's talking about. Mickey, who was born in 1928, is as youthful as ever. Mice are often used in scientific research because they have much of the same DNA as humans. Studies of aging mice show those living in enriched environments with playmates and fun things to do like running on wheels grow three times as many new brain cells as mice living in dull, boring cages. Scientists believe these studies reveal that the brains of elderly humans may also richly benefit from a variety of enjoyable activities. At every age, play is good medicine. After all, we begin aging the first second after our birth. So to avoid growing old, remember to take Dr. Mickey Mouse's prescription every day. It will retard growing old, even as you age.

While aging is the natural process of life,
growing old, grouchy and cheerless isn't.
Induce me to keep my spirits briskly alive
by fun and playing my way though in life.

January 9

Know What You Are Saying

In Lewis Carroll's *Through the Looking Glass*, Humpty Dumpty says to Alice, "When I use a word, it means just what I choose it to mean. Nothing more nor less." Rabbi Adin Steinsaltz, the renowned Talmudic scholar, believes that we are prone to do the same thing. Steinsaltz gives this example, "When you hear people, children or adults, cursing . . . they create all sorts of impossibilities, anatomical and biological impossibilities. They don't know what they are saying and they don't care, they just know that it's a curse." Is what is true for a curse equally true for a blessing? Do we know the meaning of what we say?

Perhaps the most frequent of all blessings is "Goodbye," a contracted form of "God be with you." But if it means nothing more than "See you later," then I've sadly stripped it naked of its priestly sacred power. Synagogues and church worship services all conclude with a solemn if not formal blessing by the rabbi, minister, or priest. Is not every farewell just as sacred a blessing?

> *Remind me to always stuff*
> *my greetings and farewells*
> *with juicy succulent meaning,*
> *like a Thanksgiving turkey.*

January 10

One Giant Leap for Humanity

"If you knew God," says the Prophet Mohammed, "as God ought to be known, you would walk on the seas and the mountains would move at your call." The Prophet of Islam challenges Christians and Jews as well by his words about the power of profound faith of an inner-knowledge of God. While walking on the waves requires great faith, a deeper faith exists that can perform even more amazing miracles than transplanting mountains. "I say to you," the Prophet and Teacher of Galilee said: "offer no resistance to one who is evil. When someone strikes you on your right cheek, turn the other one to him as well. . . . Love your enemies and pray for those who persecute you." Moving Pike's Peak from Colorado to Illinois would be amazing, but more astonishing would be a faith in God's desire that we never return evil for evil or injury for injury. To never respond with hostility to being hurt or offended would be a world-transforming act, an evolutionary step for humanity.

> *Whenever tempted in traffic, at work or at home*
> *to be vengeful by silence or throwing stones,*
> *increase to mountain-size my faith in God's will*
> *that I may become an instrument of peace, not war.*

January 11

Conversion of Regrets

As a child, the first poem I ever learned by heart was framed on the bathroom wall of my two unmarried aunts' home. It read, surprisingly:

> Through fear of taking risks in life,
> I have missed a lot of fun,
> the only things that I regret
> are those I haven't done.

A life without regrets seems impossible, and only the most calloused of hearts never suffers from regrets. Do not each of our life histories include occasions of selfish exploitation or neglected opportunities to assist others, to courageously stand up for our beliefs? Undoing our past mistakes isn't possible, but healing them through prayer is. Prayer is addressed to the Timeless One who dwells outside space and time. In prayer it is possible to travel backward to touch those you may have injured or wronged. Prayerfully ask God to gift those you may have wronged with the creative ability to transform whatever negative happened into something good. That living gift of God is symbolized in the cross of Jesus where something hideously evil was transformed into something good.

> *Whenever I recall any regret, remind me*
> *to fly backward in time to that incident*
> *and pray that the person I have offended*
> *can work good out of any wrong I've done.*

January 12

Wonderland

Ice crystals lacing tree branches and a soft snow create the magic of a winter wonderland. Any landscape that fills us with awe is usually considered to be some imaginary land of wondrous beauty, Yet isn't every landscape a wonderland? Regardless of the weather or the view, if a glance out your window doesn't fill you with amazement, it isn't because of any lack of wonders, but poor eyesight. You may have 20/20 vision, but you are mystically blind if you can't see that you live daily in a wonderland, amidst an abundance of marvels.

Humans have a prehistoric hunger for wonder, for the astonishing. It was this hunger that drew people to travel to far-off exotic lands, or simply across town to attend the circus. For over a century world's fairs attracted massive throngs of people seeking to see wondrous new inventions. Today, if you are hungry for wonder and you have good eyes, there is no need to travel any further than your window.

> *Cleanse my eyes, blinded by age,*
> *to see the marvels all around me,*
> *so with clean new eyes I can see*
> *my daily world is a wonderland.*

January 13

To Whom It May Concern

Perhaps you have already noticed that the prayers concluding each reflection have no salutations. In the major Western religions, ritual prayer etiquette requires that you begin a prayer by addressing God with some salutation, sometimes as if you were speaking to some grand monarch. Yet in conversation with someone seated across from you at the table you don't begin by saying, "My beloved and faithful wife Jane . . ." or "My dear and loyal friend Joseph . . ." If you believe the Divine Mystery dwells within you and is vigorously present in every situation of your life, why not simply express what is in your heart without using a salutation to greet God? In times of surprise or in times of mishap we tend to speak aloud to no one in particular. The enormous reward of praying this "To Whom It May Concern" prayer is that all of our impulsive expressions of wonder or concern become prayer. For example, "What a beautiful day!" becomes a prayer of praise and gratitude. Whether you speak such thoughts aloud or only think them, they can be prayers heard by Our Father "who art in heaven" and who is also in your heart.

May I pray to you without praying,
You who are as close to me as my skin,
and express my gratitude and needs,
confident you hear my non-prayers.

January 14

Faith-filled Atheistic Christians

Faith-filled yet atheistic Christians are those who deny the existence of God in the jobless poor, the undocumented alien, the socially downtrodden, or those with a different sexual orientation. Belief in the creed is not sufficient to be truly a believing Christian, at least so taught the Teacher who placed belief-in-action above belief-in-truths. In his Last Judgment parable, the Teacher rewarded with paradise those who unknowingly had cared for him in caring for the needs of the poor. To believe "What you do to the least of my brethren, you do unto me," requires a far greater faith than believing Mary was a virgin or Jesus rose from the dead. To treat those in the gutter of life or those guilty of sexual crimes with the same dignity you would show to Christ requires more faith than belief in any dogma. The challenge for Christianity today is to become a religion of radical believers who have faith in the invisible, if not impossible, presence of Christ among them.

Make me a believer, not an atheist.
Help my unbelief, so I may know
that you are present in all in need,
in the unemployed and imprisoned.

January 15

Go Buy a Saddle

As an old Arab proverb says, "If one person calls you an ass, pay no attention. But if five people call you an ass, go out and buy yourself a saddle." Unfortunately, four out of five people will not call you an ass to your face. So you neither buy a saddle nor tackle your imperfections! In our youth our faults appear only as faint signs, but with age they are inscribed as permanently as tattoos. Typically we turn a blind eye to our imperfections, having grown comfortable with them over time. But instead of going saddle shopping, be steadfast. Face, then change, what others leave unspoken but find undesirable. Negative character traits grow strong over the years. They are like wild asses that have a mind of their own. Rather than being saddled with your failings for the rest of your life, saddle them up! But before you can do that, you must break them and tame them. To tame these quirks is to humanize them. It requires time, patience, and a determination to be the rider and not the ridden. So if you have asinine traits, turn them into charming and gentle ones.

> *Girt up my spirit to harness*
> *my annoyances and outbursts,*
> *and saddle my fiery irritations*
> *with your gentle yoke of peace.*

January 16

Your Day in Court

Before becoming the mayor New York, Fiorello LaGuardia, nicknamed the "Little Flower," was a judge at the police court. One bitter cold day in 1933 a trembling old man in a tattered coat was brought before his bench, charged with stealing a loaf of bread. He said he had stolen the bread because his family was starving. La Guardia declared: "I've got to punish you. The law makes no exception, so I'm sentencing you to a fine of ten dollars." Then LaGuardia reached into his pocket: "Here's the ten dollars to pay your fine. Now I remit the fine," and he tossed the ten dollar bill into his famous large hat. Looking out at the crowded courtroom he declared, "Furthermore, I'm going to fine everyone in this courtroom fifty cents for living in a town where a man has to steal bread to feed his family!

Mr. Bailiff, collect the fines and then give them to the defendant!" LaGuardia's hat was passed from person to person in the crowded courtroom. Finally it was handed to the incredulous old man whose eyes glistened with emotion. The hat held $47.50.

> *Use the sharp point of a question mark*
> *to probe for my moral responsibility*
> *for those who are hungry and homeless,*
> *so to do my share to relieve their need.*

January 17

Beauty or Evil in the Eye of the Beholder

"Teacher," a student complained, "one of my brother students, whose name I won't mention, is a bad example to all of us. He loves to gossip about other students and points out their failings. And he even criticizes you! He is frequently absent from communal prayer and sleeps during meditation. I also hear that at night he sneaks out to visit the 'bad' girls in the village. Teacher, am I bound to challenge him face to face about these sins and failings? Tell me, what should I do?" "Rather," said the teacher, "go to the village and get yourself a pair of glasses." Both Jesus and Buddha spoke to the most common affliction of disciples: self-blindness. Jesus said, "First of all remove the large plank in your own eye before attempting to take out the splinter in the eye of another." Buddha said, "How easy it is to see your brother's faults, how hard to face your own." May each fault that I find offensive in another be an optical occasion for me to give myself a thorough personal eye examination.

> *Elbow my spirit when I'm disturbed*
> *by the failings and faults of others,*
> *to remind me to be more distressed*
> *about my own rather than others' failings.*

January 18

Read the Ancient Way—Like a Beginner

Small children learn how to read by reading aloud. In previous ages everyone who could read did so aloud. Today we sight read and those adults who read aloud are viewed as uneducated or mentally impaired. In our time-bankrupted society speed-readers are highly admired for their skill of skimming the text for essential information. More than a practical necessity, reading is also an essential part of a good spiritual diet. And, like food, what is read must be absorbed if it is to be nurturing. The ancient practice was to absorb what you read by using as many senses as possible. Reading aloud involves sight, hearing, and movement of the lips. If Christians, as well as Muslims, Jews, and Buddhists, wish to find the treasures hidden in their sacred texts, they should read them slowly and aloud, as if they were children once again. Read not for information but for formation, for conversion of heart. What you read aloud, hear as being spoken to you exclusively by the Divine Author of all holy books. Attune the ears of your spirit to hear God's repetitive message underlying each of the world's great scriptures, "Change. Grow up. Evolve into godhood."

> *Open my ears so to hear you*
> *speaking to me in scriptures,*
> *in everything I read,*
> *so I can grow and be like you.*

January 19

How to Avoid the Christmas Curse

Like most people, your Christmas decorations have probably all been taken down and boxed away by now. But you may want to unpack them! The custom of decorating churches and homes with holly at Christmas time is an ancient one, piously borrowed from the old Roman feast of Saturnalia. Long ago,

Christmas lasted from December 25 until January 6, the feast of Epiphany. In other places it lasted until February 2, the feast of the Purification of Mary. An old folk belief said that homes which took down their evergreens, holly, and other Christmas decorations before February 2 would be visited by misfortune and grief. As an alternative to redecorating your home to avoid that Yule-time curse, decorate your heart with the joyful spirit of Christmas by being generous and cheerful every day of this new year.

> *Help me check that I haven't boxed up*
> *my spirit of Christmas generosity*
> *with the tree lights and decorations*
> *so I can play Santa Claus every day.*

January 20

Holy Craziness

"Given a choice between a folly and a sacrament," said Erasmus, "one should always choose the folly—because we know a sacrament will not bring us closer to God, and there's always a chance that a folly will." While churches theologize if the number of the sacraments is three or seven, folly is unlimited. The fifteenth-century Dutch scholar and zealous reformer of the church, Erasmus challenges our beliefs when he says that folly, meaning craziness or foolishness, brings us closer to God than sacraments. The folly he proposes isn't the psychotic kind, but the daring foolishness to engage in those illogical, unnatural behaviors the Teacher instructed us to perform. Consider a few of the Teacher's follies that we're invited to imitate: When offended, forgive incessantly; if injured, retaliate only with kindness; when insulted, reply with a blessing; make love with your enemies, not war. To beggars—lazy or not—be generous, and be anxiety-free about tomorrow.

> *Guide me, I pray, to engage in folly,*
> *even if it be judged silly by the world,*
> *to never return violence for violence*
> *and to pardon seventy times seven.*

January 21

Personal Death Experiences

The belief in life after death seems perpetually vulnerable to agnostic doubts since no one you know personally has ever returned from the grave. Yet everyone has experienced life after death at least once. Think back to a time when you were mortified by something you did or said. Recalling that most distasteful experience demonstrates that there is indeed life after death! The word "mortify" comes from the Latin *mortificare,* "to cause to die." When you are mortified you are so ashamed you wish were dead—and so it is indeed a type of death. In everyone's personal history there are childhood memories of being mortified and ashamed that have left invisible but real wounds. With time, scabs form on those wounds. But with each adult humiliation they are ripped off again. But despite the pain, didn't you rise from that painful tomb of torment after each embarrassment and go on with life? Find hope then, if not belief, in life after death within those painful memories and subsequent resurrections.

> *I ask for the grace to see my own Easter*
> *in my humiliations and times of shame*
> *since from each I've arisen again to life,*
> *and so believe I'll arise after my final death.*

January 22

Your Worst Enemy

The nemesis of the famous Sherlock Holmes was the diabolically clever and evil Dr. Moriarty who never physically appeared in those Sherlock Holmes mysteries. His presence, however, was made known by the diabolical cleverness of the crime that would cause Holmes to say to his companion Dr. Watson: "This evil deed is surely the work of villainous Professor Moriarty!" Who is your worst enemy? Perhaps, like Holmes, you recognize your worst enemy by the cleverness of the evil you experience. Or perhaps too, as was the case with Professor Moriarty, your worst enemy is hidden in plain sight. Your worst enemy may well be yourself, your ego: that inflated self-image who hates to be wrong or contradicted, who explodes in anger when it feels it has been slighted, who always creates bogus excuses or reasons for your mistakes. This is your false self. Your false self isn't you, but a personality you constructed when young to protect you from a threatening world. Many of the world's religions teach that the way to master this enemy is self-denial. But the Teacher of Nazareth says: "Love your enemy!" So first, thank your false self for protecting you when you were defenseless as a small child. Then dismiss it with steely conviction and resolve that it is no longer needed.

> *Embolden me to say to my false self,*
> *"Childhood bodyguard—you're fired!"*
> *For it will repeatedly rob me of peace*
> *until by my loving rudeness it departs.*

January 23

Your Second Worst Enemy—Your Thoughts

Don't blame outside forces when impatience, frustration, or disappointment steal your happiness. The real culprit is you, or more correctly, your thoughts. Buddha taught, "With our thoughts we make our world. Think evil thoughts and as surely as the cart follows the ox, evil will follow you. Think good thoughts, and goodness will surely be yours." Shocking, but profoundly true! By your seemingly unimportant thoughts you personally create the world around you. By your thoughts you shape your life as pleasant or gloomy, peaceful or painful. Take for example the experience of being in a traffic jam. The real source of your irritation isn't what is actually happening, but rather your negative thoughts about being delayed or out of control. Whenever you discover that your peace or happiness has been stolen, take time to track down the real thief and you'll find it was your thoughts. If you wish to live a non-violent, peaceful life, constantly readjust your thoughts when confronted with the unpleasant realities of life or the negative behaviors of others.

Teach me that when I am thoughtless,
unaware of my thoughts, I suffer.
And when I monitor my thoughts,
I can control them and enjoy life.

January 24

What Is the Capital of Hell?

Trivia questions test your ability to remember obscure and unnecessary pieces of information. However, knowing the name the capital of Lucifer's kingdom isn't a trivial pursuit. The capital of hell is Pandemonium. Second trivia question: "Can you locate where in hell the capital city of Pandemonium is?" Even trivia fans would stumble on this question because not even Rand McNally or Google provide maps of hell. Here's a clue: For his epic *Paradise Lost,* the English poet John Milton created the name Pandemonium from the Greek for "all demons." Pandemonium is our word for any demon-infested place with chaos, uproar, turmoil, and wild lawlessness. Wherever you are dwelling in chaos and turmoil, be it your home or workplace, know that you're living in Pandemonium, the capital of hell. While living in many of the world's capitals is considered glamorous, living in Pandemonium is hell.

Where is it that you live or work?
If it is in hellish Pandemonium,
ponder moving or changing jobs.
Or redecorating your hell into heaven.

January 25

Mirror, Mirror on the Wall

If you wish to perform the miraculous works that Christ promised his disciples would do, how should you begin? One way to start might be to take an object that is found in every home, car, or purse: a mirror. The root word of both miracle and mirror is the Latin *mirari,* "to wonder at." In the days long ago, to see an image of oneself in a piece of polished metal did indeed cause wonder. Mirrors were wonder-full things for ancient peoples who could see their reflections only in pools of still water. Who among us today is ever caught up in wonder when looking into the mirror while shaving or combing one's hair? Mirrors are usually only practical necessities for those who wish to be well groomed and neat. However, your mirror can also become a rich instrument of inspiration for learning how to perform miraculous deeds. Recall the famous scene with the evil queen in the fairytale *Snow White.* She would stand in front of her mirror and ask, "Mirror, mirror on the wall, who's the fairest of them all?" A prayer exercise that I would like to suggest is a playful parallel to those words. Daily, after you have finished with the practical use of your mirror, stand for a moment in silence. Then look directly into your mirror and with great devotion pronounce this short prayer, "Mirror, mirror on the wall, may I look with love on all."

> *Remind me daily to see in a new way*
> *by always looking with loving kindness*
> *upon everyone that I see and encounter,*
> *so then to change my behavior by how I see.*

January 26

The Gift of a Mystic Mirror

"Mirror, mirror on the wall, may I look with love on all," concluded yesterday's reflection. That was written many years ago. Today I have the rare opportunity to amend what I've previously written. The person you see daily in your mirror is you, the most important person in the world. Yet that mirror image of an independent individual is an illusion! Over the entrance of the United Nations building in New York is carved a quotation from the Persian Muslim poet-mystic Saadi Shirazi:

Human beings are all members of one body.
They are created by the same essence.
When one is in pain, the others cannot rest.
If you do not care about the pain of others,
You do not deserve to be called a human being.

So when you look in the mirror, look beyond the illusion and see the other who is in pain. It is a spiritual evolution to rise above concern for your own needs and truly care for others who are in great pain or suffering.

Give me the insight to see my face
in the faces of all the human family,
to care for others as I care for myself,
so I can call myself a human being.

January 27

The Engine of Imagination

The Greek author Nikos Kazantzakis wrote: "You have your brush and your colors, paint paradise and in you go." So paint a self-portrait of yourself living joyously and—in you go. Kanzantzakis's words invite you to use your imagination as a powerful tool to create a better world for yourself and by so doing to unfold one for others. The insight of Kanzantzakis is echoed by the last master of Chabad Jewish mysticism, Rabbi Schneerson, who said: "Think good and it will be good." The truth contained in his words goes beyond the psychological influence of positive thinking to the power of imagining. It is the creative force that gives birth to something real which in time will manifest itself in the world. Place your hope for personal and global change in the dynamic power of imagination as a creative agent of true transformation.

More than a dreamer, make me an imaginer,
a cocreator working with the Divine Imager,
in creating a world of beauty, love, and peace
for myself and, by so doing, for all the world.

January 28

The Need for a Good Agenda

Busy people carefully make out their daily agenda so that all the necessary tasks get done without wasting time. Yet at the top of a truly good agenda should be appointments to waste time! The Polish poet Tadeusz Rosewicz said, "It is more difficult to spend a day well than to write a book!" As an author who knows the effort required in attempting to write a good book, I have copied his insight and keep it before me on my desk. To live well this and every day demands discipline and dedication. It's so easy to waste hours, even days and weeks. This happens not because we're lazy or disorganized, rather it's the very opposite—we're overly scheduled! How much time is wasted daily on things that seem so significant but are in reality only inconsequential? A good daily agenda is the antidote to squandering time, but planned time-outs, unscheduled times in your busy day, are essential for encountering the Unfathomable Mystery that is hidden inside every event and person of your day.

> *Confirm in my daily agenda appointments*
> *to do nothing but absorb the moment,*
> *and reminders not to rush or be in a hurry*
> *so I can meet with life's Divine Invisible.*

January 29

Life: A Mellow Drama or Melodrama?

Most of us live unexciting, humdrum lives devoid of drama. We feed our hunger for wonder with the artificial dramas of the movies or television. Since these synthetic dramas lack the enthralling power of reality, they fail to be wondrous. In our boredom we are tempted to turn our daily lives into melodramas. And so we inflate minor difficulties into major disasters—melodramas that we relish telling in detail, again and again. But there is another way to view the ongoing theater of life that isn't melodramatic. Even though you are impotent to control the sudden twists and reversals of plot in life's drama, you still exercise power over your own actions and lines. As the star of this living theater, you can play the hero or the victim. Remember, too, that every play has a stage manager who directs the actors. So if you have previously acted unheroically, listen to the Great Stage Manager of every life's drama. Listen to that soft quiet voice instructing you on how to improve your lines and actions so that your life story is a mellow drama, not a melodrama.

> *Open me up to criticism and praise,*
> *those twin voices of information*
> *required for any seeking of excellence*
> *or heroic holiness in the drama of life.*

January 30

The Endless Wars of Jenkins's Ear

In 1739, the War of Jenkins's Ear began when England declared hostilities against Spain. Jenkins was the British sea captain who claimed that the Spanish coast guard had cut off his ear in a raid on his ship. They suspected smuggling. He displayed the ear before the House of Commons, and the news of it so inflamed public opinion that the prime minister was forced to declare war. This war that lasted from 1739 to 1742 was over the loss of one sailor's ear! Don't scoff or laugh, however, for the War of Jenkins's Ear can erupt in your life today. In countless homes and offices minor wars will break out today over issues as silly as Jenkins's ear. The next time you are so inflamed as to declare a personal or domestic war over some minor injustice or personal insult, tug at your right ear and pray, "War, war, go away and don't come back another day." The cure for the main cause of war is humor and the humility to frame the offense within the big picture.

> *Only the proud go off to war,*
> *and only the foolish join them.*
> *When next the war bugle calls*
> *let me remember Jenkins's Ear.*

January 31

When Was Your Last Angelic Visitation?

If asked if we've ever been visited by an angel, 99% of us would answer never. Yet angels play an important role in the beliefs of the three great Western religions. Jesus speaks frequently about angels, Jewish piety believed every blade of grass had its own angel, and the Koran was dictated to Mohammed by an angel. Christian piety holds that everyone has a personal guardian angel. However, in our all too rationalistic world angels tend to be lumped together with leprechauns. Angel is from the Greek *angelos,* "messenger." These supernatural beings are considered God's messengers and usually are depicted artistically as human figures with wings. If you believe in a personal, loving God who is compassionately concerned with your well-being, reconsider the reality of angels. But don't expect a visit from a white-robed figure with wings. The Divine Beloved desires only what is good and beneficial for you. These desires are usually communicated not by winged beings, but by your inclinations to perform some kindness or charitable deed, and as well by apprehensive feelings of impending danger.

> *With gratitude and reverence,*
> *help me treat with angelic awe*
> *my inspirations and gut feelings*
> *as messages from you, my God.*

Month of

February

February 1

Wonder

Wonder. Besides meaning a person or thing that causes astonishment, *wonder* can also mean curiosity, as in, "I wonder what happened to January?" The answer seems obvious: the month of January has thirty-one days and when they have come and gone so has the month. Yet, to wonder what happened to January is really to ponder a great mystery—time. Does the past exit? By the same token, does the future? Time, like the Divine Mystery, is wonderment. All wondering is as holy as prayer since the All Amazing One is unbelievable yet believable, and plausible as a wonder. To be inquisitive, to question or wonder about God is not only normal, it is the royal path to enlightenment. Fear not to cross the frontier of faith and probe the darkness. Fear not the nagging or occasional doubts about God; they are divine gifts to open you to wonder.

> *Invest in me in the explorer's daring courage*
> *to wander beyond the fences of my faith*
> *with a question mark as my walking staff,*
> *and so, by wandering wonder, to love you more.*

February 2

Learn a Lesson from the Wicked

When I was a student in the seminary at Conception Monastery, an old monk and mentor was fond of saying to me, "Edward, whatever you do, do with full malice!" I found his advice puzzling at first, even sounding contrary to good spiritual counsel. Now, over fifty years later, I can unquestionably affirm the validity of his advice, as nothing is ever achieved by timidity! A frequent response when something new or different is proposed is the half-hearted, "Well, let's give it a chance." While giving a new idea a chance sounds positive, it's really the kiss of death! If any new project is to succeed, it must be begun boldly with the passion of the malice invested in evil schemes. Such wicked fervor is unstoppable as the seventeenth-century French playwright Moliere said, "There is no rampart that will hold out against malice." The master criminal's dogged determination and lavish expenditure of time plotting a crime far outstrip the efforts of the would-be saint in his pursuit of holiness! So, "Whatever you do, do it with full malice."

> *In prayer and love may I always remember*
> *what the Risen One said to the half-hearted,*
> *"I vomit you, the lukewarm, out of my mouth!"*
> *May I never love or work in tepid moderation.*

February 3

Once You've Begun, Doubt Not!
Don't Look Backward

"Once you put your hand to the plow don't look back," said the Teacher. He cleverly applies this farmer's sage advice on how to plow a straight row to anyone seriously thinking of following him in his radically new way of life. Becoming a disciple or beginning any new venture requires a departure from the known and so creates anxieties about the wisdom of such a decision. Embracing anything new always involves risk—the more novel or different is the choice, the greater the danger of making a mistake. After such a choice has been made the anxious mind whispers, "It's never too late to stop and go back," and begins to question, "Did I make the right decision?" Questioning decisions already made only jeopardizes your involvement in the new activity that requires your full, wholehearted attention. Instead of fretting over whether you made the right decision, passionately invest yourself in living out the choice you have made!

> *All too easily I can be frozen immobile*
> *by fear of making mistakes in choices.*
> *Breathe on me; defrost my icy anxieties*
> *so I can courageously be an adventurer.*

February 4

Falling in Love with Your Dragon

"I am a Chinese dragon," said the old dragon. "There's a difference, you know! In China and the East dragons are a good sign, one of blessing and good fortune. Historically, however, we do have a bad name. Heroes like Hercules, Siegfried, Beowulf, King Arthur, and even your patron, Saint George, were all dragon slayers. It's because we have bodies similar to serpents that we are considered evil. Dr. Freud would have a heyday with that fear. Indeed, all who set out on a quest go looking for a dragon or some ugly, fierce monster to kill. But the real enemies are not outside forces in some dark forest; rather, they are inside."

> *Stir me, not to slay my inner dragons*
> *but to seduce them by embracing*
> *and converting these dark urges*
> *into potent angel allies in my life.*

February 5

Mona Lisa's Smile

A sophisticated computer program designed to recognize emotions examined a scan of the five-hundred-year-old slight smile of Mona Lisa. It revealed that she was only 83 percent happy. The program also detected she was 9 percent disgusted, 6 percent fearful, and 2 percent angry. In painting Mona Lisa, the ingeniously skillful Leonardo da Vinci was able to capture the typical smile we still see daily on the faces of a majority of people. How many of the smiling people that you see are really 100 percent happy? Doesn't each of us carry at least a minimum of 9 percent of hidden disgust over something? And a 6 percent to 10 percent hidden fear seems rather low for today's crowded collection of fears—cancer, losing your job, or being a victim of a terrorist attack to mention a few. I feel confident as well that the hidden anger underneath today's smiles far surpasses the 2 percent found in smiles five hundred years ago when Leonardo painted his Mona Lisa.

> *Assist me daily in cleansing my smile*
> *of subterranean anger, disgust, or fear,*
> *and help me commit myself to keeping it pure*
> *by honest scrutiny of my every thought.*

February 6

Don Quixote de La Mancha Happiness

The gaunt, gray-bearded, gentleman knight of La Mancha is the patron saint of romantic idealists, who in the face of grim reality optimistically find life filled with promise and happiness. We easily dismiss the Don and Doña Quixotes of life as being naïve, simpleminded, or out of touch with reality. Yet recent studies have shown that those with a healthy dose of "Quixotism" have accomplished some rather remarkable things in their lives, and tend to be successful and—most of all—happy people. Whenever you're struggling with some problem, you're likely to hear that small voice telling you: "Be realistic, grit your teeth, and do what is practical." Instead, consider being imaginative and explore the undiscovered possibilities of your problem, which is to see with double vision. Look first at what appears as reality and then look for what isn't immediately visible, what is creatively hidden in the situation. Often a compromise between an optimistic and a practical solution can be the most beneficial. I keep on my desk a bit of wisdom from a Chinese fortune cookie: "In every disappointment lies hidden something of equal or greater value."

Protect me from being too realistic,
the cause of dire poverty of hope
that breeds cynicism and despair.
And keep me childlike and optimistic.

February 7

The Last and Key Piece of the Puzzle

The experiences of life zoom by faster than cars in a NASCAR race and so prevent us from seeing how each new experience is connected with previous ones. Attempting to connect the multitude of life experiences is akin to doing a jigsaw puzzle without a picture of the finished connecting pieces. A new job, moving to another city, making a new friend, or falling in love can be experiences that make life appear haphazard. However, when looking backward after the passage of years, these seemingly disconnected pieces begin to form themselves into a pattern. We might call this reflective process "jigsawing": fitting the wise choices with the wrong choices, and seeing to your surprise how each was a critical piece in the story of your life. To complete the beautiful picture of the puzzle of your life, you need the last piece, the one that always seems to be missing. Its absence is frustrating until you realize what that missing piece is. That last and essential piece that completes the jigsaw puzzle of life is death! Regardless how or when it comes, the whole beautiful picture of your life is then complete.

> *Still my anxieties over the meaning of life*
> *and the need to resolve its many complexities.*
> *Give me patience, and free me from my fear*
> *of that piece that completes my life-puzzle.*

February 8

A Stroke of Genius

"Pity me, pity me, O you my friends, for the hand of God has struck me," lamented the suffering, poor old Job. Even today God is perceived by some as being in control of every event, and so the originator of every misfortune or blessing, sickness or crop failure, accomplishment or victory. This antique belief reappears in times of tragedy and in the fine print of insurance policies defining certain disasters as "acts of God." Old Job said God's hand had struck him down in his affliction and that aged belief is still alive today as the source of the word *stroke,* the name for a sudden apoplexy, a rupture of a blood vessel in the brain.

The Creator is no puppeteer; humans and nature have been gifted with the independence to act free of divine manipulation.

Destructive hurricanes and gentle spring breezes both blow without invisible sacred puppet strings. Unlike nature we have the glorious freedom to choose to act like a destructive hurricane or behave like a gentle breeze of peace.

> *A stroke of genius was your decision*
> *to make creation free.*
> *May I use your ingenious gift*
> *in countless, clever ways today.*

February 9

The Best Way to Die Is Empty Hearted

The Teacher said, "Blessed are the pure of heart, for they shall see God." For the ancients it was not the mind but the heart that was the source of all emotion, thought, love, and desire. A pure heart paradoxically is an empty heart, yet the human heart is always filled with an endless stream of thoughts. To achieve a pure heart requires a constant flushing out of all thoughts. But does this imply being emptied of concepts of religious belief? To the religious person this seems impossible, insane. Yet is it the case? To the dying, palliative religious care offers life after death, the peaceful rest of heaven and the prospect of blissful union with God. Yet a side effect of this soothing religion is that "God-talk" can easily cause doubts of faith to arise. Death is the arch-agnostic who questions if there is really life after death or if God exists. To achieve a pure and empty heart, strive to free yourself of religious images of what awaits you after you die! The Teacher said that the eye has not seen nor imagined what awaits those who love God, so die with a pure, empty heart.

> *Empty me of all extraneous beliefs,*
> *for only one is really worth keeping:*
> *You are life—eternally vibrant life—*
> *and you and I are ever united as one.*

February 10

The Right Word

"The Buck Stops Here" was a quotation Harry Truman kept in front of him on his desk in the White House. Each of us should do the same, since denying personal responsibility is a human trait traceable back to Adam's passing the buck to Eve, and Eve's passing it on to the serpent. On President Truman's desk was also this quotation by Mark Twain: "A powerful agent is the right word. Whenever we come upon one of these intensely right words in a book or in a newspaper the resulting effect is physical as well as spiritual, and electrically prompt." Whatever we read takes us on an expedition to be electrified, to be jolted to a new level of life by the right words. No "Right Word Dictionary" exists for authors, and none is needed since words that inspire may affect one reader out of a hundred and leave the other ninety-nine unaffected. The secret of the right word is twofold: the openness of the reader to be inspired and a Ghostwriter. The Holy Ghost, that Ever-Electrifying Spirit, can radioactively infuse any word for any person at any time, transforming it into the "right word."

> *Make me ever-ready,*
> *any time or any day,*
> *so that what I read*
> *may be life-altering.*

February 11

I Wonder, What If?

What if you had lived in the days and the places where Gautama Buddha or Jesus of Nazareth were teaching—do you think you would have become one of their disciples? After hearing either one of them teaching that the path to peace and happiness was in rejecting all violence in thought, word, and deed, would you have become a believer? And what if Jesus or Buddha appeared today with different names dressed in clothing identical to what you are wearing? Would you stop and listen to what they were teaching? Don't you think after listening to them for fifteen minutes, you would walk away, finding their words far too impractical? Is today's absence of great living spiritual teachers because they are no longer necessary? Or has an era of giant spiritual masters ended because the age of eager, disciple-students willing to live their teachings has ended?

> *Frustrated desires and discontentment*
> *generate people hungering for wisdom,*
> *seeking a path to a wise teacher*
> *who's always right under their feet.*

February 12

A Merry Heart

I recently got a fortune cookie that read, "A merry heart makes a cheerful countenance." That delightful piece of Chinese wisdom should be read backward, "A cheerful countenance makes a merry heart." Our bodily expressions follow our emotions as well as give rise to them. A merry heart creates merry thoughts, and so creates a happy world. But how do you acquire a happy heart? You could practice a rite of the Egyptian priests of the sun god who began their day with a ritual of laughing in order to cleanse their souls. Laughter is a priestly soul cleanser, a holy heart enema. So whenever you feel sad about something your church does or doesn't do, or about the injustices of your government, perform an Egyptian cleansing ritual by laughing and joking about the issue. Making a laughable joke about a social evil can be as prophetic as ranting about it because laughter is the great liberating equalizer that shrinks the oppressor's power to intimidate you.

> *When next I feel I'm disheartened*
> *by the sad happenings in my world,*
> *tickle my funny bone and my heart*
> *since laughter expels sad despair.*

February 13

A Rocking Chair Pilgrim

The Muslim mystic Rumi said, "O you who have set forth on a pilgrimage, where are you going? Your beloved is here, here! Living right next to you. What a shame you've veiled yourself from your treasure." Rumi says if you wish to encounter the sacred, don't pilgrimage anywhere—just lift your veils.

Islam teaches that we have surrounded ourselves with countless subtle veils, preventing us from encountering the Divine One living right next to us. A story can hint at how to lift up those self-imposed blinding veils. There was a farmer who for fifty years had labored day and night milking his herd of cows. After half a century of laboring, he stopped and a neighbor asked him what he was going to do in his retirement? He answered, "For the first six months, I'm just going to sit on the porch in my rocking chair." "After six months," asked the neighbor, "then what are you going to do?" The old farmer smiled, "I'm going to start rocking."

> *Sit me down to do nothing*
> *but still my mind so as to open my eyes*
> *that I might see my Beloved beyond the veils*
> *here, there, and everywhere around me.*

February 14

Unopened Gifts

The German poet Rainer Maria Rilke wrote, "Love and death are the greatest gifts that are given to us. Mostly they are passed on unopened." Rilke proposes that we take love for granted, that we are unappreciative of the constancy of a love.

The Valentine's-Day custom is to send cards and give gifts to those who have given to us the greatest of all gifts—love. But instead of giving a greeting card or bouquet of red roses as a way to say "I love you," give the best gift of all: open the gift of *their* love for you. With the caress of the fingers of your soul, examine it as never before and treasure it for its preciousness. Continue opening your gift by pledging to handle this gift of love with care, great affection, and most of all daily gratitude. Greeting cards, even if they are kept, get boxed away. The most beautiful of roses quickly fades and dies. But here is an enduring gift that will enrich the life of the one you love and your own life too: promise to strive to make each day that follows this February 14 as romantic and affectionate as Valentine's Day itself.

> *May I see a small red heart*
> *on each day of my calendar*
> *so to never stop opening up*
> *the greatest gift of life—love.*

February 15

The Other Unopened Gift

Red was yesterday's festive color for Valentine's Day. Today it is black, funereal ebony black. This reflection will explore the second greatest and most often unopened gift spoken of yesterday by Rilke. If the black-wrapped gift of death comes to the door of one of your family or a close personal friend it is rarely opened. On this February day take a few moments to summon the courage to think the unthinkable. There's an old saying about the Irish that is valid for everyone: "The Irish would rather die than think about death." But obviously not thinking about death won't protect you from dying; neither will wealth, intelligence, physical strength, beauty, or fame. Even if death is personally absent today in your life right now, open that black-wrapped gift and think about it. A wholesome consciousness of your own death can enrich you with an awareness of how priceless this fleeting moment is, how magnificent the treasure of being loved. Priceless too is every unconscious breath you inhale.

> *Today inspire me to pause just to breathe*
> *slowly, prayerfully, and with gratitude*
> *so I never foolishly take for granted*
> *each precious, fleeting moment of my life.*

February 16

Saints Are Bad Role Models

Athletes, movie stars, and presidents are expected to be role models for the youth. Some are good role models, others are not. Saints, however, make bad role models since they are not playing any kind of role. Saints instead are authentic ideals. Holy people are not one person in public and another in private; they are truly who they are both on and off the stage of life. Saints set a good example by *not* trying to set an example of anything! They are simply themselves. Saints are free.

> *Remind me that halos require polishing*
> *and magnetically draw attention.*
> *Inspire me just to be your lover,*
> *faults and all, not one of your saints.*

February 17

Beware Your Primitive Wiring

Destructive house fires are frequently caused by faulty old wiring, so consider rewiring to avoid a personal disaster. Our brains are so wired that we jump first and ask questions later about what frightened us. Fear is our most ancient and powerful motivator. The body's alarm system is the amygdala, an almond shaped cluster of nerves in the temporal lobe of the brain. Structured for survival, its messages override the logical responses of the brain's cortex. For this reason it requires determined effort and persistence to think or talk oneself out of some fear. We have evolved from a fear of nature and wild beasts to a fear of other humans and their actions. Fear's stepbrother is hate, that ugly repugnance for the alien and stranger, for anyone who is not the same as us. This introduction to the brain is necessary to understand how enormously difficult it is to live Master's continuous admonition, "Fear not." If you wish to live liberated from fear, hatred, and prejudice, then unwavering, daily repeated practice is required to short-circuit your primitive brain mechanism.

> *Teach me a burglar's cunning talent*
> *of short-circuiting my alarm system,*
> *by repeated stubborn rising above it*
> *so to be free of fear and live in peace.*

February 18

Unspeakable Words

Just as *restroom* is a euphemism for *toilet,* so *cemetery* is the polite term for a *burial ground. Death* has now become an unacceptable word and is politely referred to with the euphemism *passed.* That expression reminds me of advancing from one grade in school to another or completing an exam successfully. The euphemism *cemetery* first appeared around 1387 and was created from the Greek word for dormitory, a place where a number of people slept. *Death, dying, graveyard* aren't vulgar or indecent words. They are not like *privy* or *toilet* that imply unseemly bodily functions and so require the euphemistic *restroom* for the room with a flushing device. In this age of natural foods, fabrics, and lifestyles, consider becoming more natural in your speech. Since death isn't an indecent word and dying isn't a vulgar act, consider using words that match reality.

> *Set me free of my fears of dying*
> *by trying never to think about it,*
> *so that every time I say "died,"*
> *I'm reminded I too am going to die.*

February 19

The Secret of Successful Resolutions

Reformation is not a once-in-a-lifetime act. In any good liberating spirituality, improving your self is a continuous activity. When attempting to make any changes in your life, success is more likely if you write down the changes you want to make. As the title of Dr. Henriette Klauser's book *Write it Down, Make it Happen* suggests, it's not as effective simply to think about changes we desire to make. The art of writing your desired change appears to stimulate a part of your brain called the reticular activating system which filters pertinent information to the conscious part of your mind. In writing out your goals, Dr. Klauser advises using positive instead of negative phrases. She says we should list the rewards these changes will bring. For example, one reward of achieving the goal of losing weight would be, "I would appear more presentable in my clothes and so feel better about myself." This technique also applies to the goals of a richer prayer life: a more generous spirit and greater patience.

> *With a pen or pencil reform yourself,*
> *so your own words will shout at you*
> *how to make yourself more lovable,*
> *and so make this world a better place.*

February 20

Remember the Potato

Potatoes first arrived in Europe in the early 1500s aboard Spanish ships returning from Peru. Eating this vegetable from the New World was considered stylish among the rich, but was slow to be accepted by commoners. In 1610, potatoes were actually banned in the district of Burgundy, France because "frequent use caused leprosy." The next time you enjoy mashed potatoes or French fries, recall that once they were a forbidden food. As once potatoes were legally banned out of fear of what was different or new, so today society attempts to ban certain behaviors by judging them to be as contagiously deadly as leprosy. Typically these laws are based on certain selected texts from the Bible. But those who select them ignore other taboo acts—often found on the very same page of the Bible—forbidden several millennia ago by God. Time marches on, but prejudice and fear recede at a snail's pace. So when you are asked to support the outlawing of some human behavior, remember the potato!

> *When prone to cling to past morality,*
> *remind me how morals slowly change;*
> *the once-forbidden is now acceptable,*
> *what's now-forbidden will soon not be.*

February 21

Connected to the Earth

Worldwide, millions suffer from hunger and privation; millions upon millions more lack proper housing and drinkable water, while in our country huge amounts of money are spent yearly on pets. When this expenditure is balanced against the needs of the poor, the vast sums we spend on pets is condemned as a luxury of a rich nation. Chief Seattle of the Suquamish tribe of the Pacific Northwest said wisely, "When the last animals have perished, humans will die of loneliness." His wisdom addresses our prehistoric, intrinsic need for companionship with animals and with the rest of creation. Yet day-by-day we continue to be disconnected and divorced from the natural world. Our furry, feathered, or finned pets are umbilical cords linking us to our hidden animal nature that still pumps through the veins of our human nature. Pets, even those of others, are tactile links with the animal core that is still a vibrant living part of our humanity.

> *Whenever I'm tempted to think,*
> *instead of feel—to sense my way—*
> *let me engage my animal talents*
> *so all of who I am is fully alive.*

February 22

100 Milliseconds

Studies by the psychologist Alex Todorov reveal that we form a positive or negative opinion of persons by a glance lasting no longer than 100 milliseconds! These faster-than-a-split-second judgments of others are involuntary responses of the primitive amygdala in the brain. Todorov calls them "a case of a high-level judgment being made by a low-level brain structure." Is prehistoric survival the guilty party for this instantaneous decision-making that prejudicially stains our thoughts and attitudes toward those whose faces we unconsciously find distasteful or distrustful? Like which came first, the chicken or the egg, do temperaments produce faces or do faces create personalities? Regardless, as an evolving human you must strive to follow the Teacher's difficult admonition, "You shall not judge." To achieve this requires overriding your amygdala that will take longer than 100 milliseconds!

> *Cancel my Neanderthal judgments*
> *so I can see beyond facial features,*
> *as do you, Creator and Lover*
> *of all you have so artistically fashioned.*

February 23

Your Faith Has Healed You

A thumbnail sketch of history of medicinal cures might include some interesting facts. Ketchup was sold as a patented medicine in the 1830s. Bee stings were described as a good cure for rheumatism (bees were placed in an inverted glass over the aching limbs and would sting the patient). Until the eighteenth century a general cure for all kinds of afflictions was to swallow a mixture of ground-up Egyptian mummy. Rattlesnake venom as a cure for epilepsy was not abandoned until the 1930s. Tobacco rolled into a pill or drunk as tea was a healing herb for headaches, toothaches, stomachaches, bad breath, and cuts. Until the seventeenth century in England, dressing in red colored clothing and surrounding a patient with red fabrics was considered to be medicinally beneficial to those suffering from a fever. Some of these weird concoctions did offer relief or they would not have continued to be used. Jesus, the physician of Galilee, often said, "Your faith has healed you." He typically spoke that therapeutic prescription to those he healed. Faith and medicine are powerful allies of healing, so always use them together.

If folk medicine users were healed
by belief in bee stings or ketchup,
may my faith in the medicines I use
aid my mind and soul to heal my body.

February 24

Count Your Riches and Then Invest

The Zen master Ryokan returned one night to his home to find
that while he had been away robbers had come and stolen every single thing in his simple hut. Standing in the middle of his
small dwelling, stripped of his meager possessions, he threw
his arms in the air and rejoiced shouting, "They left the best
thing, the moon at the window." Shrewd investors frequently
review their stock funds and assets as the stock market fluctu-
ates. A wise investor often finds it expedient to reinvest his or
her funds. In the spirit of Zen Master Ryokan, consider seriously reinvesting in what is always certain to return the very
highest rate of interest—the moon!

Inspire me to invest in imperishables,
investments like the pregnant full moon,
rapid rain falling on warm asphalt streets,
and the spicy smells of barbeque smoke.

February 25

Death Numb

The news of the death of someone personally known to us should have an effect upon us, but sometimes we seem to be numbed by the constant news of death on a global scale. We suffer from an overexposure to death. Psychologically, it is impossible to be emotionally involved in death as presented by the media on a worldwide scale. This overexposure by daily reports of death nationally and globally has a profound effect on our emotions when we receive news of the death of a neighbor or fellow worker. Upon hearing of the death, we may respond with a reflex-like intellectual comment of regret, and then unemotionally return to our normal business of daily life. Just as therapeutic exercise can restore the lost ability of an injured muscle, so too spiritual therapy can restore an emotion paralyzed by overexposure to death. But rehabilitation takes practice. When next you learn of another's death, pause to pray as sincerely as possible in sympathy with them and the family, for your paralyzed emotion can be revitalized by repeated compassionate communion.

Death, nudge me with your bony finger.
Remind me to be truly compassionate
for the sad loss and sufferings of others,
since by so doing I become more alive.

February 26

The Leap-Frog Creed

The bedrock of Christian faith is the Apostles' Creed. Surprisingly though, the Apostles' Creed simply leap-frogs from "born of the Virgin Mary" to "suffered under Pontius Pilate." This leap of thirty years has serious consequences, failing as it does to involve faith in the teachings of Jesus! As a result, one can pray the Apostles' Creed and feel absolutely no inconsistency with millennia of imbedded Christian belief about war or the use of violence in the cause of right. Christians have, for over two thousand years, remained adept at being deaf to violence and retaliation. The selective deafness of the Christian majority creates an elastic creed which unconditionally affirms Jesus as God's spokesperson, yet allows for patriotic support of a nation's aggression and wars. Are hearing aids the answer to this paradox of Christian belief? Or is the answer a new twenty-first century Christian creed that includes after "born of the Virgin Mary," and before "suffered under Pontius Pilate," the core teachings of Jesus?

> *Haunt me with the ancient questions:*
> *Are my flag and the cross incompatible?*
> *Can I be both a loyal, patriotic citizen*
> *and a faithful, loyal disciple of Jesus?*

February 27

Every Artist Needs an Audience

In a conversation with a good friend who is a watercolor painter, the question of whether artists ever needed to show their work arose. He answered, "It is said that every artist needs an audience, but it only has to be one person." Then followed a discussion of the need to share your artwork with another if your art is a poem or a delicious meal you've created. The next day that concept of an artist needing to share the artwork inadvertently connected itself to the Genesis story of the first, if not the primal cosmic artist, the Creator. For five days the Cosmic Artist with great imagination artistically created the sun, moon, and stars, then birds, fish, and animals. Interestingly, on the final or sixth day, only after creation in all of its splendorous beauty was completed, did God create the first humans, Adam and Eve. Did the Cosmic Artist create the first humans so as to have an audience to appreciate and share in the stunning masterpiece of creation?

> *Is my first and my greatest prayer*
> *admiring your great masterpiece?*
> *The best prayer is applauding creation*
> *and what I see in my mirror.*

February 28

The Three Things Required

In one of her poems, Mary Oliver says that three things are required in life. To sum them up in a single sentence: love what is mortal, hold it against your bones knowing your own life depends on it, and when the time comes let it go. This trinity of life's requirements begins with passionately embracing what you love as if it were immortal, yet knowing it is fleeting. Cling to what you love as tightly as you would a life preserver in the middle of an ocean. Then, when that inevitable day comes, readily release your love. This last of the three requires living with a consciousness of one of life's eternal laws: "Everything changes and nothing remains forever." In the face of reality, this infallible law of life is daily denied because our mind weaves the spidery web of the illusion of permanence over whatever one loves: a spouse, a child, health, or mental abilities. Live in reality, so you can love with intensity.

> *Cripple me from only half-loving*
> *out of the fear of the pain of loss.*
> *For the pains of loss are but brief*
> *next to years of extravagant loving.*

February 29, Leap Year

Soulful Praying

Prayer is generally considered an activity of the heart and mind. In fact, the classical definition of prayer is lifting up one's heart and mind to God. Yet praying, we use the pronoun I. Good prayer should strive to be as integrated a human act as possible, and not simply limited to head or heart. So consider in your praying replacing the pronoun *I* with the word *soul*. Using *soul* can help you visualize your prayers originating from a deeper place within you. The more you involve your soul in daily life and prayer, the more it will grow toward being a *mahatma*. This Sanskrit word from India means "large or great soul."

My soul aches for all of me to pray,
Not just using my often distracted mind,
Or relying upon a frequently fickle heart,
So my soul can grow larger, more beautiful.

Month of
March

March 1

Why Be Good?

A parable that reappears in various forms in different religions tells the delightful story of a peasant who encounters an archangel hurrying toward him on the road. The angel is carrying a flaming torch in one hand and a big bucket of water in the other. The puzzled peasant asks, "Where are you going with that flaming torch and bucket of water?" "With this torch," the archangel shouts as he hurries past him, "I'm going to burn down all the mansions in heaven and with this bucket of water I'm going to quench all the fires of hell. Then we'll see who really loves God." Reward and punishment, the promise or the threat, are basic motivators for small children. Religion adapted this primal behavior modification tool with the promise of long-range consequences: heaven for the good, hell for the bad. Yet, it is by our choices that we create our own hell or own heaven here and now. Mature lovers are good and decent, not out of fear of the stick or hope for a carrot, but simply for the joys of being good.

> *May I love as you love me,*
> *even if not loved in return.*
> *I hunger to be like you,*
> *a true unconditional lover.*

March 2

Become a Wonderworker

The first miracle performed by Jesus in John's gospel was at a wedding party in the village of Cana. At the height of the merrymaking there was a disaster: They ran out of wine. The Teacher, being informed of their plight, took large jars of water present for purification rituals at meals and changed them into gallons and gallons of wine. That wonder generated a second one as the gloom at the wedding was miraculously changed into intoxicating joy. The miracle-working Teacher promised us, his disciple-friends, that we would perform even greater wonders than he. So experiment with making miracles like his at Cana. Change a bland dinner into a festive occasion by infusing it with pleasure and enjoyment. Whenever a job, a social gathering, or a personal encounter seems as common and plain as water, be a wonderworker and change it into the wine of festivity by your good humor and love.

> *Remind me that, even lacking mystical powers,*
> *I can still perform miracles if my desire is great,*
> *if I have a healthy forgetfulness of myself*
> *and a hefty appetite to make others happy.*

March 3

Elastic Values

"A tree that is unbending is easily broken"—wise words for this month of March from the *Tao Te Ching,* the ancient holy book of China. The word *March* comes from the name of the Roman god of war, Mars. The Old Saxon name for this month was *Hreth-monath,* meaning rough-month because of its boisterous winds. So in this month of war-like winds, reflect on how flexible your standards are when facing life's turbulence. Are you among those who maintain that no matter how strong the headwind or opposition, you should always be unbending in your principles and beliefs? A touch of humor and wisdom can often add a little warmth to the chill of severity. Here are some more words of wisdom for this stern month from Groucho Marx: "These are my principles. If you don't like them, well, I have others!" Flexibility instead of rigidity is an infallible sign of the presence of life. What is rigid and unbending is dead.

> *Nature constantly compromises,*
> *creatively adapting to change.*
> *Inspire me, too, to be naturally elastic*
> *and flexible in my beliefs.*

March 4

A Way to Stem the Increasing Violence

Escalating violence is a problem in our society. Civil and religious groups aggressively lobby the networks and Hollywood to remove or drastically limit the violence in television programs and movies. Violent computer games are likewise targeted as the cause of many of the brutally vicious acts of youth. No one will deny that in our society aggressive behavior and violence has increased; when searching for its source, there's another place we ought to look. In an article entitled, "Another Inconvenient Truth," Jack Nelson-Pallmeyer documents the numerous references to violence in the scriptures of Judaism, Christianity, and Islam. He concludes by saying, "The widespread acceptance of violent images of God solidifies the relationship between violence and the divine so completely that functionally, violence is the real religion in the world today."

> *Yearning as I do for peace in the world,*
> *should I take up scissors*
> *and cut from every bible all its dreadful*
> * violence?*
> *Or should I be blind to everything but your call*
> * to love?*

March 5

Thank God for Turning a Deaf Ear to My Prayers

If we were to thoughtfully review our personal life stories, I am confident most of us would agree with the British writer C.S. Lewis who claimed he was grateful that God had not answered all of his prayers. Lewis said that later in life he saw how disastrous his life would have been if God had granted some of his petitions. I find it amazing how, in the mysterious process we call prayer, we are somehow given what we need for the long journey of life, but not what we crave at this or that moment. A common theme in fairy tales is the youth who is given three magical wishes. The stories focus on what or what not to wish for. So it is with prayer. If some of our youthful wishes had been granted they might have detoured us from the joy and happiness of our lives today. Perhaps then the old saying is true: all prayers are answered. Sometimes the answer is that we get what we ask for, other times the answer is we don't.

> *Teach me not to weep*
> *over my many unanswered prayers,*
> *but rather to discover your love*
> *in them being unanswered.*

March 6

Pockets of Faithful Disciples

In Reinhold Niebuhr's book *Moral Man and Immoral Society* he wisely says that only individuals can sacrifice themselves, not groups. Likewise he says that only saints can truly practice the admonitions of Jesus such as never to return evil for evil. Because of this Niebuhr asserts that there can be nonviolent individuals, but not pacifist religions. While "pockets of pacifists" such as the Amish and Quakers can practice the nonviolent teachings of Jesus, an entire religion such as Christianity cannot. Two thousand years of history appear to confirm Niebuhr's view of the impracticality of the gospel for the majority of Christian believers. Perhaps the most frequently heard complaint about churchgoers is that they are hypocrites. Is that a valid accusation if only saints can embrace all the Master's teachings or be true pacifists? Does the world expect too much of the average Christian? Do churches expect too little from their members? Or are individual Christians guilty for not expecting greatness of themselves? Perhaps the answer lies in a new name: The Church of *Aspiring* Christians.

May my ears echo daily with your call,
"You shall love your God passionately,
with all your heart, soul, body, and mind,"
for fiery zealous love prevents hypocrisy!

March 7

How to Enlarge Your Faith

Do you believe your religious life can benefit from the teachings and spirituality of Muslims, Jews, and Buddhists? Or do you believe your religious faith is superior to that of other Christians and of non-Christians, and you have nothing to learn from them? Sir John Sacks, the chief rabbi of the British Commonwealth, wrote, "Those who are confident of their faith are not threatened but enlarged by the different faiths of others." It is exciting to think about enlarging your faith since with age it can often feel like it is stagnant or even shrinking. As love grows with the years so also should faith. To expand your faith, explore the rich spiritualities of other Christian traditions and of non-Christian religions. No need to go to Tibet, just go to the religion section of your local bookstore. Browse the shelves with a hungry appetite for God.

Embolden my faith so it can be fertilized
by the teachings and zeal of other faiths,
so I can better love, serve, and pray to you,
the mystic destination of all the many paths.

March 8

Freedom Requires Constant Vigilance

The Exodus is a liberation story of the great escape of the Israelites from their Egyptian slavery that fused them together as one nation, one people, under God. Yet their shouts of victory were soon replaced by snores as they abandoned their Exodus freedom to become subjects of a king and the temple priesthood. As the old Irish expression goes, "From clog to clog takes only three generations," clogs being the heavy wooden-soled shoes worn by indentured servants. Indeed, freedom from both political and religious enslavement requires constant vigilance. Jesus admonished his disciples to stay awake, to watch and pray.

Let me pray with one eye open,
as cautious as a cat half-napping,
so as not to be caught slumbering
when they attempt to enslave me.

March 9

Reverencing the One in All

The Yupiit people of Alaska refer to the spirit that they believe inhabits all things as *yua*. They believe that *yua* is just as present in a sled dog, a bear, a fir tree, and even a rock as it is in a human being. As a result, they treat all beings and all things with respectful reverence. When they move a stone from one location to another, they do so with reverence as if bestowing upon the stone the blessing of a new place to dwell. We are more surrounded by manufactured objects like computers and automobiles than natural ones like rocks and trees. Instead of treating them as inanimate objects, imagine that you can see a *yua*, a spirit, dwelling in them. How different would your interaction with them be? Could this recognition of the *yua* spirit dwelling within all things assist you in reversing the growing tendency to treat people as robotic objects?

> *Open my soul to see your Spirit,*
> *invisible and dwelling in all persons,*
> *creatures, and things in the cosmos,*
> *to treat all of them with veneration.*

March 10

St. Jacob, the Wrestler

If wrestlers needed a patron saint, it would surely be the patriarch Jacob who in the book of Genesis wrestled all night with a divine being at a crossing called Penuel. The ancients believed that to cross any frontier it was necessary to engage in combat with the divine beings that guarded every boundary. Jacob, the alien intruder, desired to cross over into the land of Canaan. He is thus also patron of border crossings. Life is a series of frontiers. Some we are eager to cross. Others we are dragged up to by circumstances that demand we cross them. Every frontier requires wrestling with mysterious forces, desires, and fears. All frontiers—be they physical, emotional, or spiritual— require that we change. They involve wrestling with our fears, doubts, and desires. So the next time you find yourself in an inner tug-of-war, consider if you are resisting some new frontier in life that has to be crossed. If that is the case, then know your struggle is one of prayer. The reason to pray is that you are grappling not so much with an emotional or psychological issue, but, like Jacob, you are wrestling with God.

Frontiers frighten me, I confess.
Help me to overcome my fear
of what is new and unknown,
of what awakens sleeping inadequacies.

March 11

Who Lost Who?

Today, a majority of churchgoers are not only dissatisfied with their churches, they have departed from them. They came thirsty for God, but found only bone-dry wells. They've stopped searching. If you are among this ever-growing majority, know that you didn't lose your faith—rather your faith lost you! If you can't find a well with living water, dig your own! Build your own inner church out of the wreckage of your once dynamic church. If this sounds inviting but intimidating, remember that after centuries of being spiritually fed by ordained others, we have become ritually disabled and worship handicapped. Don't be afraid! It isn't as difficult as it first appears. Trust the Master who said, "Where two or three of you are gathered in my name, there am I in your midst." To experience "church" you only need two people coming together in his name—any one of countless names. Gathering in his name means coming together in the name of Love (his favorite name), or in the name of Meal (a sensually delicious name), or in the name of Peace (his most beautiful name).

> *Open my eyes to the cistern of grace*
> *hidden under my home and daily life,*
> *so to pull up buckets of Living Waters*
> *of your presence, love, pardon, and joy.*

March 12

Getting Close to God

Seekers of every religion have shown great ingenuity in discovering ways to get closer to God, but St. Simeon Stylites seems to have taken that challenge literally. Simeon lived in the fourth century near Aleppo in Syria and sat in solitude for thirty-nine years on top of a sixty-foot tall stone pillar. When asked why he lived on top of the pillar, he answered that he was doing penance for people's sins and wanted to be closer to God. While esteemed as a holy man, blessedly bizarre is the idea that to reject the sharing of daily life with others (a holy hiding away still common) brings one closer to God. The Teacher said the opposite: God is found in others, especially the poor and needy. It isn't possible to have insights today into the various psychological problems of men and women mystics who lived unnatural and often tormented lives. But it is possible to not envy them or attempt to imitate their abnormal bizarre spiritualities.

> *If you want to be closer to God,*
> *just rub shoulders with the crowd.*
> *If you want to do penance for sins,*
> *just rub shoulders with the crowd.*

March 13

Tailoring Your Prayers

For Jewish mystical masters, praying was no casual activity. Entering into communion with God required the same abandonment as if, in the midst of prayer, you were to die. For them, it was not only the words of prayer, but each letter of each word of prayer that was significant. These holy men of the Torah said: when you pray, you enter into every letter of a word with all your strength and soul, for God dwells within each letter. Some Jewish spiritual masters referred to the words of prayer as the garments of God, and spoke of praying as the joyful task of making garments for the king of kings. What an intriguing image, God wearing my prayers! If you pictured in your mind God dressed up in your prayers, such an image would transform you into a conscientious prayer-tailor, painstaking-ly meticulous to make each prayer as beautiful as possible.

> *Cure my racing through the words of prayers,*
> *hop-scotching toward the Amen finish line.*
> *At each word, stop me to fill it with myself,*
> *then sew it to others in a robe fit for a king.*

March 14

Prayer Flowers

In the ancient Zoroastrian religion, worship was liturgically connected with flowers. Flowers in Christian worship are only used for decorations, especially at weddings and funerals. Yet flowers are to the soul what food is to the body. A bouquet of flowers in the house or even a single flower is not a luxury, but a sacrament of soul food. Blooming flowers are typically objects only for the eyes to behold, but the next time you are near a flower pause to smell its scent and let your nose pray. An inexpensive spiritual exercise is to obtain a single flower and to engage in a conversation with it. Flower talk requires sensitive ears. If you are patient it can be a rich discussion, especially if you ask your flower how it feels! You might be surprised to hear it say, "I'm dying you know, since I'm a cut flower. Yet I feel it's a gift for me to give my life to make yours more beautiful and to bring you closer to nature—and so to God."

> *Open me up to the art of flower listening,*
> *so to hear some truly inspiring sermons*
> *on how to make the world more beautiful*
> *by dying gracefully to give life to others.*

March 15

Needlework

By the middle of March, Christians are in the midst of the Lenten season of personal reform. This is an ideal time for annual spring-cleaning, regardless of your religious beliefs or lack of them. Since bad habits, unhealthy diets and lifestyles, like dust, have a way of cleverly and slowly drifting back into our lives, we all need a personal spring housecleaning. Resolutions to make changes in life patterns and major or minor addictions require determined endurance and patience with slow removal. Whatever your springtime cleaning task, resolve to tackle it with the dogged determination of digging a well using a needle as your shovel! The Turkish have a saying, "To dig a well with a needle." That proverb gives a vivid image of the painstakingly slow and determined effort required to accomplish certain tasks, especially personal or social reform.

> *Grant me the patience to needle away*
> *microscopically at the difficult tasks*
> *necessary to accomplish real reform*
> *in my personal life and in my society.*

March 16

Eyeservice, the Old Slave Master

Mrs. Byrne's Dictionary describes a well-known activity by use of the word *eyeservice.* She defines it as, "Work done only when the boss is watching." The boss, for those who do eye-service, can be your work supervisor, your peers, your friends, your bishop, your pastor, and even your parents regardless of your age. *Eyeservice* is also done by a surprisingly large number of people who are dominated by an invisible overlord, their inner-critic. This boss demands you attend to the most unimportant, even trivial tasks like cleaning off the speck of dust on the chair rung or straightening the picture frame that's but a centimeter crooked. We all, to a greater or lesser degree, are saddled with a harsh taskmaster of our own creation as our overlord. This most fascinating form of slavery, where one is both the slave and master, began in our childhood to gain the approval and love of our parents. Unlike other slave revolts in history, escaping from this slavery can be almost impossible unless you are dedicated to tirelessly digging day-by-day your own escape tunnel.

> *Each time I hear that inner voice*
> *demanding that I do more or do better,*
> *prompt me to be a naughty child,*
> *to rebel by doing the very opposite.*

March 17

The Wearing of the Green

This green feast of St. Patrick's Day gives everyone, regardless of whether they are Irish, German, Japanese, or Lithuanian, a chance to wear the green of spring and new life. Four days from now old, dreary winter will lose its grip on us, pack up its ice, snow, and frosty breath and depart for another year—and we all say, "Good riddance!" Let the color green of this holiday be like the Groundhog, a weather forecaster who proclaims that the rich green of new vegetation will soon grace the land. It's only right and proper that today's marching bands and gala parades joyfully announce that old man winter is on his deathbed. This festive emerald-green holiday anticipates the changing of the seasons. However, having become an indoor, computerized, denatured people, this change of seasons can easily elude us unnoticed. Today, even if you're not Irish, wear a bit of green, if only in your heart, to rejoice that spring will soon be here.

> *Halter my workaholic tendencies,*
> *shatter my shackles, so that work-free*
> *I can celebrate by merrymaking and parades*
> *this birthday feast of a new holy season.*

March 18

Negative Gratitude

The polite response when you've had enough food or anything else is, "No thank you." It can also be an escape clause when viewing an ad for new clothes, "No thank you, my closet is already full." You can delightfully say, "No thank you," to the itch to have a larger house, adding, "I have all the rooms I need." If ever tempted to have a new spouse, say, "No thank you, I don't need a new lover; I'm still finding great delight in exploring my present love." When facing an avalanche of advertising, you can say, "No thank you" to more and more and more, adding,

"I have more than I need or can use." To live a simple life is a most attractive ideal, yet in our affluent society it seems a daunting if not impossible task. Don't be intimidated; a simple life is really very easy—all you have to do is make "No thank you" one of your most frequently used expressions.

> *Grant me daily the grace of gratitude,*
> *to be thankful for all my many gifts,*
> *and so be freed from artificial needs,*
> *that I might lead a joyful, simple life.*

March 19

What Do You Do?

Perhaps the first question upon meeting someone new is to ask what do you do? This question about another's occupation or work is a social mechanism for knowing how to relate to the person. If they answer, "I'm a brain surgeon," you treat them in a certain way, and if they answer, "I'm a garbage collector," you respond accordingly. As far as possible, refuse to let yourself be defined by the work you do. That is, unless you've chosen a mystical profession. If your life work is gracefully accepting whatever life presents to you—the good, the bad, and the ugly—then you have a mystical profession, regardless what you do to earn money. Mystical mechanics, when presented by life with something ugly, are able to ingeniously turn that gift inside out into some good. Mystical engineers, when given something beautiful, never clutch it to themselves but hold it in their opened palms. They ravish it to the fullest with delight, and then install wings on it so it can fly away.

> *Coach me to practice the trade*
> *of an accomplished acceptor;*
> *skilled at heartily embracing*
> *whatever life delivers this day.*

March 20

I Grew Up in a Two-Story House

As a child I lived with my family on the ground floor of a two-story house. At my mother's knee I learned my catechism's first exciting theology lesson, "God is everywhere!" But when I played hide and seek with God in our house and was frustrated, I would ask my mother, "If God is everywhere, why can't I ever find him anywhere in our house?" Tenderly she would say, "Eddie, you must have faith; God is everywhere," and so I became a believer. At about the age of seven I learned a new lesson at church that God lived up in heaven. Heaven was a mystery, and all I knew was that it was up. Logically, I concluded God must be the never-seen mysterious resident on our second floor. This childhood deduction was based on watching adults pray—they always looked up at the ceiling when they prayed. One day my uncle came to our house tearful that he along with others at the factory had been laid off work. He looking up at the ceiling and wailed, "Why, God, has this happened to me?" I was never able to hear the replies of that mysterious second floor resident, but I presumed others did.

> Remind this hearing-impaired believer
> to read your messages you've scattered
>   everywhere
> in sign language that thunders
> "I am here!" "I am here!" "I am here!"

March 21

Spring Equinox

Prehistoric priesthoods set this day apart as sacred, as a feast to celebrate the resurrection of the earth. The sun, radiant and healing, revitalizes the dark and dormant. The days and nights are again of equal length on this day of the equinox. A true planetary pilgrim experiences this feast not as a spectator, but as a concelebrant with the earth and all creation. This day is both holy and magical, filled with hidden spirits and sounds. May your ears, eyes, and nose be attentive to the rebirth of green life pushing up through the earth, even if still hidden from view. The ancient ones lit great fires to banish the tired, aged spirits of winter and darkness. They built bonfires to ward off the half-hidden fears that perhaps this time, this year, winter would not leave and they would die in the barren, icy darkness. With reverence, let yourself be touched by this hidden memory as you respond to the gravitational tug of the planet Earth on this feast.

> *On this Spring Equinox day,*
> *as this new season is birthed*
> *from old winter's tomb-womb,*
> *birth a fresh new spirit in me.*

March 22

The End Times, or the Beginning?

The brilliant Jesuit theologian and paleontologist, Teilhard de Chardin, who died in 1955, wrote years before his death, "Once upon a time everything seemed fixed and solid. Now everything in the universe has begun to slide under our feet."

Amazing. If this insightful visionary sensed that the universe was shifting under his feet back in those relatively calm times in the middle of the last century, would he describe what is happening today as an earthquake? For Teilhard de Chardin, however, this cosmic displacement wasn't some apocalyptic collapse of the once stable realities. It was rather a beginning breakthrough birthing of an ever-evolving creation that requires frequent upheavals of the fixed status quo.

> *Banish any temptation to judge*
> *these evil times as a breakdown,*
> *for they are breakthrough times*
> *of promise arising out of chaos.*

March 23

How to Prepare for Armageddon

The Prophet Mohammed said that if the end of the world, the Day of Judgment, should arrive as you are planting a tender young seedling, you should continue planting it. The basic challenge of holiness is striving daily to live each moment with grace-filled attention. God dwells only in the present moment. The Prophet Mohammed was inspired to emphasize this divine reality by saying that even if the world and all the heavens were to come catastrophically crashing down around you, continue doing whatever it is that you are doing. Don't fall down on your knees crying out for mercy; just continue with confidence being fully absorbed in what you're doing in that God-soaked moment.

> *Plant me firmly in the present moment,*
> *the everyday temple in which you dwell.*
> *Glue my gypsy mind to the here and now,*
> *so in whatever I do, I shall find you there.*

March 24

Do You Want to Hear a Good Dirty Story?

Before you prudently look to see if anyone is reading over your shoulder, allow me to say that this dirty story isn't new, it's the most ancient of all dirty stories. One day in paradise, God, having grown lonely, decided to create a companion, and took some plain dirt and shaped it into the form of a human. God found this newest of creatures to be handsome, if inactive, and so leaned over and breathed the breath of life into its nostrils. Included in the divine breath was consciousness, intelligence, and spirit. A true work of art was this animated clay in the shape of a beautiful human infused with almost unlimited potential, yet designed to disintegrate back to dust. Art museums do everything possible to preserve their great works of art from the ravenous hunger of time that slowly consumes them, leaving only dust. Not so the Great Artist who created all the uniquely beautiful masterpieces to recycle themselves back again to rich, fertile, and creative dirt.

> *While my mind plays out among the galaxies,*
> *my body ages racing to return again to dust.*
> *May I then embrace this divine contradiction*
> *by enjoying today the touch of tomorrow—dirt.*

March 25

A Good Day to Begin Anew

In the Middle Ages, this was New Year's Day. Because today is nine months before Christmas, in the ancient medieval calendar it was the feast of the Conception of Jesus and also the legal New Year's Day. Since 1582 we have celebrated the new year according to the Gregorian calendar created by Pope Gregory XIII to correct the old outdated Julian calendar. This day of March 25, according to legend, was also the first day of creation, the day on which Adam and Eve left Eden to begin a new life, the day of the Exodus from Egypt, and the day on which Jesus was crucified. New Year's Day in this current year is only eighty-two days ago! How easily does a new year become old, and even more easily do we slip back into the routines of daily life as prisoners of habit. Your New Year's resolutions are now an aged eighty-two days old, and typically forgotten. Use this original new year's day, once famous for so many important events, to make a springtime resolution of newness. Let today be a new personal exodus from some personal slavery, a new beginning for your marriage, or a good day to die to old habits.

> *I too easily procrastinate beginning anew,*
> *so help me to become a continual reformer.*
> *Rally me to choose to correct one fault this week;*
> *then next week another, and so on, till I die.*

March 26

Soaring to the Stars

The English poet William Blake said, "No bird soars too high, if he soars with his own wings." But how much higher could you fly with a second pair of wings! Be grateful then if in life you've been miraculously given another pair of wings—the love of another, grafted on to you who naturally should have only one pair. The traditional image of love and friendship is two hearts united, but for accomplishing greatness in any activity imagine this love more dynamically as two pairs of wings. Birds and angels use their wings to escape earthbound gravity. Wings are for flying, so in your marriage or committed friendship know that another pair of wings has been sewn onto your soul. Rejoice with angelic confidence that because of love you can soar ever higher and higher.

> *Thank you for my extra set of wings,*
> *gifted to me from my spouse or lover*
> *with which I am able to dare to soar*
> *into the stratosphere powered by love.*

March 27

God Windows

Buildings are like persons; they also have eyes that are called windows. One function of windows is to allow us to look out at the world that surrounds our homes. Church buildings have eyes as well, yet typically they are closed with stained glass eyelids. But those beautiful eyelids painted with images of saints and holy symbols on them shut out the surrounding environment. Why? Why also do we close our eyes when we pray?

Is it for the same purpose, to shut out distractions and sights that might take our minds away from God? For at least a millennium Christian churches have preached the world is evil, so it's only logical then to shut out evil from your prayer and from places of worship. But is that what we truly believe? Or do you believe that your eyes are actually divine prayer portals by which to pray the prayer of visual awe and adoration?

> *Thank you for my two God-windows,*
> *your gift of inspired holy prayerscopes*
> *by which I can both simultaneously*
> *see with awe and pray with wonder.*

March 28

Spoon Teachers

In the *Dhammapada*, the wise teachings of Buddha, there is the following powerful question, "Does the spoon know the taste of the soup?" These brief nine words contain great wisdom about teaching, whether you are a parent or a professional educator. So reread them again slowly to soak up their implications. At first reading they appear obvious, but we know from experience they are not. Every teacher must personally know the taste of the soup of advice, instruction, or preaching he or she is ladling out to others, since listeners, even children, have keen taste-bud-ears. They perceive easily those who attempt to teach without having tasted the soup, especially sacrifice, personal discipline, moral integrity, prayer, and the difficult struggle for holiness. Taste the soup, then teach what you know, not from books or norms of social morality but what you know personally by the taste.

> *Hold my tongue before I give advice,*
> *to ask, do I know the taste of the soup*
> *that I'm eager to generously dish out?*
> *If I don't, with silence glue my lips.*

March 29

Lex Talionis—the Law of Tit for Tat

Three thousand years ago or longer, the law of Exodus restricted Israelites in their pursuit of revenge. A tooth for a tooth was a greatly evolved moral law for its day when wholesale slaughter often was the revenge taken for a single offense. Only one life could be extracted for the single loss of a life, one eye for a single eye taken, and so on. This ancient law was called *lex talionis,* and it outlawed giving your enemy a lesson by retaliating with excessive retribution. This three-thousand-year-old desert law, known by heart to most, still remains the basis of today's primitive, capital punishment system. The next verse in the *lex talionis* of Exodus 21, "a wound for a wound, a stripe for a stripe," is today almost universally used in domestic retaliation in our personal lives. Whenever we are wounded by others' unkind words or actions, we wound them back. However, the Galilean Teacher gave us a divine law extremely superior to the *lex talionis,* "Never return a wound for a wound. If someone strikes you, respond by striking them back—with love."

> *Let me gauge my degree of evolution*
> *by how I respond to injury and offense.*
> *May I embrace your eternal call to evolve*
> *upward from the primitive to the divine.*

March 30

Rudely Ignoring the Holy One

Pearl Bailey, in a single sentence, said a profound and mystical truth, "People see God everyday; they just don't recognize him!" In the catechism, at the bottom of the page on which is found the lesson that God is everywhere, there is a footnote in tiny, almost microscopic print: "But God is invisible." Pearl Bailey, along with other mystics, apparently wasn't able to read that infinitesimally small print. The spine-chilling, scary line of Pearl's statement is that while people see God every day, "they just don't recognize him (or her!)." Her observation causes a landside of haunting questions: Did I walk right past God today on the sidewalk or in my hurried trip out of the supermarket, but didn't know it? Did I fail to see God in that joyously noisy crowd at the wedding reception because I am used to looking only in church where people whisper quietly? Was I blinded to God in the falling white snowflakes, being conditioned to only see God in small, white communion breads? An early childhood lesson was never to be rude and always greet your neighbors. So, God, were you offended by my rude behavior of not saying "hello?"

> *Open wide my heart to recognize you*
> *in a hundred thousand different forms,*
> *by a holy nod of the head to one and all,*
> *greeting you whom I see in blind faith.*

March 31

The Passing of March

Today, the month of March, having grown old these past days, will die. No wake or funeral is planned. However, the brief thirty-one-day life of March provides a good occasion to reflect on progeria, a rare disease compressing a person's entire life cycle into a few brief years. A victim of this affliction, while only seven or nine years old, will look, act, and actually experience the physical pains of a very old person. Progeria victims die of advanced old age by the time they are twelve, or even younger. There is also a progeria of the spirit. While not a disease, it is a condition that inwardly ages those suffering from it. Outwardly they appear their actual biological age, perhaps thirty or forty, while their thinking and behavior is that of a very old person. The causes of this type of progeria could be a subterranean fear of life itself, homesickness for a bygone era (even if the afflicted never personally experienced it), unhealthy parenting, or self-imposed, protective religious rigidity.

> *Inoculate me from progeria of spirit*
> *that would antique me into a reliquary of the old,*
> *nostalgic and wistful for past days,*
> *by fully embracing the newness of today.*

Month of
April

April 1—April Fools' Day

Comical Communion

Fools, clowns, and jesters invoke laughter. The mystic Meister Eckhart was fond of saying that when he laughed his soul was laughing together with God. If on this classic Feast of Fools a joke or something funny causes you to laugh, rejoice that God is laughing in your soul with you. Unfortunately, there's not much frivolity any more on this ancient feast of foolishness, or on any day in our grim work-addicted culture, or in our solemn, staid churches. Encountering a laughing soul is as extraordinary as finding a diamond in your dishwater. It requires a flying leap of imagination to conceive of something as inconceivable as a laughing soul. Souls pray. Souls meditate. Souls weep. Souls certainly don't giggle or laugh. Grateful then for Meister Eckhart's gift of awareness of comical communion with God, go to communion giggling frequently.

> *Tutor me to consciously remember*
> *with my every laugh and chuckle,*
> *I'm in holy, humorous communion*
> *with God who's laughing in my soul.*

April 2

God Save the Fool—You

No one wants to appear foolish, yet the playwright Theodore Rubin wrote:

> I must learn to love the fool in me, the one
> who feels too much, talks too much, takes
> too many chances . . . lacks self-control, loves
> and hates, hurts and gets hurt . . . laughs and
> cries. It alone protects me against that utterly
> self-controlled, masterful tyrant whom I also
> harbor and who would rob me of human alive-
> ness, humility, and dignity, but for my fool.

Your inner fool is also your inner saint whenever you do as the Teacher taught—even if by doing so you appear foolish to our ever-practical world. Your inner fool is reluctant to show itself in public out of fear of appearing weak or being shamed, and so needs to be coaxed out of the closet. To overcome this fear of appearing foolish, play the clown with yourself when you are alone and laugh about your dumb mistakes and blunders. And be vigilant, for your sleeping tyrant dictator will rob you of your humanity and godhood. Attend to life's duties, but be constantly alert for sneak terrorist attacks of your sleeping tyrant by keeping at your side your inner fool as your personal bodyguard.

> *Challenge me to never fear to cry,*
> *to appear weak or unsophisticated,*
> *so my inner clown can protect me*
> *from becoming a tyrannical dictator.*

April 3

A Mirabilary

We are wonderstruck when we're caught off guard by some amazing or surprising thing or person. Unlike being lightning-struck—which is lethal—being wonderstruck is life-giving and spirit-arousing. If God is the Wonder of Wonders, then to witness any wonder is to have a divine visitation. These are more common than is believed. Admiration is to wonder, to be awed when people act heroically, selflessly, or generously. Normally, we have low expectations of our fellow humans. The unexpectedness of such behaviors are visitations of wonder. We capture this by calling them a "bolt out of the blue," linking them to lightning. Become a bolt out of the blue yourself by being a mirabilary, an uncommon synonym for wonder-worker. Today, surreptitiously plot to be a mirabilary by being a one-person divine visitation. In unexpected places and times, act in a surprisingly unselfish, noble, or heroic way.

> *Inspire me to perform surprise deeds*
> *of unexpected kindness and generosity*
> *for strangers, friends, or family,*
> *and so be your wondrous bolt out of the blue.*

April 4

Where You Find Pardon and Peace

One hundred and eighty years before the birth of Jesus of Nazareth, a Jewish wise man named Sirach wrote: "He who takes vengeance will suffer vengeance from the Lord . . . forgive your neighbor . . . and your sins will be pardoned when you pray." Was Jesus familiar with these words of Sirach, whose full name was Jesus ben Sira? If so, perhaps he was also familiar with another rabbi from Sirach's time who taught: "Transgressions between a man and his neighbor are not expiated by the Day of Atonement, unless the man first makes peace with his neighbor!" Like these two, Jesus taught that freedom from your sins is not experienced in religious rituals of atonement or reconciliation. Liberation comes only when the offender goes to the offended and seeks forgiveness. If you

are seeking pardon and freedom from guilt, find it by heroically embracing the challenge that predates the teaching of
Jesus of Nazareth, by making peace with the one whom you
have offended.

> *Embolden me to bravely face the one*
> *I have offended and ask for pardon.*
> *Let me receive peace not in ritual confession*
> *but from the person whom I have hurt.*

April 5

Precarious

Life is precarious! We live in a world filled with potential dangers. Militants with suicide bombs target civilians in crowded
places. Every day we hear of natural disasters or deadly diseases that kill thousands. Life is indeed precarious, but thank
God for that! The next time you find yourself in a precarious
place, be grateful! Did you know that *precarious* means "full
of prayers!" *Precarious* is Latin and means "prayer or begging." We adopted it from its original Latin into English as a
descriptive adjective for any dangerous, life-threatening situation. Not only is walking all alone down a dark alley in some

big city slum—or along the narrow fragile ledge of a high cliff—precarious, paradoxically so is sitting in church!

> *When all is calm and peaceful,*
> *inspire me to be precarious,*
> *since being full of prayer*
> *is being filled full of God.*

April 6

Uncage Your Animal

The renowned Swiss psychologist Carl Jung said, "It is difficult to say to anybody, you should . . . become acquainted with your animal." Jung was aware that we associate the animal part of ourselves with being wild, even acting insane. As a result, we aren't inclined to become friendly with our animal nature. Begrudgingly, we acknowledge we have an animal nature. We are ashamed of its primitive instincts and hungers. We take great pride in our IQ, our human intellectual abilities. We enjoy stimulating ideas and mental activities, yet do not find the same pleasure in our animalness. However, to become fully human requires bringing to full maturity both our animal and human natures. Perhaps someday psychologists will create a test for measuring your AQ, the degree of your animal quotient! Just as those with a low IQ are excused for their stupid or inappropriate behaviors, perhaps we will do the same for those with low AQs. Regardless how high their IQ, we will excuse their lack of naturalness and their inability to lustily enjoy the sensual delights of being a human animal.

> *Stir me to express my animal-hood,*
> *to eat with non-human sounds of joy,*
> *to howl with delight in a hot shower,*
> *so to feel all of me that God has made.*

April 7

Your Enemies Are Your Best Friends

Jesus, the Galilean teacher and sage, called his disciples to the seemingly impossible task of loving their enemies. One possible rationale for this radically impossible teaching could be that we are all one, and therefore your enemy is *you*! Another could be that your enemies are good mirrors. They tend to be frank, to be bluntly truthful. The novelist Stephen King said, "Only enemies speak the truth; friends and lovers lie endlessly, caught in the web of duty." Comments from friends like, "You look great" or "You haven't aged, you look the same as you did ten years ago," can easily be loving lies. Sharp as barbed wire but authentically useful are the opinions of those who don't love us. So listen to and seriously ponder the truthfulness of what your enemies say about you. If their words are true, then take action to correct them.

> *Embolden me not to cringe about*
> *what I hear is said behind my back,*
> *and help me receive the naked truth*
> *my loving friends can't say to me.*

April 8

Awakening the Third Eye

The Zen tea ceremony began to flourish around the twelfth century as a ritual drinking of tea that employed reverence and tranquility as a means of awakening the third eye of insight. One aspect of the tea ceremony is the inspection by the guests of the ceramic teacups, spoons, and other objects to be used in the tea ritual. These are viewed not as we Westerners would see them for their practicality, but instead as visual objects of beauty to be appreciated as part of the total experience of the tea ceremony. We eat our meals on mass manufactured dinnerware that we typically treat as purely functionary objects.

Even if they are not as artistic as original crafted Zen tea-cups, look anew at your dinnerware with reverence for its beauty as a way to open your third eye. Daily life is crowded with ordinary objects dismissed as merely functional, but they can become gateways to insight. In the eyes of the ancients, dining was a sacred event. So before placing food on your plate, pause to gaze reverently at the plate and admire its beauty. Through this mini-ritual, you help to open your third eye to a visual and spiritual feast.

> *Third eye, the eye of my heart,*
> *be opened as I reverently handle*
> *the common objects of my meals*
> *so I can see far more Life in life.*

April 9

Jazz Up Sacred Scriptures

To find peace, happiness, and God in the inspiring words of the Bible, the Koran, or the teachings of Buddha, don't memorize them. Instead, like a jazz musician, approach these inspired texts and see them as musical scores to be jazzed up by extemporizing on them with the notes of life. Then, as would a jazz musician, improvise the words of scripture by playing the inspired text with your right hand while with your left you play the jazz and joys of daily life. Life is a song, so learn to play it by ear without a printed score that must be rigidly followed. Playing with life or scripture implies playfulness, the creative source of jazz. Those who play their lives instead of just living them find each day to be melodically joyful.

> *To make your words live, show me how to play*
> *with one hand "Seek first the Kingdom of God,"*
> *while the other improvises by jazzing it up with*
> *"Seek life. Seek love. Seek peace and harmony."*

April 10

Post-Crowd Traumatic Stress

A good friend, a psychologist, says that my PCTS (Post-Crowd Traumatic Stress) can result from two causes: the first is just the energy required to be fully present to those to whom you are speaking; the second cause, interestingly, of this stress after attending an event can be the energy expended from suppressing what you would really like to say to some people! This polite suppression is an especially likely suspect for PCTS when you've reached a ripe age, since by then you have little patience for religious fakery, and political or social hypocrisy.

Also, with older age, that youthful addiction to approval diminishes, so the truth more easily wins in a wrestling match with politeness. Was the Galilean spiritual master, Jesus, suffering from PCTS when he boldly called the Pharisees hypocrites to their faces? Or was he trying to awaken them by using a type of provocative shock treatment?

> *Since I am not indifferent to being loved,*
> *teach me when to speak*
> *and when to keep silent*
> *with those sadly stone deaf to hearing the truth.*

April 11

The Great Untruth

Shakespeare places a commonly held belief on the lips of his King Lear, "Let not women's weapons, water drops, stain my man's cheeks!" Instilled in boys since childhood is the untruth that to weep is a sign of weakness. Babies cry, big boys don't! Infants are usually twenty weeks old before they laugh, but they cry with their first breath. Infants, being unable to express their needs to their parents with words, communicate them by crying. Women and children are given license to legitimately cry in public, men are not. That's macho mischief, since tears, like laughter, are human emotions that say what is beyond the power of words to express. Tears and laughter result from an overflowing heart occasioned by some deeply moving experience: agonizing pain, a theatrical drama, grief, great joy, or immense beauty. It is not a sign of weakness but of strength for a man to weep openly in public, since only a strong, mature man isn't ashamed of his humanity.

> *Remind me, male or female, that no license*
> *is required to allow my soul and heart*
> *to express my full humanity by weeping*
> *tears of sadness, joy, delight, or wonder.*

April 12

Escaping the Blue Dragon of Gloom

When gloom moves in, we should move out! Dr. Martin Groder, a psychiatrist from Chapel Hill, North Carolina, suggests an immediate change in environment. He encourages doing such simple things as rearranging the furniture or pictures in your home. Move out of doors and allow yourself to be responsive to the vast world of creation so Dr. Nature can chase away the Blue Dragon. Groder also encourages spending time with the arts: listening to classical music, visiting an art gallery, even flipping through a book of beautiful paintings. Engage life creatively, not only by enjoying the art of others but also by creating your own: drawing and painting, playing a musical instrument, or preparing a creative meal.

> *As the Blue Dragon whispers, "Roll in a ball,*
> *close the shutters, brood alone in your gloom,"*
> *inspire me to unroll myself outward into life,*
> *art, or nature, and so escape out of my gloom.*

April 13

A Gift to Accomplish the Seemingly Impossible

Back in the 1950s when the Roman Catholic Mass was in Latin and I was a young seminarian, I recall being terrified when I was told that I was assigned to read the Epistle in Latin at High Mass. As a struggling Latin student I knew my Latin pronunciation would be terrible. I agonized at having to read in front of my professors and the other monks, as well as several hundred fellow seminarian students. When I shared my sweaty anxiety with a wise teacher, he said, "With the mission or task comes the grace to execute it." Inwardly I chanted these words over and over as I read my Latin scriptural reading. To this day I don't know what it sounded like since my heart was pounding so loudly I couldn't hear myself. But those words remain a powerful source of strength for me even now, so many years later. "With the mission comes the grace to execute it." If you are anxious about raising a teenager, performing some public role or church ministry, or whatever difficult task is before you, don't be! Trust that whatever graces or powers necessary to accomplish that task will be given to you, if you but ask.

> *Trusting, I lower my empty bucket*
> *into you, the mystic bottomless well,*
> *filling it full of whatever I truly need*
> *to accomplish the task you've given me.*

April 14

Collecting Garbage

An important and necessary social occupation is the collecting of garbage. This profession is unfortunately not viewed with esteem or respect. When asked what they want to do when they grow up, few children would proudly announce, "I'm going to be garbage collector!" However, a child who announces to his or her parents that their goal in life is to become a banker will be warmly praised. Is collecting money really any different than collecting garbage? Doesn't money, when valued more than family, friends, or morals, become just trash? Jesus warned against the craving for money, a substance of artificially inflated value, and instead urged the zealous collection of what is of real value.

When they arrived at the site of Custer's Last Stand, the relief army troopers sent to his aid found all his troops dead and stripped naked of their clothing and possessions. Over that Little Bighorn hilltop littered with dead bodies the prairie wind was hauntingly blowing the soldiers' paper dollar bills like autumn leaves.

> *When I am anxious about money,*
> *tell me again, that it is transient wealth.*
> *Inspire me to be rich in what*
> *can't be stolen, taxed, or depreciated.*

April 15

Tax Day

If you are disgruntled today at paying the government your hard-earned money in income taxes, blame Mars, the god of war! Income taxes were created in 1861 by Abraham Lincoln's administration as a temporary measure to pay for the Civil War and eventually became a permanent yearly taxation. Americans

are urged not to begrudge paying taxes, but rather to see them
as a civic duty, a just debt for the services the government provides. At the time of writing this reflection, according to the
Center for Arms Control and Non-Proliferation* nearly half
(49 percent) of all our taxes go to support old Mars, the military! America not only spends more money on the military
than any other nation, but more than all other nations com-
bined! The humorist Will Rogers once accidentally overpaid
by very large amount the income tax he owed. When he tried
in vain to claim a rebate, his many letters to the IRS were never
answered. In his next income tax form, in the section marked
"Deductions," Rogers listed the amount of his overpayment as
"Bad Debt, United States Government." When almost half of
my tax money is used for war weapons, I also consider that to
be a "bad debt."

> *Any spirituality of God lies*
> *if void of the affairs of state.*
> *Taunt me to work to change*
> *the way my taxes are spent.*

---

* Source: The Center for Arms Control and Non-Proliferation quoted in
Labyrinthine, Indestructible Economic Force, by Jeff Severns Guntzel. National
Catholic Reporter, March 9, 2007.

April 16

Hanging on a Cross of Iron

Today your wallet or purse still feels the painful extraction of your money to pay your income taxes, so it is a good occasion to reflect on the following words from 1953:

> Every gun that is made, every warship
> launched, every rocket fired, signifies, in
> the final sense, a theft from those who are
> hungry and are not fed, those who are cold
> and are not clothed. The world in arms is not
> spending money alone. It is spending the
> sweat of its laborers, the genius of its scientists,
> the hopes of its children. . . . This is not the
> way of life at all, in any true sense. Under the
> cloud of threatening war, it is humanity
> hanging on a cross of iron.

These are not the words of an anti-war radical; they belong to that distinguished soldier and American hero, President Dwight D. Eisenhower. Take time to reread his words again, and ponder the immorality of your government that spends almost half of your taxes on weapons! Eisenhower did not call these huge expenditures of our taxes on the war establishment a civic duty but a "theft" of money stolen away from the poor, elderly, unnourished, and impoverished.

> *Remind me that my silence is consent!*
> *Open my mouth to loudly object*
> *to this sinful thievery of my country,*
> *else I'll be guilty as an accomplice!*

April 17

A Built-in God Finder

It is calculated that our brains possess a catalog of over fifty thousand different smells! Ah, your nose, what a marvelous gift that you easily take for granted, even if its powers aren't what they once were. Scientists speculate that since prehistoric times humans have lost at least 80 percent of their originally sharp sense of smell. Multiple are the reasons, among them society's recent anti-odor bias, an overly sanitized deodorizing of life. Add to those, "keeping our noses to the grindstone," resulting in smelling only industrial grindstone! Animals, especially dogs and cats, continue to have superior gifts of smell that serve as key sources of information and as their early-warning systems. According to Dr. William Fliess, a friend of Freud's, your nose, even with its diminished powers, is your most important sexual organ. If Fliess is correct, then your nose is a great God-finder, so use it for something more than breathing. Like a bloodhound, use it to sniff out your home, workplace, and neighborhood for the ever-elusive Presence of the Divine Mystery.

> *May I go sniffing my way to heaven,*
> *tracking your strong, pungent scent*
> *in all the 50,000 fragrant, aromatic,*
> *and exotic places you hide from me.*

April 18

Nose Alert

Commercials were once aimed for the eyes; now retailers are targeting your nose! To attract customers, Westin Hotels recently installed air-filtering machines that discharge into their hotel lobbies fragrances that are a mixture of green tea, green ivy, geranium, and black cedar said to create feelings of tranquility and peace. Westin should prudently monitor these fragrance releases lest their guests become so tranquil they insist on sleeping in the lobby instead of going to their rooms! This new scenting of America includes various upscale stores. Some stores are releasing the smell of baby powder in their infant wear departments, and in departments selling intimate and swimming apparel the alluring aromas of lilac and coconut. The common folk wisdom is that the best way to sell a house is to create the aromas of freshly baked chocolate-chip cookies or bread. If synagogues and churches, desirous of attracting more worshippers, installed fragrance machines, what smells should they use?

> *Looking heavenward I ask,*
> *"God, what do you smell like?*
> *Baby powder, bread, or wine,*
> *coconut, sweat, or sacrifice?"*

April 19

The Benefits of Becoming a Passalorynchite

Whenever you find yourself in a difficult conversation, or at other times when you are reluctant to respond sincerely, consider becoming a vowed *passalorynchite*. They were members of an early church sect who took vows of perpetual silence. We all talk too much—with our lips! While complete silence is impractical, consider just talking less by becoming an associate member of that old religious sect. As an associate *passalorynchite* you might find it beneficial and pleasant to communicate at certain times only with smiles of approval, or frowns of questioning or disapproval. As an associate *passolorynchite* you might also discover that a simple nod of your head contains wonderful, expressive eloquence.

> *Teach me silence, the global language,*
> *that speaks volumes*
> *and wordlessly refutes arguments.*
> *Teach me your sacred language.*

April 20

Become a Writer

One of the more magnificent miracles of the Spirit of Creativity is the telephone. Yet it, along with instant messaging and e-mail, appears to be responsible for the demise of letter writing, if not of writing itself. Once everyone who could write was a writer; they wrote letters to one another and kept hand-written diaries or journals. In Egypt, ancient ages ago, this ability to write was considered a gift of the gods to humans, and appropriately was named hieroglyphics—*hiero* (sacred) and *glyphics* (writing). The gods, being divine healers, hid a therapeutic medicine in that gift of writing. To write heals by allowing you to rethink your scattered thoughts in order to put them into words and then to allow you to see in print your thoughts. To see thoughts in print heals by shrinking fears connected to them, as it also allows dreams to become blueprints. To achieve a resolution, write it down. Seeing it in print almost magically energizes you to achieve it. Writing a daily journal transforms your life into a personal adventure by which you can escape from being lost in the faceless mass of an impersonal, technological world.

> *Keeping a daily journal, as do explorers,*
> *makes daily life a grand adventure;*
> *sketching rough maps of treasures found,*
> *even if I venture only around the block.*

April 21

A Gypsy Heart

Beloved by pilgrims in medieval England was the great shrine of our Lady of Walsingham. To the English faithful of the middle ages, the sparkling sky path of the Milky Way pointed the way to the shrine. This gave birth to the following words:

> O stars that point to Walsingham,
> O roads that lead to Rome,
> what can you offer a gypsy heart
> that's forced to stay at home?

Pilgrims believed that pilgrimage was a pious practice that gave healing to both body and soul. America, being such a young country, lacks authentic shrines, believed to be radioactive with God's graces to heal bodies and inspire souls. Since a vast ocean separates us from the centuries-old medieval shrines of Europe, we keenly feel the ache of a gypsy pilgrim heart that's forced to stay at home. Cure your aching gypsy heart, and go on a pilgrimage.

> *Anoint me as a homebound pilgrim,*
> *to tread the prayer paths of my heart,*
> *visiting shrines in my neighborhood*
> *as a content gypsy in your company.*

April 22

Dishonorably Honorable

When is it honorable to be dishonorable? Honor, once described as "an instinct of incomparable beauty," was the most precious possession of a gentleman or lady. Duels with swords or pistols were fought between men because one of them felt the other had cast doubts upon his honor. "It is the honorable thing to do," could mean marrying a woman you didn't love but whose pregnancy was your shared responsibility, or marching off to be killed or wounded in some war. Not to loyally defend the actions of your government, be they right or wrong, is viewed as being dishonorable. Refusing to continue to wage war is grounds for a dishonorable discharge from the military and the source of life-long shame. And ordained ministers are expected to be honorable, to always loyally endorse their church's teachings and rules. So when is it honorable to be dishonorable? As you prepare to answer, remember that imprinted on the military belt buckles of Heinrich Himmler's S.S. troops was the slogan, "My Honor Is Loyalty."

> *Whenever someone offends your honor,*
> *do the truly honorable thing—do nothing!*
> *For evil, Jesus taught, do not return any evil,*
> *so in God's eyes you will be honorable.*

April 23

A Closet Mystic

You were born a latent mystic and a soul explorer. Developing this vocation is indispensable to your spirituality. Yet, if you believe that "mystic-hood" is only achieved by meticulously following exacting methods in ever-escalating stages, you will never leave home for Home! Being your primal vocation, mystic-hood requires an everyday expedition to discover the Divine Mystery hidden incognito in the commonplace. Your soul is safari-ready, yet you are apt to dillydally with daily demands. While exciting, this greatest of all quests can also be exhausting and frustrating. Nothing defies penetration like the familiar, as John O'Donohue says. The familiar tends to be immensely numbing, and so can paralyze your soul's spirit of discovery. Be hopeful, however, for the Invisible aches to become visible; the Holy Hidden cave to be revealed. Pray for the grace of a soul explorer willing and eager to struggle to break open and re-mystify your domesticated, mundane world.

> *Make me a blind seeker who*
> *by longing and faith touching*
> *finds you, the Unseen Mystery,*
> *in whatever and whoever I touch.*

April 24

Wondrous Envelopes

While not invented until 1839, nothing is so common in our lives as a paper envelope. Previous to that inspired invention, people simply folded their letters over and sealed them shut with wax, often adding in it a seal of their initials. Then the folded sealed paper was turned over and the address of the person to whom the letter was written was printed on the front side. The envelope itself being part of the letter made it feel a more intimate connection with the sender. Envelopes contain more than letters and bills. Adventures, people, and even God come in envelopes! God seems to enjoy employing the use of the widest possible variety of envelopes in all shapes, sizes, and colors. Just as we say to never judge a book by its cover, so too never judge an envelope by its appearance. The Inexplicable Mystery defies all containment. Yet God delights in coming to you in all kinds of envelopes: strangers, oak trees, and letters from friends.

> *Ricochet me back to my childhood*
> *and awaken my delight in surprises,*
> *so I can thrill when unexpectedly*
> *I find you inside a common envelope.*

April 25

Boomeranged

Whenever you say anything that contradicts something you previously said, boomerangs inscribed "BYS" can come flying back to strike you saying, "But you said." Some people

make a sport of boomeranging. They enjoy flinging statements back at those who have changed their opinion on any
subject. Boomerangs are weapons that leave bruises, and they
can be embarrassing. To avoid boomerangs we are tempted to
keep our opinions to ourselves. After all, contradicting yourself implies you are a flip-flopper, a windsock thinker whose
opinions change with the wind's direction. Don't give in to that
temptation! Abraham Lincoln was a popular target for B.Y.S.
boomerangs. When struck by one he would reply, "Yes, that is
what I said yesterday, but I hope that I'm smarter today than I
was yesterday."

> *Daily may I grow smarter and change*
> *my mind, and so contradict myself.*
> *Inflexible easy chairs or pulpit dogmas,*
> *like old Egyptian mummies, are dead.*

April 26

Too Late

All disasters in war could be explained, General Douglas
MacArthur said, by two words: *too late*. Not only in war,
but in marriage, religion, and in every aspect of life can disasters be explained by the words *too late*. In war the needed

reinforcements arrived too late. In marriage reconcilable differences are faced too late to avoid the disaster of a divorce. By not repairing a small leak on your roof or inspecting that minor noise in your car engine, disasters occur because costly repairs arrived too late. Religion, that holy inflexible protector of the past, begrudgingly and tardily changes her rules and teachings too late to prevent the departure of many believers. If what needs attention is your marriage or your lifestyle, do it before it's too late. If what needs changing is an addiction or health condition, do it now, today, or else it will all too quickly be too late.

> *Castigate me for procrastinating,*
> *lest I continue inventing excuses,*
> *"tomorrowizing" what cries out*
> *to be done today, without delay.*

April 27

Compulsive Addiction

The Sufi spiritual master, Rumi, a devout alcoholic-abstaining Muslim, used wine frequently as a metaphor for spiritual ecstasy. Here is one of my favorite sayings of his: "Two strong impulses: one to drink long and deep, and the other, not to sober up too soon." This is poetic insight about a deeply religious experience in which one is swept away by a transcendental tsunami and wishes it would never end. The mystical occurrence could be the awesome birth of a child, escaping some disaster by a hair, or being swept aloft to the stars while hearing the music of Bach played on a massive pipe organ. Addiction doesn't happen with just one taste, but only after numerous uses of the substance. However, with the intoxicating Divine Substance one hit can hook you for life, so beware. Cautiously remember that old saying from the Orient, "If you don't have room in your living room for an elephant, then don't make friends with an elephant trainer."

> *Grant me a hawk's eyesight to recognize*
> *in a crowd of licensed elephant trainers,*
> *the real dangerous ones, lest I foolishly*
> *become hooked on divine elephantitis!*

April 28

The Best Pentecostal Fire

An eager student tingling with excitement asked, "Teacher, what do you think about charismatics? Last night at a Pentecostal prayer meeting I had hands laid on me, and now I'm filled with the fire of the Holy Spirit!" "As there are many roads to God, so too there are many ways to be gifted by the Holy Spirit," the teacher replied. The baptized-in-the-Spirit-student then asked, "Teacher, don't you think speaking in tongues and the fiery enthusiasm of charismatics are wonderful?" After several moments of silence, the teacher said, "Prairie fires are exciting and colorful, but alas, they're usually short-lived. The best fires are those in kitchen stoves."

> *In my ordinary heart,*
> *build a hidden inferno*
> *to produce fiery acts*
> *as my tongues of love.*

April 29

An Upside Down Victory

During the dark days of World War II, Sir Winston Churchill popularized the "V" for victory sign. To properly make this sign, spread the first and second fingers of the right hand apart in a "V"shape with, most importantly, your palm facing toward yourself. When President Ronald Reagan came to England to visit the Queen he gave the crowds the "V" sign with his palm facing the people. Unfortunately, no White House assistant had informed him that the British consider giving that hand sign with the palm facing others to be a vulgar, offensively derisive sign. There is also a third and non-offensive way to use that "V" sign. Instead of pointing your two extended fingers upward, point them downward with your palm outward. An old belief held this upside down "V" sign insured triumph over evil. It possessed the charmed power to drive the Evil One back down into hell! Evil diabolically visits us on numerous occasions. Awareness protects us, so when next you're in the presence of evil, discreetly make an upside down "V" victory sign.

Whether dressed in pure angelic white with a halo,
riding by in a black bulletproof limousine,
or clutching a big bible while ranting hate,
beware; dark and sinister evil is ever near.

April 30

Changing Behavior

Per Olofsson of Stockholm has created a novel solution to global warming with his solar-powered heating and air-conditioning unit. His invention will allow the average home to reduce its release of carbon dioxide by thirteen tons a year!

However, Olofsson realizes that while his new technology will greatly benefit the environment, it will not be easily embraced by society. He says, "Changing behavior is more difficult than changing technology." Tomorrow you will change your calendar from April to May. If only changes in our behavior were as easy as flipping a page of the calendar. The media enthusiastically announces each new breakthrough in computer, industrial, or medical technology. Could we be inspired to personally change if the media, along with news of new technological advancements, had parallel stories of women and men who had achieved significant behavior changes? We need role models, enticing pioneers of self-reinvention to respond to the radical technological and sociological changes of our rapidly changing world. We desperately need new people for new inventions.

> *Inspire me to be a self-reinventor,*
> *to banish fears of being different*
> *and break old habits inhibiting me,*
> *so to redesign myself as a new me.*

Month of

May

May 1

Merry May

Today begins the "Merry Month of May," an expression no longer frequently heard as a description of this new month. The term *merry*, as in "God Rest Ye Merry Gentlemen" or "Merry Christmas," was once a popular adjective in England. It was also applied to the companions in arms of a knight or outlaw, as when Robin Hood's companions were called his "merry men." Obviously, Robin's companions were famous for being robbers, not jolly. The Old English expression "merry" meant pleasant, delightful, and even holy. In today's world of instant global communication, disasters around the world are almost daily events, so any pleasant news is indeed merrily delightful. After a cold snowy winter, followed by a blustery March and chilly, rainy April, the flowers, songbirds, and sunny warm days of May make it a truly merry month. If only we could match the merriment of May in our attitude toward life and our fellow humans, what a difference in our world it would make.

> *"Rejoice always," said old St. Paul.*
> *Live in a merry mood so you will be*
> *living advertisements of the Joyous One*
> *within you, who is eager to be experienced.*

May 2

Crowded Conversations

It is believed in certain cultures that when two people are engaged in a conversation, they are not alone! The belief is that whenever two are engaged in a conversation—there are at least six other persons present! The first two are what each person actually says to the other. The next two are what each of the two meant to say, and the final two are what each of them understood was said by the other, so making a conversational crowd of six. To be a good listener in a conversation, empty yourself of yourself. Strive to return to the present from frequent audio absenteeism so you can be consciously attentive to what the other is saying. Attempt to plug your ears so as not to hear the haranguing voices of your thoughts endlessly engaged in filibustering. Finally, glue the ear of Sherlock Holmes onto your head so you can decipher the other's unintended encrypted messages. Do these things so as to enjoy a private conversation with only two persons present.

> *Please graft on to my head a third ear,*
> *to hear better what is trying to be said,*
> *to uncover what is actually being said,*
> *and so be a loving, understanding listener.*

May 3

Fat Plump Prayers

An admirable ritual observance worthy of your imitation is the Muslim practice of praying five times a day. But the duty is more than to pray, since the Prophet Mohammed taught that for the five prayers to truly be prayer they had to be accompanied by *hudhur*, presence. For the prophet, as it was for all great spiritual teachers, the validity of each prayer required that it be filled with one's substance, the presence of the person who was praying. Jewish spiritual masters spoke of this necessity as well, saying that each word—even each letter of each word—should be filled with substance, with fire and love. So the next time you pray, even if you are not especially religious and are attending a funeral or wedding where the pastor says, "Let us pray," don't pray skinny prayers! In fact, don't pray at all! Believer or not, it is better to say nothing if you are only mechanically mouthing empty or halfhearted words. Silence is golden, valued by God infinitely more than empty, unoccupied prayers.

> *Call me to a halt before I pray,*
> *to inhale deeply, then breathe out*
> *into my prayers all of who I am,*
> *making them precious as pearls.*

May 4

Fast-Love

The popularity of fast-food dining and eating on the go would have been as unimaginable to ancient peoples as making love on the go. To them, today's hamburgers and fries eaten on the run would be a truncated meal. Yet fifty years from now it may well be called an old fashioned meal! It may take even less than fifty years to realize a secret desire of overworked, busy Americans to get rid of the time wasted preparing meals, eating them, and having to clean up afterward. Science may gift us with such a time-saving miracle: the ability to nourish our bodies quickly by swallowing a handful of pills. But in previous ages meals were more than nourishing the body. They were events to be leisurely enjoyed, where the food was properly seasoned with time, conversation, and stories. If you are hungry for a spiritual renewal, there is no need to go to a monastery or a lonely mountaintop—go to your dining room table. Hungry for a mystical experience? Go to your kitchen and prepare with love and delight a delicious meal.

> *Arouse my appetite for leisurely eating,*
> *remind me that all meal times are sacred,*
> *daily seders and luncheon Last Suppers,*
> *so to rescue an endangered sacred species.*

May 5

A Clandestine Method to Holiness

"Teacher," a student proudly proclaimed, "every day I strive to learn something new and to take on some new spiritual task so I can quickly become holy." "No one becomes holy in a hurry, " replied the teacher. "The best way to become Godlike is not to take on some new work each day, but instead, to drop something daily." The ancient scriptures of China say that in the pursuit of learning, "every day something is acquired." In the pursuit of the Way, the Tao, "every day something is dropped." If you had a seven-day drop list, what might it contain? Make a pledge to take the most difficult step of all—drop part of yourself. If a daily drop is not possible, then seriously consider a pledge of a once-a-week disposal.

> *As a clinger-on, encourage me*
> *to drop whatever is holding me back*
> *from being a better, kinder,*
> *and a more patient, loving person.*

May 6

Only a Breath's Difference

In the rainforest of northwestern Brazil, along the banks of a tributary of the Amazon called the Maici River, lives a small tribe of hunter-gatherers called the Piraha. Their language is one of the simplest known, based on just eight consonants and three vowels that are expressed with a complex and rich variety of tones and inflections. It reflects the great simplicity of their customs and living conditions in which they speak only in very brief sentences exclusively in the present tense. After many years of missionary effort, the simplicity of their language has to this date prevented a translation of the New Testament into their native tongue, and their conversion to Christianity. Perhaps no conversion is needed! Unlike in our language where there are two distinct words for *enemy* and *friend*, the Piraha have only one word whose meaning changes with the changing of a single syllable! Jesus of Galilee taught, but we refuse to learn, that an enemy is to be loved as oneself. Could that mean that in the beginning the words *friend* and *enemy* were spoken by God in the same breath as one word?

The next time when hurt or offended,
when the word enemy comes to mind,
inspire me to pause, take a deep breath,
and exhale, "enemy-me, me-enemy."

May 7

The Doctor

A ship's cook was once known in naval parlance as the "the doctor," since the crew believed he doctored up the food. As a ship's cook had to doctor up spoiled food, so also did peasants and the poor. Without refrigeration, cooks in previous ages attempted to disguise rotting meat by the use of sauces, wine, and potent herbs. In some churches today, the minister with a doctorate in divinity or theology is called doctor. Any good pastor, rabbi, or mullah could merit the title of doctor in a medical sense if he or she astutely diagnoses the real pains and afflictions of the congregations. And if they are authentic soul-doctors, they don't doctor up struggles and sacrifices with pious placebos. Religion is ancient medicine, but it can cause painful afflictions as well as cure them. If you are suffering from some type of spiritual affliction and can't find an authentic spiritual doctor, follow the old Palestinian proverb, "Physician, heal thyself."

Seeking healing for my soul afflictions,
and failing to be cured by professionals,
come heal me. And even if I am not licensed,
together we will be spiritual physicians.

May 8

Every Breath a Lesson

The holy sixteenth-century rabbi Isaac Luria of Safed pro-posed a solution to an ageless rabbinical problem arising from the principle that God's presence is everywhere. If this was so, how was there any room left to create the world in a cosmos filled with the divine presence? Rabbi Luria proposed the mys-tery of *tzimtzum,* the contraction of God having to make room for the world. If you compared this divine contraction to what you are doing at this actual moment, *tzimtzum* isn't as mystify-ingly inexplicable as it first appears. The act of breathing first requires a breath that must be exhaled before another can be inhaled. Like the first creation, daily life requires continuous creativity to find solutions to a variety of issues. Being creative and inspired requires inhaling, withdrawing into yourself. When forced to face your next difficulty, don't face it, retreat! Draw into yourself, do nothing, then out of nothing can come something new and creative.

Let me live the old catechism lesson
that God made the world out of nothing.
Let me face any predicament inspired
to inhale, then breathe out the solution.

May 9

A Tailless Cow

When confronted with some difficulty, concerned friends often say, "Trust in God. Pray. Don't worry. Everything's going to be OK." Their intentions are good, and they are only trying to be helpful by encouraging you that the situation isn't helpless if you leave everything in God's hands. Whenever we are hurting or feel impotent in responding to what's beyond our control, we can go for help to the Fixer-Upper God. We prayer-dial 911, wanting the Magician God to work wonders on our shaky marriage by making it honeymoon stable again, or cure our baby clinging to life in an intensive care unit. Instead of turning over your problem to God to solve, you might find it helpful to ponder this African proverb: "God will not drive flies from a tailless cow."

No situation is out of my control.
I am never impotent or powerless.
My fate's form is in my control,
if I have the willpower to adjust to it.

May 10

Don't Use a Secondhand Nest

"There are no eggs this year in last year's nest." This old proverb is worth contemplating in this month when birds are building new nests to lay their eggs. Unlike birds, we humans return to old solutions that formerly worked to find resolution for today's difficulties. We also presume since there were eggs last year in that nest, why shouldn't we find new eggs in the same nest this year? Be practical; why build a new nest when the old one is still useable? As creatures of habit in our marriages we tend to resort to former ways of loving and interacting, and in life employing the same old patterns to accomplish our dreams. Eggs are ancient spring symbols of new life. For your marriage, work, or prayer life to be fresh requires a different nest to birth the new. Lovebirds know that the secret of fresh love is variety! Unlike birds, we don't need to find new nesting materials. Simply take whatever you used to build the original nest now in need of new life and creatively rearrange those twigs into a new nest with affectionate loving.

> *Ancient is the lure to use old solutions*
> *to solve our new problems and trials.*
> *New tribulations need fresh solutions,*
> *and nests to incubate new egg-ideas.*

May 11

"Schaff" It

Schaff is German for sleep, but also actually means loose or relaxed. To relax or hang loose by taking a nap could get you fired in our very uptight, pressurized working world. Naps are for retired seniors and nursing home residents. Naps are illegal activities for any up-and-coming dynamic worker in our always-on-duty, 24/7, cell-phone world. *Schaff* is also the secret of Judo, the Eastern discipline and art of self-defense: *Ju* means soft, and *do* means art. The soft art of Judo is responding in a loose, relaxed, and even care-less way. In the art of Judo you remain loose so your enemy's aggressive angry energy becomes the force that overcomes him or her. Instead of assuming a rigid defensive position, a Judo master is loose and moves gracefully with the aggressor's force allowing his aggressive energy to flip him over in defeat. The next time you feel you must take some defensive position, respond instead with the *schaff* of a Judo artist. Or when pushed to work more to get the job done, instead take a nap or hang loose. You'll accomplish more work.

> *Wise are those caught napping*
> *when tension ties them in knots,*
> *for when they are relaxed and loose,*
> *tangled knots untie themselves.*

May 12

Heaven Bound, We Hope

Sermons on hell outnumber those on heaven ninety-nine to one. Since heaven is the destination of all believers, people ask, "What is heaven like?" Heaven is described as dwelling in the presence of God in a place of eternal rest and peace. Yet perpetual rest implies doing nothing! Doing nothing sounds at first like an eternal vacation for those who have worked eight hours or more a day for their entire lives. Yet a paradise of eternal rest that means no cooking, no laundry, no gardening, no trips to the grocery store, no sports, and no television sounds boring! When you've had to sit in a doctor's waiting room with nothing to do, haven't you found that experience boring? Once a small child died a sudden death, and of course went directly to heaven. After several days in heaven the small child went to God and said, "If I'm good today, may I play in hell tomorrow?"

> *As much of our busy work is worthless,*
> *practice your heaven by doing nothing;*
> *enjoy just being in the present moment,*
> *and find having to wait to be heavenly.*

May 13

Speak Little, Listen Much

President Calvin Coolidge was famous for his limited use of words. On one occasion when he was given a walking cane to commemorate his visit to a city, the presenter went on and on. He spoke lavishly about the merits of President Coolidge and all he had accomplished. He finished by presenting Coolidge with the walking stick saying, "This beautifully fashioned mahogany cane is as solid as the surf-sprayed coast of Maine. This mahogany walking stick is as beautiful as the shores of the great state of California." President Coolidge stood up and smiled as he acknowledged the presence of the gathered crowd, and upon accepting the cane he simply said, "Birch." Then he sat down.

> *Help me ration my words as wisely*
> *as if each one cost a hundred dollars,*
> *so others have ample time to speak*
> *and I have time to truly listen to them.*

May 14

A Prayer to Begin Your Day

Since humans first began to pray they have greeted each new day with a prayer. In all religions you find these sunrise or beginning-the-day prayers. Charles de Foucauld, a former French Foreign Legionnaire, had abandoned the practice of his faith in his youth. Later in his life he became a deeply religious man who wrote the following prayer to begin his day:

> Father, I abandon myself into your hands.
> Do with me whatever you want.
> I will be only grateful for whatever you
>   choose to do.
> I am prepared for anything; I accept
>   everything.

It isn't easy to pray this prayer wholeheartedly. Yet those who can live this prayer are able to accept unexpected misfortunes graciously. Empowered to greet disappointments with gratitude and prepared for anything, they will not be among the victims of life's emotional Pearl Harbors or 9/11 attacks. Such total abandonment is only possible for those who see God as their beloved, and themselves as beloved by God.

> *Life is crowded with unexpected events,*
> *so let me live the Coast Guard motto,*
> *"Semper paratus," always be prepared,*
> *by abandoning myself into your hands.*

May 15

Ancient Arithmetic

The Piraha, a small tribe of Brazilian hunter-gatherers mentioned in the May 6 reflection, retain a tribal culture and simple language that remains basically unchanged since primitive times. Their uncomplicated arithmetic, also found among pre-industrialized native peoples elsewhere in the world, amounts to counting "one, two, many." This easy computation that uses "many" to mean anything more than two would be judged a simplistic exaggeration by industrial cultures that require the use of precise computation. Yet the measurement of "many," even if inaccurate, is a poetic and encompassing way to count the years you've been married, lived in the same house, been friends, or worked for some company. The lavishly generous word *many* is also a marvelous measurement of the abundance of good things of life you've been given.

> *I am grateful for my heart's many beats*
> *that have pumped life into me,*
> *for the many times I have been loved,*
> *and my many mistakes pardoned.*

May 16

Well-Maintained Antiques

Antiques are beautiful, but being old like them isn't! Billions of dollars are spent annually on hair dyes, hairpieces, facial creams, and skin tucks attempting to camouflage an antique look. It is natural and psychologically healthy to want to look as good as possible. But attempting to camouflage the effects of growing old or reversing the aging process can be a type of idolatry, especially in a culture that worships slim-bodied gods and goddesses of youthfulness. Exercise is a necessary good, and physical fitness is important for healthy bodies and souls and for well-functioning brains. But it can slip into the idolatry all too easily. Engage in the exercise of inner aerobics if you desire to age gracefully but not grow old: think radical new ideas, dream of new adventures, embrace newness, and discipline yourself to find the same beauty you see in the most costly antiques—and also in aging, old people.

> *Inspire me to be an artist of aging,*
> *using my own body as my canvas*
> *upon which to paint beauty, vitality,*
> *enthusiasm, and joy by my thoughts.*

May 17

I Can't Remember

To remember, we need to forget; and when we forget, we need to re-member. The mind's function of memory is marvelously well-suited to daily life. Imagine how difficult grocery shopping would be if you never forgot your previous grocery lists. To remember where you parked your car at the crowded shopping mall requires that you forget where you parked it the last time. According to Dr. Neil Macrae, a psychologist at England's University of Bristol, this automatic, unconscious process called *temporary forgetting* is essential for remembering life's daily events. This unconscious, automatic ability can become conscious and intentional when we prayerfully intend to forget in order to forgive. When we are engaged in such holy forgetting, we re-member the body of Christ. Through reconciliation we rejoin two members of the Body who have been separated.

> Give me your miraculous eraser
> to scrub away again and again,
> Seventy times seven times seven if necessary,
> what love demands be forgotten.

May 18

No Idle Wish

Scripture abounds with persons giving blessings and others asking to be blessed. The biblical theologian Walter Brueggemann described a blessing as an act, gesture, or word whereby one person transmits the power of life to another. The blessings of God are usually envisioned as ethereal, otherworldly. Perhaps this is because after having been blessed abundantly in a church service, it is rare for any tangible benefit to be experienced. Those of past ages knew curses and blessings were not idle words. Just as you can unknowingly be infected by a virus, so your life can be unknowingly recharged by a blessing.

The one who is blessing is an instrument of the transmission of divine life, so take every blessing seriously. Pause before a blessing at meals, blessing your children, or the indirect blessings of saying "goodbye," a contraction of the blessing "God be with you." Envision yourself as a lightning rod through which a mystic lightning bolt is about to pass, down and outward. Life offers ten thousand occasions to secretly bless. Use them.

I raise my hand, palm outward,
pausing to allow your lightning
to invisibly flash down into me
and out through my hand into all I bless.

May 19

A Long Line Is a Dead Line

Life is precious. Don't waste it, even though sometimes you can't help it. A recent study showed the average amount of time the ordinary person spends waiting in line is five years! You can wonder if five years is accurate, since you likely are convinced that the correct number must surely be more like ten or fifteen years! The loss of those years is one reason for being angry when someone cuts ahead of you in a line of traffic. Another reason is the Anglo-Saxon cardinal rule that to cut into the line ahead of others is the mortal sin of cheating. Those who rudely violate this unspoken cardinal rule are judged as discourteous, even uncivilized. In this age where courtesy is considered an antiquated virtue and more and more people commit this mortal sin, how do we respond to uncivilized, impolite behavior? Begin by asking yourself: Is some emergency the reason for them cutting in line? Are they perhaps late for an important commitment? Is waiting actually a negative activity? Living peacefully in a chaotic world requires living in reality. Accept the reality of waiting and the reality of humanity as it is, not as it should be.

> *Tattoo on my heart the desire to be*
> *like you, Eternally Patient One,*
> *who never wearies waiting for me*
> *to grow up as a living image of you.*

May 20

God Bless You!

For millennia, whenever someone sneezes it has been customary to offer a blessing. Arabs traditionally clasp hands and reverently bow, while Italians say *"Felicita"* and Germans respond *"Gesundheit."* Ages ago the Roman custom was to say "Congratulations," since the sneeze was seen as the body's attempt to expel sinister spirits, and those about to sneeze were blessed with "Good luck to you." Our English sneeze blessing of "God bless you" began in the sixth century as a papal command by Pope Gregory the Great. At that time Italy was beset with a virulent pestilence, and one of its symptoms was persistent sneezing. From expelling evil spirits, a prediction of your death, to a symptom of a plague, sneezing was seen by the ancients as a deadly if not dangerous act. Don't smile—it seems those of previous ages were correct to judge sneezing as deadly. Science informs us today that when you sneeze all your bodily functions including your heart cease! When all bodily functions cease, you're dead, even if only for a microsecond!

> *Awaken me to my minuscule deaths,*
> *to my many heart attacks upon sneezing,*
> *After each sneeze, let me have*
> *a little Easter and come alive again.*

May 21

The Speechless Wonder of Awe

The great genius Albert Einstein was nicknamed by his parents as a child, *der Depperte,* or, the dopey one. Albert was so unusually slow in learning that his parents consulted a doctor about their young son who had such difficultly in speaking. Einstein later explained that his slow verbal development actually was an advantage since it allowed him "to observe with wonder" the everyday things that others took for granted. He said that unlike others who puzzled over mysterious things, he was awestruck over the most commonplace. This exploration of the common paradoxically led Einstein to do the same with the cosmos. When asked, he defined his faith as a reverence for the creation of the universe and its laws, and the mysteriousness of their nature. If, like Einstein, you wish to experience the mysteriousness of life, then practice being slow to speak. Even if you appear to be *der depperte* by lacking words to describe or name some commonplace thing, you may discover the awe of its wonderfulness.

> *Make me a scientist of the commonplace*
> *puzzling over the mystery of daily stuff,*
> *wordlessly probing for the Great Mystery,*
> *the Mother of wonders and the awesome.*

May 22

You're Welcome

The polite English response to "thank you" is that strange and puzzling reply, "You're welcome." If taken literally it should be followed by a question: "Welcome to where or to what?" After searching through countless resource books of English expressions, I was unable to find any source for our polite acknowledgment to being thanked. So let's play with the mystical meanings of that expression. When you say thank you for some kindness, some act by a family member, waitress, or clerk, you acknowledge their action isn't something that is due to you—it is a gift. To habitually say thank you to others is to humbly consider them more important than you. Failing to say it implies you are superior and have no need to thank servants who are only doing their duty. Addiction to being grateful is an imperial way to dwell in the presence of the Giver of all Gifts. So, "you're welcome" can be a marvelous acknowledgement that the speaker is an usher who welcomes you into the mystical presence.

> *Don't limit gratitude to humans;*
> *machines untiringly serve us,*
> *all creatures confer on us gifts,*
> *so thank tirelessly each of them.*

May 23

The Urge to Be a Hero

Youth feels the urge to be heroic, and this desire lures many into dangerous occupations, especially military service. True, wars offer a fertile field to act heroically, yet Buddha offers another and better field. He says even if you were to conquer in battle a thousand times a thousand men, the one who conquers oneself is the greater warrior. Self-conquering comes only with self-control. Disciplining of self is essential for anyone seeking to heroically confront life's unfortunate circumstances, be they physical drawbacks or powerful emotions. Raised a Hindu, Buddha's words about conquering yourself rephrased the ancient teaching of Hinduism: "The one who restrains his anger from bolting within him is the true hero and charioteer, not the one who slays in battle many foes." Such true heroes and heroines are urgently needed in our violent world that glamorizes brute force. It requires courage and true heroism to be a peaceful, nonviolent person. Town squares don't have statues that commemorate heroes of nonviolent peace, but they should if we are ever to ban that uncivilized behavior we call war.

Challenge my hero hunger
by battling my selfishness,
by controlling my passions
to become a peace warrior.

May 24

Comforting Delusion

There is a negative side to the self-control encouraged in yesterday's reflection. Sometimes the practice of self-control can lead to someone being addicted to control—of everything and everyone. Controlling persons are usually skilled manipulators, an ability that is essential to being in control. These addicts attempt to control every aspect of their lives, usually as protection against what they fear, but their excessive control is an illusion. Self-control is expedient, yet there is very little else in our conscious control. We have no control over our dreams, our digestive, cardiovascular, or neurological activities, the weather, the stock market, and most of all, our security. The vast military might of all the armed forces, triple locks on every door, a maze of iron bars over all your windows, smoke alarms, and wearing seatbelts—while all useful—do not guarantee your security from injury, harm, or death.

May I find security in uncertainty,
like an acrobat walking gracefully
on a high wire with no safety net,
secure only in being loved by you.

May 25

Toilet Wonder

While many are obsessed with the prevailing fear of a terrorist attack, what you really need to be afraid of is going to the toilet! A recent statistic reported that each year forty thousand Americans are injured by toilets! While the report didn't elaborate precisely how toilets injured so many thousands, it does provide food for wonder. Consider using this unknown bathroom threat not to raise alarm but awareness. Instead of exploring the hazardous aspects of toilets, consider how easily outside, foreign dangers are exaggerated while simple household ones are ignored. Perhaps the reason for the lack of orange alerts about toilets is they would not benefit the political party presently in power, the budget of the vast military-industrial complex, or the sale of handguns. So the next time you approach a toilet, let that innocent flushing apparatus awaken your resolve not to allow fear to victimize and exploit you with fears.

"Fear not," taught the Teacher.
So let me not be a disciple of media
and live in the kingdom of fear,
but to live as his bold fearless disciple.

May 26

Unintended Unattractiveness

The famous phantom of the opera was a man whose face was accidentally deformed, making him so ugly that he wore a mask to conceal his appearance. Fires and other accidents often leave their victims with disfigured, ugly faces. Accidents are not the only sources of disfigurement; you can also disfigure yourself! Face experts say when you daily wear a frown or a worried expression, those wrinkled lines of irritation begin to permanently etch themselves into your face. A cosmetic rule for a beautiful face is: don't be grumpy, angry, or combative since these will damage your complexion. To also be more beautiful, smile as frequently as possible. Science has proven that a self-induced synthetic smile produces the same chemical changes in your brain that occur at those moments of delight that cause spontaneous smiles. Each of us is a divinely designed interlocking reality of body-brain-spirit—that means beauty is more than skin deep!

Do frowns make wrinkled souls?
Does anger construct ugly faces?
Help me be beautiful inside-out,
smiling often to be happy of heart.

May 27

Maybe Tomorrow

Professor Harold Hill is the dynamic, flamboyant salesman in Meredith Wilson's musical, "The Music Man." Professor Hill attempts to get Marian, the librarian, to go on a date with him, asking her with all his charm to meet him by the footbridge in the city park. Marian wants to go but is fearful and refuses, saying, "Please, some other time. Maybe tomorrow." Hill, the ever-persistent salesman, continues but fails to tempt her to agree to meet him at the bridge. At that point, exasperated, he says those marvelous words worth remembering, "Pile up enough tomorrows and you'll find you have collected nothing but a lot of empty yesterdays."

Inspired, I will boycott tomorrows,
in favor of my todays and tonights,
pledging to procrastinate no more
in living out my dreams and hopes.

May 28

Insurrection in an Unlikely Place

An open invitation to all peoples is Isaiah's call to civil disobe-dience, "Why do you spend your money for what is not bread, and your labor for that which does not satisfy?" Aware that the secret police have undercover agents everywhere, don't read these words out loud to others. To our giant corporations and industrial rulers nothing is as threatening as questioning the nourishment promised, not in bread but in your new car, larger television screen, or the latest fashions. Never openly question the consumer's dogma that the reason you labor so hard and for so many hours is to make the required money to buy stuff—stuff that fails to truly satisfy. Ancient as the sun is the oppressive deception that old rebel Isaiah challenged when he said, "Come, buy wine and milk without money and without price." What are the bread, wine, or milk that can be obtained without money? It is a haunting question that only revolutionaries can answer.

> *Everywhere is propaganda*
> *in loud, flashy, four-colored lies.*
> *Deafen me! I am an explorer seeking*
> *lasting, enjoyable, true satisfaction.*

May 29

Happiness, Here and Now

The poet John Keats sought his happiness only in the present mystery of that which was directly before him, as he said, "Nothing startles me beyond the Moment; if a sparrow come before my window, I take part in its existence and pick about the gravel." Notice Keats capitalized the word "Moment" as one would speak of the Divine. Instead of bee-like buzzing here and there busily collecting honey, he instead advised one should be like the blooming flower, passive and receptive. Keats believed if one could learn to be flower-like, "Sap will be given to us for meat and dew for drink." Recall Isaiah's riddle of yesterday about where you go to "buy wine and milk without money and without price." Keats would say, go nowhere! What will truly satisfy your hungry heart is to be found by immersing yourself in the present Moment, your personal Divine Visitation.

> *May I deeply plunge myself in the Moment,*
> *into that overflowing Grail of the Holy.*
> *Not to just look at things, but become them,*
> *so to stumble into a mystical encounter.*

May 30

Soul Food

The Inuit Native Americans of Northwestern Canada and Alaska, whom the Europeans named "Eskimos," engage in a very discerning ritual before they eat. In their meal prayers they give thanks to the seal, salmon, or elk for the gift of their soul present in the food that they are about to consume. Think about the fact that all meals are a sharing of souls. First, be conscious how at any meal the food has been invested with the soul of the person who prepared it. Be aware of how those who share a meal also share their souls with those at that meal. Pausing to pray before you eat means taking time to look meditatively at the fish, animal, or vegetable on your plate. Then be filled with gratitude and the consciousness that if the food you are about to eat wasn't sharing its soul, its vital life force, with you, it wouldn't be food!

> *All meals are holy soul-sharing times,*
> *dining upon the soul food of plants,*
> *fish, fowl, and animal in what's eaten,*
> *and sharing the souls of others at table.*

May 31

A Good Irish Wake

Once again we have come to the death of another month, and so it's an appropriate time to reflect how quickly time comes and goes. Instead of simply letting May pass away without recalling memories of her gifts and her gracious presence in our lives, hold an old fashioned Irish wake for her. As is the custom at Irish wakes, say farewell to this fifth month of the year by telling stories about beautiful Miss May, the flower bedecked bridal Queen of Springtime. A good wake should awaken those attending to ponder the shortness of life and wonder about what happens when someone or something they love dies. Not simply months, days, and weeks, but flowers, lovers, and friends die as well. At your Irish wake for the deceased month of May, take a moment to reflect on a common saying expressed at the death of a Muslim, "We come from God, and we are perpetually returning to him."

> *If it is you, the Impenetrable Mystery,*
> *O God, whom I shall return to at my death,*
> *by romancing life's impenetrable mysteries,*
> *may that ambiguous darkness not scare me.*

Month of

June

June 1

Wonderworker

As body-spirit beings, among our many hungers is the desire for wonder—to be surprised by the breathtaking—to be "wonderized." Wonderworkers are discoverers or creators of wonders or marvels such as scientific discoveries or technological, almost magical, achievements that awe us. There are other wonderworkers who perform not magical but miraculous feats by giving someone the "benefit of a wonder." When another person does (or fails to do) something, we can either quickly judge them or we can give them the benefit of a wonder. Examples of this are, "I wonder if she is out of town and that's the reason she hasn't answered my call," or "I wonder if they misunderstood my invitation and thought I said tomorrow instead of today." Who doesn't long to be "wonderized" in this way? Each day provides new opportunities to work wonders by postponing condemnation whenever others inadvertently step on your toes or rub you the wrong way.

> *Stall my ever-eager desire to judge blindly*
> *without sufficient evidence,*
> *the motives and intentions of others*
> *by wondering up possible excuses.*

June 2

Fear of Change

Was anyone frightened by yesterday's change from May to June? For many, change is a cause for fear-laden anxiety, in particular for some religious people. The sociologist Richard Antoun, author of *Understanding Fundamentalism: Christian, Islamic, and Jewish Movements* (Atamire Press, 2001) defines fundamentalism as "an orientation to the world, both cognitive and affective . . . [that] indicates outrage and protest against (and also fear of) change." Fundamentalists in every religion cling to the old forms of worship and oppose the changing of social morals. Yet for Darwin, adapting to change was critical: "It is not the strongest of the species that survive, nor the most intelligent, but the ones most responsive to change." More than in prehistoric times, to creatively embrace change is a more critical ability with ever-new technologies, ever-speedier modes of communication, and evolving social attitudes. For the marketplace, change is essential to success, as customers don't desire old models but the newest improved designs. God also desires the new, according to Isaiah and Jesus who said, "Behold, I make all things new!"

May the sight on my calendar
of new June not frighten me,
but rather call me to find delight
in life's recurrently new changes.

June 3

June Weddings

This is the matrimonial month. But have you ever wondered why June was chosen instead of September? One theory is that June became the most popular wedding month because of what used to happen in May. In the medieval times, May was bath month. Weddings, if celebrated a few weeks later, were more pleasant after the bride and the bridal party had their annual bath. The weather being warm in May, it was ideal for the annual family bath. First in the tub was the father, then the mother next stepped in the same tub of hot water, then, beginning with the eldest, one by one the children. Last of all into the now gray with dirt bath water went the baby. Some think that this hierarchical family bathing ritual is the origin of the old expression, "Don't throw out the baby with the bathwater." In our time, brides and grooms smell good regardless of the month, but June has remained the classical month to be wed. June can also be a month-long rededication of renewing and rejoicing in the love you share with your spouse, companion, or partner.

> *Pull tightly as possible that knot*
> *binding you to the one you love*
> *that time and routine can loosen;*
> *retie it again and again with love.*

June 4

Beware of Standing Still

Today people are in a hurry, even to become holy. The most important wedding of virtues in the quest for holiness is the marriage of patience to passion. Seekers rarely have both the perpetual passion to be godlike and the patience to wait a lifetime to achieve their goal. Both qualities are learned in the shadow of the cross. Medieval writers often compared the cross to a ladder, and in this spirit Saint Bernard of Clairvaux, the great spiritual giant of the twelfth century, wrote, "Either you must go up or you must come down; you inevitably fall if you try to stand still. It is certain the man [or woman] who does not try to be better is not even good; when you stop trying to be better, then you cease to be good."

Shout loudly, "Don't stand still,
climb higher and ever higher!"
Be more loving and patient
lest you die of laziness of spirit.

June 5

I Wonder If . . .

Besides its meaning of being astonished by some person or thing, the word *wonder* can also mean curiosity. Blessed are those who seek wonderment for it has given birth to new inventions and fresh solutions to old problems. Necessity has been called the mother of invention, but the true mother of inventiveness is wonder. Those who create new solutions to old problems and improvements on existing inventions are those who say to themselves, "I wonder, is there a better way to do this?" To wonder is a divine activity since it imitates the Divine Creator who wondered the world into existence, even if the design required billions of years of wondering. When faced by some thorny problem, instead of repeating what you've tried in the past, wonder about the difficulty. Allow your curiosity to lead you in and out of various doors of possible resolutions until you find the right door.

I wonder why I'm not a saint?
Is it because I settle for less
when capable of being more?
I wonder what God thinks of me?

June 6

Traveling Machines

"Which machine shall we go in, yours or mine?" This was how my first pastor would inquire about whose car we should take to go somewhere together. My pastor was a New Yorker, and I, his young Midwestern assistant, found his use of "machine" quaint, like calling an airplane "a flying machine." Some people think that automobiles have personalities. They even name them, as is done with ships. But my pastor was right, I think. In reality automobiles are no more than a piece of machinery to transport you from one point to another. A recent study of psychologists showed that those who give their cars a name or a gender are more likely to express road rage. "Anything you do to make your car feel like your territory," says Jacob Benfield, a coauthor of that study, "will make you upset when someone steals your parking space." So, be cautious of vehicles with personalized license plates since that may indicate the driver has a belligerent and aggressive personality.

Let me not over-identify with my car
or glamorize it to improve my image.
Devoid of my self-image, I'm free to go,
joy riding in my traveling machine.

June 7

Einstein's Uncle

Albert Einstein, while Jewish by birth, had little interest in religion itself. However, he found God in wonder, in the awesomeness of the universe and its hidden secrets. When asked about religion Einstein was fond of telling a humorous story about his agnostic Jewish uncle. Paradoxically, this uncle was the only one in his family that went to synagogue. When the agnostic uncle was asked about this religious practice, he would smile and say, "Ah, but you never know."

Despite my beliefs or lack of them,
inspire me to be like Einstein's uncle:
to worship, live a good moral life,
and to hold to the creed, "Ah, you never know."

June 8

Don't Travel With a Fool

June typically begins the vacation travel season and asks not only where shall I go, but also with whom? That question is likewise an excellent one for the journey of life that requires both a destination and companionship. Good advice for traveling life's path comes from Buddha. In his *Dhammapada* he says, "If the traveler can find a virtuous and wise companion, let him go with him joyfully and overcome the dangers of the way. If you cannot find a good friend or master to go with you, travel alone rather than in the company of a fool. Do not carry with you your mistakes. Do not carry with you your cares. Travel alone."

> *Failing to find a wise master or friend,*
> *lonely as it may be, may I travel alone.*
> *Most of all help me to not lug along*
> *cares and past mistakes, so to travel light and free.*

June 9

In God We Trust

The Persian proverb, "Trust in Allah, but always tie up your camel," is worthy of pondering each time you see this motto on your money, "In God we Trust." Indeed, trust in God, but be leery of your government and mistrustful of your elected politicians, especially those who patriotically wrap themselves up in the flag of your country. "Trust in God," but always be skeptical, even hesitant to accept pronouncements of your church about what is, or is not, the will of God. "Trust in God," but always lock your doors. "Trust in God," but have a reliable retirement fund and medical insurance. In every aspect of your life "Trust in God," but be as shrewd as serpents and innocent as doves striving to balance between being trustingly carefree and suspiciously cautious.

> *As a trusting Muslim ties up his camel,*
> *as a trusting Christian, I lock my door,*
> *welcoming but cautious of strangers,*
> *may I live trusting, prudently, in God.*

June 10

The Song of Silence

Once upon a time in ancient Japan a mighty warlord greatly desired that his young beautiful daughter should marry. She rejected all her suitors. When the old man pressed his daughter about how she would choose a husband, she replied, "I will make a drum of silk stretched on a bamboo frame and the man who hears the music I play on my drum will be my husband." The old warlord lamented, "What foolishness," knowing he would die without seeing his grandchildren. As countless suitors came and departed, the disappointed old man moaned, "Oh, daughter, I told you so." Then one day, a richly dressed, handsome young prince came and asked to marry the old lord's daughter. The old man informed him she would only marry the man who had heard her playing her silk drum, and, smiling, the prince said, "In my far-off kingdom I heard her drum!" The shocked father asked, "Young sir, how is that possible; she plays upon a silk drum?" The young man replied, "My Lord, I heard its silence!" That day the daughter of the old warlord put away her silk drum for she had finally found a husband.

Amidst the noise and racket,
teach me to hear the silence
of the love ballads you play to me
on your silken drum.

June 11

Living Deliberately

Henry David Thoreau said that the reason he went off to live alone in a small hut near Walden Pond in Concord, Massachusetts, was "to live deliberately." Thoreau provides us with a marvelous compass for how to experience this June day, or any day, by living it deliberately. This calculated living begins at sunrise with the deliberate intention to absorb every crumb of the day or as Thoreau said, "I wanted to live deep and suck all the marrow out of life . . . to know it by experience." Few of us live this way. Instead, we allow ourselves to be swept along by a tidal wave of activities that result in accidental, inadvertent living. Sadly, we are trapped inside our heads. The escape route out of this half-living is to become a master criminal. Courts make judgments about whether an offense is a deliberate act, i.e., intentionally calculated and premeditated, and therefore more severely punished than those committed on impulse. Premeditate how you will cleverly pilfer all the delights, pleasures, and life out of this day by living it deliberately.

> *Shock me out of shallow living,*
> *to deliberately commit myself*
> *to dive deep inside this gifted day,*
> *tasting, sensing each of its gifts.*

June 12

Stinginess

Among pre-industrial people, being stingy was the worst of all moral failings. The vice of stinginess applied not only to possessions but to one's thoughts as well. This vice of all vices included meanness and rudeness in speech and acts toward others and even toward nature. In ancient societies rudeness was correctly seen as the enemy of both community and communication. Richard Nelson, a student of the ways of Native Americans, said a mother might tell her little daughter, "Don't point at the mountain! It's rude." Gary Snyder, in his book *The Practice of the Wild,* gives the Native American code of conduct: "One must not boast, or show much pride in accomplishments, and one must not take one's skill for granted. Wastefulness and carelessness are caused by stinginess of spirit, an ungracious unwillingness to complete the gift-exchange transaction." Snyder adds, "These rules are also particularly true for healers, artists, and gamblers!"

> *Sensitize me to rudeness,*
> *contagious among hurrying, busy people,*
> *ego-blind by their stingy mirror eyes*
> *that reflect only themselves to them.*

June 13

The Mysterious Revolving Door

In the first stage of the Islamic rosary, a Muslim repeats ninety-nine times, "May Allah forgive me." The purpose of this prayer is found in its name, *tawbah,* meaning turning as an expression of a wish for change. Christians also express this desire for ongoing self-change before they come to Holy Communion saying, "Lord I am not worthy" or "Lord have mercy on me." While these prayer expressions can easily become rote, they still possess the power to awaken worshippers to the necessity to be emptied. The Spanish mystic Saint John of the Cross referred to this type of death as, "to die before you die." The spiritual path in every great religion begins with a conversion, a reformation intended not simply as a first stage but as a lifelong process of changing. The symbols of religions are many—the Muslim crescent, the Buddhist wheel, the Jewish Star of David, and the Christian cross—but an encompassing religious symbol for all of them would be a revolving door!

> *Yesterday, did I have a little death*
> *as I turned around from good to better?*
> *Inspire me to will to die a little today,*
> *so death by death I may grow in love.*

June 14

Heretical or Here?

The sixteenth-century German Lutheran mystic Jakob Boehme labored as a shoemaker and lived with a profound sense of the presence of God. His mystical writings were condemned and not published until after his death. In one of these he wrote, "Most have been under the impression that heaven is many hundred, nay, many thousands of miles distant from the earth and that God dwells only in that heaven. . . . If our eyes were but opened we should see God everywhere in his heaven; for heaven stands in the innermost moving everywhere." This humble German shoemaker's insight that heaven and God were all around us in the innermost workings of the world was judged heretical. As a mystic, like poets and mystics before and after, he told us that heaven and God aren't up, they are all around us. Today his concept isn't heretical, intellectually. The work of twenty-first-century mystics and believers is to *realize,* to make real, that all around us is heaven and the Presence. How radically different the land, water, the wild and tame creatures, and all of us would be treated if we lived out his vision of heaven.

> *May I imitate the carpenter of Galilee,*
> *who found heaven and God among us*
> *by seeing, feeling, and even tasting heaven*
> *camouflaged cleverly in the commonplace.*

June 15

"Up Anchor"

Rita Klarer, an old friend, wrote to me saying she was making a book of the favorite quotations of her friends, and asked me for mine. After pondering several favorite quotes, I sent her the following one from Shakespeare's *Julius Caesar,* Act IV:

> There is a tide in the affairs of men,
> which, taken at the flood, leads on to
> fortune.

Omitted, all the voyage of their life
is bound in shallows and in miseries.

I have personally used this Shakespearian quote many times. I have found it so affirming of acting on your intuition, even if what you do is contrary to logic and common sense. To pull up anchor and set sail whenever you feel the flood is sweeping underneath you is to follow the voice of what the Buddhists call "your belly brain."

Dare me to trust my feelings,
those inner wisdom whispers,
that while lacking common sense,
make sense, being soul fed.

June 16

Catholic Smells

Regardless if you are a Christian, Buddhist, Muslim, Jew, or agnostic, this reflection is for you. A recent study of the most pleasing smell to American males stated that it wasn't the smell of home-baked bread but of a new automobile. According to the Chicago Research Foundation on Smell and Taste, the smell of apples makes a room seem larger. The next time your world begins to feel cramped, try eating an apple and sniffing each piece with every bite. Interestingly, the aroma of barbecue smoke makes a room seem smaller. But barbecue smoke isn't the only thing that shrinks the size of your world—so do the smells of nationalism, religious superiority, and the foul stench of racial and sexual discrimination. Divinely aromatic is the smell of unity, and when expanded to include universal, global, and even cosmic dimensions, it is an invigorating fragrance. It is the intoxicating scent of God.

> *I've only one nose, but one is enough*
> *to sniff like a bloodhound your presence*
> *in the poor and needy, the underpaid and*
> *exploited aliens, and the lonely-hearted.*

June 17

A Cause for Wonder in a Lost Ministry

In England, until the end of the eighteenth century, there was a liturgical, lay ministry with the most unusual function— keeping order among the dogs in church! In previous times it was common for the faithful to be accompanied by their dogs when they came to church for worship. Since dogs will be dogs, the dog warden used a whip to maintain order among the barking, naughty hounds, and tongs to remove those trouble-making dogs that refused to be disciplined. The disappearance of church dog wardens prompts me to wonder if the faithful stopped bringing their dogs to church, and if so, why. Or perhaps the ministry of the church dog warden ceased because the dogs' owners began to discipline their misbehaving dogs on their own or remove them from church? The next time crying and misbehaving small children in church cause you distress, remember the "good old days," and be grateful your fellow parishioners no longer bring their barking hounds to church.

> *Longing to return to the "good old days"*
> *is a dangerous, short-sighted religious ache.*
> *These days are tomorrow's good old days!*
> *So be free of nostalgia and find joy in today.*

June 18

A Smiling Terrorist

The most efficient way to exorcise evil is with joyful humor. Joy and humor are the Molotov cocktails, the makeshift incendiary bombs of Blessed Bolsheviks, who toss these hand grenades of delight into the Evil Empire's drab work camps. As a holy terrorist, your mission is to set off such ticking, tickling time bombs in depressive meetings and when you are confronted with gloomy, authority-thumping bureaucrats. When those seated on their rickety thrones of power attempt to intimidate you, just explode a smile in their direction. The Enemy's henchmen/women hate smilers who by such revolutionary acts silently rob them of power. Laughter is the best device to explode the solemn respect that religious authoritarians demand for themselves and their ideas.

> *I enlist as one of your underground agents*
> *a covert God-spy and a blessed terrorist,*
> *who by good humored silliness and smiles*
> *sabotages grumpy bureaucrats' machinery.*

June 19

Fully Alive

"The glory of God is a human fully alive," said Saint Irenaeus, the second century bishop and martyr. His famous dictum is worth recalling whenever we humbly stand before some magnificent Gothic cathedral, some giant mosque covered with gorgeous blue mosaics, or any religious structure that gives glory to God. I believe that the Creator would agree with Saint Irenaeus and say, "As for glorifying me, I would far rather see one fully alive human than a thousand splendorous cathedrals or blue domed mosques!" If you feel the urge to be fully alive, be forewarned that you are setting out on a dangerous journey. On every mile of that road there are yellow warning signs, "Danger! Being fully alive requires plunging deeply into every sorrow as well as every joy." Living lavishly and not halfway requires exposure to those excruciatingly painful feelings that we dread. Saint Irenaeus was a martyr who died for his faith. Those who seek to be fully alive will likewise endure the martyrdom of full emotional exposure.

> *I care not how high the cost*
> *of loving with all my heart,*
> *gladly gambling for love's joys*
> *far surpasses the agonies of loss.*

June 20

Being Human

The anthropologist Frances Harwood asked a Sioux elder why his people tell stories, and he answered, "In order to become human beings." Harwood then asked, "Aren't we all human beings already?" The old Sioux smiled and answered, "Not everyone makes it." Have you? Are you a human being or even in the process of becoming human? We rarely if ever ask ourselves what makes one truly and fully human. We may not ask that question but we do acknowledge that the brutal, sadistic behaviors of fellow humans is inhumane. To be a human being is to be a member of the species *homo sapiens*, as distinguished from lower animals. But it means more. To be a human is to be humane—civilized, compassionate, charitable, and kind. The opposites of these humane attributes are cruelty, selfishness, rudeness, and lack of caring. Reflecting that such antisocial behaviors are becoming increasingly commonplace in our society gives validity to the old Sioux elder's words, "Not everyone makes it."

> *Angry in traffic or irritated at home,*
> *spur me forward in ongoing evolution,*
> *outgrowing harmful, unkind behaviors*
> *to more resemble my Creator's image.*

June 21

Summer Solstice

Today is the summer solstice, so take a moment to wave at the sun and say, "Thanks, old-timer!" Our sun is a middle-aged star. To the young, middle-aged is old. Like many middle-aged folks, our sun is healthy. But like them our day-star is also halfway to the grave. No need to panic; it will require another five to six billion years for the sun's core to run out of hydrogen. Then it will begin to burn helium causing it to expand quickly to over one hundred times its present size, making the sun a red giant two-and-a-half times brighter than it is today. As the sun expands to this gigantic size, it will inflate outward beyond earth's orbit with intense heat that will melt the continents, boil away the oceans, and finally vaporize the entire planet! Then the sun will end its ten-billion-year life in a cosmic death. The sun's death was unthinkable to those of previous ages who considered it to be eternal. Pondering the fate of the sun is a good reminder that you will die in a blink of an eye compared to the five billion years before the sun's death date.

> *What's five billion years in cosmic age?*
> *Oh, here today and gone tomorrow sun,*
> *teach this earthling the needed lesson*
> *that "all life's brief, so enjoy today."*

June 22

Trust Your Soul

"My soul doesn't want to be here." This is a valid reason for leaving a party, a movie, or some religious service before it is over. If we could listen carefully to the inner radar of our souls, we would politely excuse ourselves or sneak away from events that are unhealthy for either our souls or our bodies. These two are one, infused with a unity that influences both. Gatherings that are disagreeable to your soul should be avoided like toxic radioactive landfills. When you are invited to something, first say to yourself, "Let me check my inner radar before I reply." If your soul radar warns that you shouldn't attend, don't. If obligation requires you accept, go, but do so eavesdropping on your soul. If you are in the wrong place at the wrong time, politely leave as quickly as possible, whispering to yourself, "Sorry, but my soul doesn't want to be here."

> *Soul-bodyguard protect me*
> *from those dangerous places*
> *requiring counterfeit kindness*
> *and smiling polite hypocrisy.*

June 23

You May Never Know

At the beginning of the Second World War, a large number of bombs dropped by the Germans on France did not explode. French bomb experts defusing them were curious about what caused this malfunction. They discovered small handwritten notes tucked inside the bombs. French prisoners of war doing forced labor in German munitions factories had written on tiny pieces of paper, "We're doing the best we can from where we are with what we got, every chance we get." That simple message could be the motto of anyone seeking to make this world a better and more just place. We can mistakenly believe that to leave the world a better place than when we were born it is necessary to do something grand or perform some great service. To make the world a better place, simply do the best you can just where you are—your neighborhood or workplace—with the talents and resources you have, as insignificant as they may seem. Do it every chance you get! As Mahatma Gandhi said, "You may never know what results come from your action. But if you do nothing, there will be no result."

How awesome is creation's design,
nothing is purposeless or useless.
So too your actions, even if minor,
influence the world for good or evil.

June 24

An Educational Toy

The yo-yo, whose name in the Filipino Tagalog language means "come-come," is worthy of meditation. Introduced in 1929 to Americans by the toymaker Louis Marx, the yo-yo was well known in antiquity. It even appears in Greek paintings eight hundred years before the birth of Christ. Originally, it was a stone hunting weapon. It weighed four pounds and was attached to a twenty-foot cord. With this stone-thrower's boomerang, hunters would climb out on a branch of a tree and patiently wait for game to approach. Slinging the stone weapon attached to its long string at their prey allowed hunters to retrieve their weapon without having to climb down out of the tree. Ancient spiritual masters used the yo-yo too. They warned that all words and deeds were yo-yos that would always come back to you. So don't be a fool. When you're tempted to use the weapon of angry words or actions against another, don't do it! If you do, they will come spinning back to strike you.

Unless I want to be the target
of my anger flung out at others,
Let me not be violent in thought or word,
as they recycle always back to me.

June 25

Trailblazers Needed

Prophet is a dusty word from antique Bible times and far-distant lands. Prophets, it is thought, belong to an exclusive club whose members are chosen by God. Institutions do not create or license prophets, especially not religious institutions. Like pigs, prophets are only honored after they are dead! To invigorate the needed and noble profession of prophet, replace the term prophet with that of trailblazer, and suddenly it's no longer antique. The Prophet of Galilee, who interestingly never objected to being called one, was a trailblazer who cut a pathway right through cultic religion and blazed a trail through inflexible, prejudicial social conventions. He did away with the exclusive prophetic club by bestowing his prophetic spirit on all of his followers. Each follower was to be a trailblazer, charged to cut a new path through the wasteland of social injustices and through the battlefields of old problems to new solutions. Every profession, every art, and especially every religion, needs prophetic trailblazers!

> *Innovative spirit of the new,*
> *my gift of Galilee's Prophet,*
> *impel me to cut new paths*
> *across old, tired boundaries.*

June 26

Being Turned Inside Out

Disaster brings out the best and the worst in people. And what is true for large calamities seems true for minor, personal ones. When confronted with sickness or some physical or emotional suffering, some remain cheerful as they silently tackle their afflictions. Others react to their suffering by being irritable, grouchy, surly, and impatient. We can now rephrase the saying about the two responses to a disaster: disaster brings out the best and the worst in people. Ageless wisdom tested by time shouldn't be contested, yet is the old adage really true that tribulations bring out the best or worst in you? The answer it seems is that they only bring out what is already in you!

I believe you reside within me;
may my belief in your presence
saturate me with a cheerfulness
that radiates my every activity.

June 27

Wondrous Nasal Communion

According to the magazine *Scientific American*, the odds are that if you live in the northern hemisphere, every time you fill your lungs with air you breath in at least one molecule of the same air that once passed through the lungs of Socrates! An amazing bit of information, since if you've breathed the air used by Socrates or Plato you must also have inhaled a molecule of air once breathed by Jesus of Galilee! Stop now and slowly breathe consciously. Be aware that each breath you inhale contains a mystically saturated molecule of air breathed by Jesus. In the Judeo-Christian scriptures, God's breath is identical with the spirit of creative life and inspiration. So consider using your plain old everyday breathing as nasal communion! Be aware that you are inhaling the Spirit, the wind-breath of the Divine Mystery.

O my nose, either long or short,
source of my holy communion
with the sacred breath of life,
may I breathe my way to heaven.

June 28

Come Hell or High Water

In 1738 Jonathan Swift of *Gulliver's Travels* fame wrote this in another book called *Polite Conversations*: "Promises and piecrusts are made to be broken." A question at the conclusion of this customary month for marriages and their promises of love unto death: was Swift correct in comparing piecrusts and promises? It is naive to expect politicians to keep their campaign promises, but we do expect marriage partners to keep theirs. This romantic idealism defies the reality of today's statistics, yet at each wedding we again trust that the power of love will guarantee the keeping of those until-death-do-us-part promises. Realism asks if anyone can promise anything about the unknown future. The ageless ritual promises of marriage and love therefore need to be translated as, "I will do everything within my power, come hell or high water, to keep these promises of love and fidelity to you, so help me God." This is an astounding promise requiring the guts to face even a tsunami of bad times by placing your love and trust in the hands of the Match Maker.

> *Help our promises of love*
> *To grow slowly year by year,*
> *So that like the tree trunk with many rings,*
> *We become ever larger and stronger.*

June 29

From Bridal White to Bridal Blues

Americans spend fifty billion dollars each year on weddings. And at the end of this month of weddings the bills for them fill the mailboxes of countless brides and grooms. Also occurring at about this time is a common affliction for June's new brides: bridal blues. Psychologists say this post-marriage bridal depression results from the absence of attention that had been focused on her. A marriage requires months of hyperactivity: planning the wedding ritual and music, purchasing a wedding dress, sending invitations, bridal showers, the rehearsal, and more. At each of these events the bride-to-be is the center of attention. Immediately after the honeymoon, however, the queen-for-a day status vanishes and she experiences the effects of the law of gravity: "What goes up must come down!" So if you are a relative or personally know a woman recently married, be seriously concerned that she might be suffering from this hidden affliction. Consider ministering to her as friends do for those who suffer post-funeral grieving or depression; give her a call to drop by for a visit or perhaps take her to lunch.

May I become especially sensitive
to that lonely vacuum that follows
significant events in others' lives,
and forget myself to care for them.

June 30

Light as a Feather

Today, as old June dies, take a few minutes to wonder about your own death by recalling Maat, the Egyptian goddess of the final judgment, whose symbol was a single white ostrich feather. The Egyptians believed that after they died their souls were led into the Judgment Hall of the Dead where the goddess Maat stood holding the scales of justice and eternal life. In one of the two pans of her scale, the goddess placed the heart of the deceased. In the other she placed her white ostrich feather. If the dead person's heart was heavier than her white feather, then the deceased was forever banished from immortality. However, if the heart of deceased had been made light as a feather by a lifetime of kind deeds, love, and care for the needy, they were ushered into paradise. A good motto for any day, and to prepare for death, is "to lighten up." Prepare to die by throwing off weighty burdensome worries and heavy grudges grown gray-haired by your years of nursing them. Your last day is coming, so begin dropping your dead weight, a term the Egyptians would have found most significant.

> *Old resentments are dead weight*
> *that drown the soul. So free me*
> *by thoughtfulness and generosity,*
> *to be soulfully light-hearted.*

Month of
July

July 1

Holy Wow

A new month provides a chance to revive the prehistoric quest for wonder as you search for signs of the Astounding One, often referred to as God. The most common expression of someone who has an epiphany of the Awe-Inspiring One is, "Wow!" Besides being an expression of wonder and amazement, it can be a prayerful proclamation of the Divine Presence. Whenever you are caught up in something so wonderful that it causes you to spontaneously respond, "Wow," know that the Almighty can't be far away. Even if this little, three-letter word is slang, it's the most frequent prayer of mundane mystics—ordinary folks overcome with wonders of God. "Wow!" is also a one-word prayer of adoration, a nonreligious single word abbreviation of the prophet Isaiah's ecstatic cry, "Holy, Holy, Holy," when he experienced the presence of God awesomely filling the temple.

> *"Wow, Wow, Wow," I cry in awe,*
> *aware I am in your holy Presence.*
> *What an experience! What a stunning sight*
> *and marvelous gift I've been given.*

July 2

Role Models

Spain's Queen Isabella, who reigned from 1451 to 1504, is known by all American school children because she supported and financed the voyage of Christopher Columbus to sail west to India across the yet-to-be-crossed Atlantic. Isabella is typically presented as a far-sighted woman worthy of imitation, yet in her entire lifetime she only took a bath twice! There is a yellow-brownish color akin to soiled calico that is called Isabel, and according to legend it is named after Queen Isabella of Castile who made a vow not to change her underwear until the city of Granada fell to the armies of Spain. If we knew the whole truth, perhaps Isabella, like other role models in sports, the military, or even the saints, had a hidden shadow side that was hardly worthy of imitation. Unfortunately, role models are often like others who play roles—actors and actresses. What is seen in the famous and great is only half of who they are, simply the role they are acting out in public. You need no role model to imitate to become who you were uniquely created to be. All you need is the courage to be you.

When I am tempted to imitate another,
arouse me to be more than average,
and dare me to be the one
and only whom you made.

July 3

Wondering About Miss Liberty

A good way to prepare to celebrate tomorrow's Independence Day is by wondering about the Statue of Liberty: What if she were to be dressed as originally designed? For the 1870 celebration of the opening of the Suez Canal, the French sculptor Frederic Bartholdi designed a giant sculpture to stand at the entrance of the Suez Canal. The statue was of an Egyptian peasant woman of the Nile wearing a Muslim face veil! She held her torch high, symbolic of Egypt bringing light to Asia. When the wealthy Arab prince benefactor financing the statue went bankrupt, Bartholdi was forced to inventively redesign his statue. Removing her veil, he made her into the Statue of Liberty, whose torch was now to enlighten the world. Ponder what the effects would be if tomorrow a Muslim-veiled Miss Liberty would appear on patriotic floats in countless parades, and in displays for Fourth of July sales. Could Miss Liberty as a veiled Muslim jar us, then liberate us to desire our freedom

and a veil-less equality that would be a worldwide experience
for all peoples?

> *Don't just celebrate your freedom on the Fourth,*
> *but patriotically invite others to celebrate their*
> *   freedom too.*
> *Don't back those forcing democracy on others;*
> *instead by justice and peace ready the soil for it.*

July 4

Land of Wonders

In *Democracy in America,* the French historian Alexis de
Tocqueville recorded his impressions of America in 1835 based
on his fact-finding tour of our country. He wrote, "America
is a land of wonders, in which everything is in constant motion and every change seems an improvement. . . . No natural
boundary seems to be set to the efforts of man; and in his eyes
what is not yet done is only what he has not yet attempted to
do." Along with the fireworks, picnics, and parades of this July
Fourth, take time out to reflect on Tocqueville's insight that
we Americans have set no boundaries on what we can accomplish. Imagine health care for all citizens similar to the way we
have universal education, freely available to all. Think not of

a minimum wage, but of a truly living wage for all workers. Consider new prison systems that ensure reform, not simply the warehousing of criminals. Celebrate the Fourth by patriotically dreaming of making America once again the land of wonders.

> *Today, awaken me to my American duty*
> *to vote, pay taxes, and work for equal*
> *taxation of all citizens and corporations,*
> *so the American dream is possible for all.*

July 5

A Blessing, Not a Curse

The Fourth of July holiday is over; today it's back to work. As millions return to their jobs, they can easily dream of life as one long holiday, without having to work. Is that a dream of paradise or of hell? We humans are designed for work, and by our work we find perfection. The Hindu Bhagavad Gita tells us, "Man (woman also) finds perfection by the intensity of his devotion to his own tasks, which means working not for his own glory, but for the good of the work to be done." In the Hindu religious philosophy of work, the joy of any task is not in completing it, but rather in the doing of it. In the American philosophy of work, the joy of it comes only upon finishing the task. This view is strongly influenced by the Judeo-Christian story of Eden, where having to work was one of God's curses. The Industrial Revolution added to goal-directed work by exploiting workers and turning them into mere cogs in a giant manufacturing apparatus. In our society where work is a chore, even a drudgery, our time spent with God is only on nonworking days, which says a lot. Divorce God from your labor and your life will be joyless, since most of daily life is work.

> *As I work, help me to find*
> *my joy in the doing of the task,*
> *whether it is at my job or home,*
> *so that I may work in holy communion.*

July 6

Scandalous Worship

Appearing sixty-six times, the most frequently used term in scriptures for worship is the Greek *proskkyneo,* translatable as "adoration" (prostrating oneself or some submissive act). Humans have considered this subservient conduct only proper in the presence of the Divine Mystery. However, Patricia Sanchez writes that the Greek *proskkyneo* can also be translated,

"I come forward to kiss!" She says in worship we come forward not only to kiss, but to be kissed by God! Such intimate affection is appealing! In the depths of every soul there is a desire for deep intimacy with the Divine Beloved. Yet, such intimacy also causes dread, for we fear that the moist touch of God's lips upon ours can be the kiss of death, as it was for the prophets. The greater the intimacy, the more vulnerable one is to be given a special divine assignment. So we shrewdly keep a safe distance away from being kissed by God, successfully hiding behind barricades of ageless ritual, filling up our worship by piling up words upon words interspersed with hymns of pious platitudes.

> *Dare me to discard my hymnbook.*
> *Discard the protective ritual barriers,*
> *and draw near to kiss, and be kissed,*
> *by you, O passionate lover of lovers.*

July 7

Watermelon Wisdom

In these summer days when you next enjoy eating watermelon, recall a saying of the followers of the Prophet Mohammed: "A watermelon produces a thousand good works!" This Islamic saying originated when watermelons were mostly eaten out-of-doors so their seeds dropped to the ground to become the source of countless new watermelon plants. Seeds are messy, so modern scientists have created seedless watermelons. While appearing to be an innocent folk proverb, this Islamic saying about watermelons contains superior spiritual advice. Our good works, like watermelons, also contain seeds, invisible yet richly fertile with potential for more good. Watermelon wisdom says to be lavishly careless in doing good deeds so that the tiny invisible seeds within your works will be generously scattered everywhere. Pray that as you leave the scene of your crime of kindness, you will leave behind you a long and broad trail of tiny fertile love seeds.

> *Insure I do all my good deeds secretly,*
> *being sloppily careless in my generosity,*
> *so I'll scatter everywhere the rich seeds*
> *inside the love gifts you have given me.*

July 8

Don't Complain . . . Unless

After discussing the weather, the second favorite subject in conversations is a long litany of woes: complaining about how corrupt the government is, how ineffective congress is, how sad the level of education in our schools is, the reckless driving of young people, and on and on the Wailing Wall litany goes. Eric Gill, the English artist, once said, "It is no use, and no good, complaining about the world we live in and vaguely wanting something better, unless we are prepared to review the grounds of our life and its real meaning." The place to begin to deal with the woes of our world, Gill said, is to review the ground or the basis of your own life, and the meaning of why you are alive. Complaining about what's wrong with any institution or bureaucratic agency is a waste of time, unless you personally are willing to remove whatever is wrong in your own life. The Teacher said to first take the two-by-four out of your own eye before you try to remove the splinter in another's eye. Resist the temptation to engage in the great spectator sport of complaining . . . unless there is truly nothing about yourself to complain about to yourself.

> *Silly to think I'm infallible*
> *with nothing to be corrected.*
> *Made aware of my many faults,*
> *I'll not complain about others.*

July 9

The Vow of Holy Abundance

Poverty of possessions is a highly promoted religious ideal. It can include a vow of poverty and disciplines of self-denial of physical luxuries, fine foods, and drink. The spiritual path of asceticism especially targets a poverty of possessions where the ideal is to have none! Religious poverty easily gives rise to guilt over material possessions, as when Gandhi rightly said, "If you have clothing in your closet that you don't wear, then it is stolen goods. Stolen from those who lack clothing." Extreme poverty can be a spirituality of denial that idealizes stark, barren living quarters, that abstains from physical comfort, delicious tasting foods, and owning material things. The Teacher of Galilee never promoted a lifestyle of material poverty! Instead, he called his disciples to simplicity of life by sharing their goods with others in need and by being liberated from artificially created cravings. He taught holy abundance instead of holy deficiency saying, "I have come that you might have life and have it in great abundance." His abundance of life didn't require owning many possessions, but rather in being possessed by God. Seek first an abundance of Divine Mystery, and simplicity of life will naturally appear in your life, and in great abundance.

Fervently I desire to be possessed
by you, the Giver of all good things,
so to enjoy the great glut of wealth
and happiness of those totally yours.

July 10

The Womb of Wonders

The Englishman Richard Blechynden ran the tea concession at the St. Louis World's Fair of 1904. On one very hot Missouri summer day, not a single fairgoer stopped to purchase a cup of hot tea at his stand. This ingenious Englishman decided to solve his predicament by creatively defying history, not to mention all previous tradition, by offering his customers ice-cold tea! Unthinkable in his own tradition-bound England, his insane concoction of ice and hot tea was immediately adopted by try-anything Americans and remains popular to this day. So on this hot July day, if you quench your thirst with a glass of iced tea, raise your glass in a toast to Richard Blechynden for his courage to think outside the box. After setting down your glass of iced tea, take a moment to survey your life and your problems, most of which likely will seem insolvable and beyond your control. But don't give up, be inspired by your drink of iced tea and, like Blechynden, think the unthinkable.

Help me turn my problems upside down,
forgetting the rules of logic and tradition,
my fears of what the neighbors will say,
to be inspired by the Mother of Invention.

July 11

A Cure for Your Secret Addiction

Our childhood fear of ridicule and teasing has tattooed us with a lifelong addiction to being respected and taken seriously by others. This subterranean addiction surfaces whenever we commit some blunder in front of others and their laughter at the mistake stings like burning acid. To address this addiction, strive to correct it by making fun of yourself when alone and with others. Regardless of failures, continue to at least chuckle at your spiritual clumsiness when you're impatient or uncharitable with others. Wholesome self-humor—being a holy work—requires the grace of the mirthful Spirit. If you pray seriously to this Muse-spirit of life's divine comedy you will be given the grace to be silly. Yes, silly! In Anglo-Saxon times, a "silly" person was one who was blessed and innocent . . . and so holy.

Tickle me to work to triumph over
my addiction to be taken seriously.
Chide me to poke fun at silly me
when I blunder and stumble like a fool.

July 12

Cause of Death: Ran Out of Words

The Native American Cheyennes believe that at birth each child is given so many words, and when he or she has used up their allotted amount, they die! Recently, studies may reveal a divine partiality in word generosity since they show that an average American woman utters around seven thousand words in a day, while a man uses just over two thousand. Man or woman, and regardless of whether or not you believe the Cheyenne about being given only so many words to use in life, consider speaking less and listening more. A major childhood achievement is when parents are able to teach their child how to talk. Sadly, no one at any age teaches us how to talk less and listen more. Therefore, the art of being silent must be a self-taught talent, and it may become a most enjoyable talent. The Yugoslavian news agency reported Peter Mustafic of Botovo, Yugoslavia, after not saying a word for forty years, suddenly began talking at age ninety. When asked about his silence, Mustafic said, "I stopped speaking in the 1920s in order to escape military service, and then I simply got used to it and enjoyed it."

> *Within your reach are the hidden, rich rewards*
> *of peaceful enjoyment and insights into others,*
> *if in every conversation you have the strength*
> *to hold your tongue and quietly pay attention.*

July 13

Jazz Up Your Life

Our lives are crowded with old routines that we play out each day note for note just as we have done for countless yesterdays. Daily habits, of course, make life easier since no thought is required to do the next task, but habits also deaden. So consider improvising on your daily life. Improvisation as a way of life is based on the musical theory, "No music can be imprisoned by marks fixed upon a page." Improvising isn't just straying off the straight and narrow; it is creatively straying, like when one plays jazz. In this uniquely American music, one hand plays the melody as initially written, while the other hand improvises with notes to accompany and harmonize with the original score. By improvising, an old, familiar musical theme is creatively transformed into something new. Today, as jazz musicians would play an old song in a new way, do the same with some old daily routine and prayer. Jazz it up by harmonizing old routines with new twists, and you'll find your actions and prayers are suddenly fresh and alive.

> *Since habits deaden the soul,*
> *inspire me to jazz up my life*
> *in how I do the dishes and how I pray,*
> *and in my ways of loving you!*

July 14

Artificial, but Very Real Prisons

On this date in 1789 the citizens of Paris began the French Revolution against the tyranny of their king by storming the Bastille, the royal prison. However, the Bastille held only seven prisoners! And a couple of them were lunatics imprisoned for their own and society's safety. On this historic liberation day, examine if you are living in a prison. Culture defines an elaborate system of arbitrary boundaries for nations, social classes, political parties, and religions. When someone says, "I am a Republican or I am a Democrat," they state an artificial boundary that easily can imprison. To say, "I am a Christian," can also mean limiting yourself to an invisible but real wall that incarcerates you as easily as if you were inside the Bastille. To Australian Aborigines, our idea of boundary lines that separate nations and ownership of land doesn't exist. On this French Liberation Day, consider becoming an Aborigine who does not recognize artificial walls separating countries, religions, classes, races, and sexes, and so enjoy a new freedom.

> *To see as you see, a world undivided,*
> *may I see no divisions . . . of religions,*
> *nations, sexes, or social classes,*
> *and so be freed of ancient imprisonment.*

July 15

Neanderthal Fears

In Hebrew the word for stranger is *zar*. It is also the root of the word for border. The existence of borders, both in the ancient world and today, creates the existence of strangers. Someone from the other side of your border is a person beyond your range of sight, and so is seen territorially and theologically as a potentially dangerous threat. Early peoples often would kill strangers on sight for no other reason than they were strange, other, different, and foreign. Neanderthals, it seemed, were so afraid of what lay beyond the familiar that they would never cross a body of water too large for them to see the opposite shore. Is it possible that after countless millennia since the existence of these primitive peoples we still harbor Neanderthal fears of the unknown? If so we have a serious problem since to advance spiritually requires encounters with the Ultimate Stranger—God! These encounters require risking crossing all known boundaries, going beyond what is seeable or understandable into the divinely dangerous unknown.

> *Am I like the Exodus Hebrews,*
> *afraid to go up Mount Sinai to see you,*
> *so from my desert place I send Moses and*
> *   mystics?*
> *To know your love, dare me to meet you!*

July 16

An Ebony Experience

Thomas Fox, the Protestant mystic and founder of the Quakers, lived in seventeenth-century England. One day Fox was on his way to visit some friends in the Coventry prison who had been incarcerated there for their beliefs that were considered too contrary to the official religion of England. Fox said that as he approached the prison:

> The word of the Lord came to me saying,
> "My Love was always to thee, and thou
> art in my love." And I was ravished with
> the sense of the love of God and greatly
> strengthened in my inward man. But when I
> came into the prison where those prisoners
> were, a great power of darkness struck me;
> and I sat still, having my spirit gathered up
> into the love of God.

This mystical experience is unique and of great assistance to us. Thomas Fox reported, ". . . a great power of darkness struck me!" We are conditioned to expect visitations from God to come with blinding light, not darkness. Yet Fox says he sat silently in the darkness, absorbed in the ravishing love of God. So the next time you find yourself enveloped in darkness, as helpless as if you were lost, just sit in silence and allow yourself to be ravished by the love of God.

> *Your darkness is light turned inside out,*
> *so may I on my dark days Braille-feel*
> *your presence and luminous affection*
> *making my gloom a lover's rendezvous.*

July 17

A Good Batting Average

Summertime is baseball time. The best hitters in baseball history only got a hit once for every three times at bat! The extraordinary players do a little better: Ty Cobb's average was .366, Rogers Hornsby's was .358, and Joe Jackson's was .356. But most professional players do worse! We all come up to bat each day. When I attempt to write a new reflection and swing with all my might and miss, I try to remember that a really good player gets a hit only one out of three times. So if on a certain day a reflection in this book doesn't inspire you, consider the odds! Or think about your own plate appearances. When you try to be kind to some rude or disagreeable person, and fail twice to get a good response, don't stop trying. You may get a hit on your third try. The fact that the best baseball players in history had a sixty-seven percent failure rate can actually be encouraging for you and me. So relax, be patient if you strike out the first couple of times you try to be accepting and tolerant of those with political or religious beliefs different from yours.

Remind me whenever I fail
two or more times, to try again
and pray with faith that midget prayer,
"So help me God!"

July 18

So Help Me God

The short four-word prayer that concluded yesterday's reflection is actually borrowed from the courtroom: "So help me God." This traditional conclusion to the oath of truthfulness that includes placing the right hand on the Bible can be an ideal prayer reminder. This short "hands-on prayer" has great possibilities for awakening you to an essential and undeniable reality: your absolute dependence upon God. To help awaken you to this reality, you might try beginning each task that involves your hands by saying, "So help me God." Use that four-word prayer as you grasp the steering wheel of your car, finger the keyboard of your computer, or place the kitchen pot on the stove for the evening meal. "So help me God" is both a prayer to God and a reminder to yourself of your absolute dependence upon God.

When I face some difficult task,
and know well that I need help,
may I pray, "So help me God,"
and then try to do the undoable.

July 19

The Man Who Didn't Answer the Call to Prayer

The great Sufi saint Sarmad of Gwalior was once invited by the Emperor Aurangzeb to attend prayers with him at the grand mosque of the state. When the hour for prayer arrived, Sarmad wasn't anywhere to be seen in the mosque. Everyone was shocked since any invitation from the emperor was a royal command. When the time of prayer was over, the emperor's escorts eagerly tried to explain the absence of the holy man. "Perhaps old Sarmad is sick," said some. Others said, "Maybe since he is so old, his memory is failing and he forgot your royal invitation." The Emperor Aurangzeb left the mosque smiling and said, "No! Sarmad isn't sick and he didn't forget to attend this hour of prayer! Sarmad is a mystic; he lives every hour in Allah's presence and so an appointed hour set aside for prayer means absolutely nothing to him. Everywhere and every time of day for a man such as he is the place and time for prayer, and his every breath amazingly is a prayer. Should not we be like Sarmad?"

> *Holy times for prayer and worship*
> *are only reminders to pray always.*
> *Protect me from minimum loving,*
> *so we too can make love always.*

July 20

Look at the Moon

On this day in 1969 the American spacecraft Apollo 11 landed on the moon. While millions of Americans rejoiced in this great feat, the Native American Zunis of New Mexico were stunned at such an unspeakable sacrilege. In the Zuni religion the moon is sacred, a divine being. As they saw television images of astronauts walking, even jumping with glee, on the moon, they saw a sacrilege. For poets, lovers, and songwriters the moon is a lunar sacrament, and for many great religions it is a sacred clock proclaiming feast days such as Easter, Passover, and Ramadan along with the arrival of the new year. The next time you look up at the moon, take a long loving look, for she is about to lose whatever is left of her lunar magic and sacred nature. Scientists have announced that the soil of the moon can be a limitless source of clean, safe energy. The moon rocks the astronauts brought back to earth contained Helium 3, a potential fuel for fusion reactors. It is estimated only forty tons of moon soil could provide all of the electrical needs of America for a year! As you read this, the Chinese are designing the first lunar mining machines to turn the moon into a strip mine.

> *Old moon, never lose your magic,*
> *to awaken the poet and lover in me.*
> *Keep me a primitive child of wonder*
> *so to be stunned at your pale beauty.*

July 21

New Amazement

We suffer today from the banishment of mystery and wonder. Everything must be logically verified by testing. The need to appear sophisticated is replacing childlike astonishment. Only the simpleminded stand and gape open-mouthed at some modern marvel that the rest of us hurry past without a second glance. Deprived of wonder, life sadly becomes a giant labyrinth of torturous, twisting, interlocking, unconnected pathways that create confusion and alienation. The labyrinth is a fitting image for life today, because the original purpose of a labyrinth was to confuse, amaze, or bewilder. The word *bewilder* once carried the sense of being lost in a wilderness. So the next time you are lost in a contemporary labyrinth and feel you're "in over your head" or "out of your league," don't despair! Rejoice that you've been dropped into wonderland.

> *Lest I be seen as sophisticated,*
> *never drunk on awe in wonderland*
> *where I dwell, I am soberly suave;*
> *so come, heal my silly stylishness.*

July 22

The Pyromaniac Prophet

In the course of his life numerous attempts were made to murder the notorious rabbi Jesus of Galilee. Yet each time he escaped by eluding his enemies. So before they came to arrest him in the Garden of Olives, why then didn't he attempt to escape from Jerusalem to the safety of Galilee? The most frequent answer to such a question is, "It was God's will that he die." But why would God desire the death of anyone, especially a man as holy and good as Jesus? A possible way to understand this comes from a belief in Greek mythology: It is necessary for the gods to die or disappear since only then could humans inherit their intense interior fire. Sparks flew whenever godly heroes died. This is because death released a fiery whirlwind of the sparks of their divine fire that blew outward over those left behind. If this is the implication of the death of Jesus, each disciple should check within themselves to see if they have a low-burning pilot light or a blazing fire.

> *Your cross shouldn't grieve me but incite me*
> *to wildly fan the feeble fires of my heart*
> *enkindled by the blizzard of sparks flying*
> *off your cross and over the world to me.*

July 23

Jiffy Speed

When you tell someone, "I'll be with you in jiffy," you might more accurately say, "I will be with you in a couple of hundred jiffies!" A jiffy is an actual measurement of time that stands for one one-hundredth of a second. This faster-than-an-eye-flicker jiffy may be a prophetic word about our lives in the near future. Contemporary life is increasingly approaching jiffy speed. We grow ever more impatient with the speed of our electronic gadgets and computers. Jiffy time leads to the extinction of time prophesied in 1848 with the invention of the telegraph and the rapid expansion of the first railroads. These time-saving marvels caused people to speak about "the annihilation of time and space." Love causes imitation of the beloved, and being enamored with instant communicating machines results in attempting to imitate them. While appreciating the convenience of e-mail and the instant communication of cell phones and other electronic wizardry, beware of their effects on how you eat, visit, and make love!

> *Inoculate me against the plague of jiffyism*
> *by self-placed prophylactic speed limits*
> *on my meals, leisure, prayer, and visiting,*
> *lest by becoming swifter I lose my soul.*

July 24

Left With Only the Bones

The religion of the American Navajos has parables, and among them are wisdom stories about Coyote, known as the trickster or evil one. He is depicted as a selfish, gluttonous, oversexed, foolish, and dangerous trickster. In one of their parables, Coyote works his magic and causes it to rain in torrents, creating a flash flood that forces the prairie dogs out of their holes. With a promise to his stooge, Skunk, of a share in the catch, old Coyote rounds up and kills a large number of prairie dogs and puts them in a fire pit to cook. As the prairie dogs are roasting, Coyote schemes how he can cheat Skunk out of his share of the feast. But as usual in these Navajo prairie parables Coyote's plan backfires by a twist of fate, and he is left to chew on only the leftover bones of the prairie dogs. Unimportant are the details of how he lost out, since the truth of the tale is valid for each of us: Personal loss always comes to anyone who attempts to gain something only for oneself without regard for the needs of others. So don't be enchanted into playing the game of greed, since you'll always, always lose.

> *Greed notoriously produces scarcity,*
> *never bounty, so if tempted to be greedy,*
> *never give in to getting more, since now*
> *and hereafter, you'll be a loser.*

July 25

When the Messiah Comes

"The person who is awake finds joy in the stillness of meditation and in the sweetness of surrender. Hard it is to be born and it is hard to live, but it is even harder to arise, and be awake." So said Buddha in the fourteenth chapter of his *Dhammapada*. It is appropriate then that the name *Buddha* actually means "the awakened one." There is a similar emphasis on awakened living in Judaism. In a collection of tales by Jewish mystics known as *Tzaddiks,* there is a fascinating story about the Messiah. It tells how when the Messiah comes, nothing in life will change or be different. People will do what they have always done, except that they will be awake! This tale wondrously homogenizes two religious beliefs, as it creates Kosher Buddhists and Buddhist *Tzaddiks.* For Christians who believe that the Messiah has already come in the person of Jesus of Nazareth, it raises a major question. In today's world where things really haven't changed that much in the two millennia since the coming of Jesus, the Christian Messiah, are Christians awake?

> *Alarm-clock, awaken me*
> *to realize God's kingdom*
> *present here, all around me,*
> *so that I will live accordingly.*

July 26

The Lone Ranger

The Lone Ranger is a great American myth. His story embodies the idea of a lawman (a ranger) being ambushed and left for dead, but who is nursed back to life by a faithful companion.

In countless movies this mythic hero, portrayed as a masked stranger, rides in alone from outside of a community to rescue it from some great peril or evil. But the true hero is never a loner, and even though he was called the Lone Ranger, he wasn't actually alone. As unconventional as his mask was his faithful companion, Tonto. In the culture of the Wild West, Tonto was a despised outsider because he was a Native American. This ancient mythic theme is repeated again and again with stories of this masked stranger who rescues the settlers but never settles down himself, never marries or becomes part of life. When his task is completed, he rides off before he can be thanked, always causing someone to ask, "Who was that masked man?" His deathlike rejection of a comfortable life was essential to his being the Long Ranger, and the reason for it may provide an insight into the departure of Jesus. The scholar of mythology, Joseph Campbell, writes in his *The Hero with a Thousand Faces*, "The hero of yesterday becomes the tyrant of tomorrow, unless he crucifies himself today."

> *When I act heroically,*
> *like the Lone Ranger,*
> *let me be dead to all praise*
> *and depart un-thanked.*

July 27

Impossible, But Not Really

If forced to make a difficult decision where any possible option seems unthinkable, consider toothpaste. Historically, the first toothpaste was an Egyptian creation of ground pumice and strong wine. Early Romans used human urine to brush their teeth and as a mouthwash! Urine continued to be used until the late eighteenth century as an ingredient in toothpaste and with good reason—the ammonia in it has a powerful cleansing power. Today it is unthinkable that anyone would use their own urine to brush their teeth or as a mouthwash. Or consider Pablo Picasso. The impoverished young painter once burned his own paintings to keep warm in winter. Impossible to imagine! If you are facing a truly difficult choice, consider all the alternatives. Perhaps it is the absolutely unthinkable option that has the most positive benefits. If so, consider doing the unimaginable.

> *Become my consultant as I ponder*
> *an impossible solution to a problem.*
> *Remind me, as the angel said to Mary,*
> *"With God, nothing is impossible."*

July 28

Flabbergasted

If June is the month of weddings, then July is the month of revolutions and of the birth of that delightful word, *flabbergasted*. To be left speechless, struck dumb with wonder, is to be flabbergasted; a word delightful to the ear and one that goes all the way back to the American Revolution. Perhaps the American colonists were left joyously speechless when their rag-tag army of amateur soldiers defeated the most professional and powerful military force in the world. Without question, King George of England was surely flabbergasted when he learned that the undisciplined, poorly equipped, colonial rebels had defeated his magnificent army. Typically we are not left speechless by experiences of wonder, so only the fortunate know the taste of being flabbergasted. Ask yourself if you have ever in your life had an experience so wondrous that it left you not only wordless but breathless? If you have had such an experience, be abundantly grateful since that means you had an epiphany, a manifestation of the divine mystery.

May I be lucky enough to have an epiphany,
to be left tongue-tied and breathless,
in awe before something too wondrous
ever to be expressed in words or prayers.

July 29

An Eyeful

Wonder, like gratitude, is the diving board from which to plunge into prayer. Usually wonder is short-lived and soon fades away as the wondrous person, event, or thing becomes humdrum. In the early eighteenth century, London had a Hum-Drum Club, composed, it was said, of very honest gentlemen of peaceful dispositions. They would sit together in the posh club smoking their pipes and saying nothing until midnight. As the clock struck twelve, I wonder if they said good night to one another! If, like those honorable members of the Hum-Drum Club, you find you lack anything worth pondering or discussing, consider this fact: As you are reading this page, the retinas in your eyes are performing ten billion computer-like calculations every second! And as your eyes focus on the words of this sentence, they blink every two to ten seconds, and swing back and forth one hundred times each second!

> *Eyes have not seen what wonders*
> *have been created in each of us;*
> *awesome abilities we yawn over,*
> *blind to their incredible functions.*

July 30

Anonymous Wonder

You and I are known by name to only a small circle of family and friends, but to the rest of earth's billions we are anonymous. So why not be buried anonymously? The renowned English poet John Keats, as he was dying in 1821, requested that he be buried anonymously with his tombstone inscribed, "Here lies one whose name was writ on water." Scholars speculate Keats' epitaph was to arouse wonderment about who was buried in the mystery-shrouded tomb, and so enhance his legacy. Tombstones primarily are for those still alive who knew the deceased. For those who will see your tombstone a hundred years after your burial, it might just as well be nameless. Today, pause to consider your future burial by asking why you would purchase an expensive granite tombstone. Wouldn't a simple wooden cross with your name inscribed on it be sufficient to mark your gravesite for the years remaining for those who knew you by name?

> *I am no president who needs a grand tomb,*
> *so bury me in the hearts of those I've loved.*
> *Let my epitaph not be chiseled, but cherished*
> *memories of me, treasured by those I've loved.*

July 31

The Secret of the Quest

Jewish mystical spirituality is expressed in the *Zohar*, a text that expounds on the mystical insights of the Torah. The *Zohar* says that for each of us there is a light burning in heaven, and the All Holy One has made the light of each person distinctively different. When, for example, two friends share a meal and conversation, their two lights above are fused as one and out of this union of two lights is born a luminous angel. This gleaming angel however has been given the strength to survive only for one year unless the two friends meet again. If by some unfortunate circumstances the two friends are separated for longer than a year, that shining angel slowly weakens until it fades away. This same wisdom about friendship is found in Islam where it said that if a person prays all day, meditates in caves for decades, and give alms to the needy but lacks brotherhood of friendship, he is of no good to himself or to others. In Islamic mysticism there is no greater healing power in the world, no greater happiness, than brotherhood or friendship.

Challenge me to preserve good friendships,
spending hours and efforts enhancing them
in a society greedy about its time and energy,
that judges friendship to be far too expensive.

Month of
August

August 1

Turn on the Light—and Wonder

The next time you flip a switch and an electric light comes on, pause to wonder. As you turn on that light, what you are witnessing is matter being liberated into energy. Einstein discovered that light sometimes behaves like a particle and sometimes like a wave. Today contemporary scientists tell us that there is no such thing as a wave or a particle of light; we can only treat light as if it were a wave for some purposes and as a particle for others. Yet, actually it is neither. Rather light is something beyond the grasp of our minds, an unexplainable mystery and a cause for wonder.

> *As I touch my arm, open my mind.*
> *This flesh I touch is matter patiently waiting,*
> *not to return to dust again,*
> *but to be freed into the Mystery of Light.*

August 2

A Practical Treasure From Your Old Toy Box

Pretending is a wonderfully useful ability that shouldn't be left in your old toy box in the attic. To "pre-tend" is to pre-care-for, to pre-arrange or to look after some future event. Woe to those who recklessly plunge unprepared into the next important event in their day without pre-tending. Just as a skilled actor or public speaker practices by pretending to give a speech to an imaginary audience, so you should use childhood pretend-ing to prepare yourself for some difficult personal task, such as apologizing for a mistake. To pretend is to "make believe" (with an emphasis on *believe*). It means practicing for some-thing important with the conviction that it is real. When you practice pretending with enough faith and conviction, you will be surprisingly changed inwardly and given new powers by the magic of your imagination.

> *When faced with a difficult task*
> *may I be childlike and pretend*
> *I'm doing it with graceful ease,*
> *and find the difficult now easy.*

August 3

The Worship of Pain

Oscar Wilde once commented, "It is rarely in the world's history that its ideal has been one of joy. The worship of pain has far more often dominated the world." The cult of martyrs in both Christianity and Islam could be used to illustrate Wilde's point. In both of these religions sainthood is the glorious reward for those dying painfully for their faith. Halos are rarely, if ever, bestowed on those who live a long, joyous life, since living happily isn't often recognized as a religious ideal. Silent endurance of physical pain and suffering is an ideal regularly held up for imitation. When suffering enters people's lives, they are frequently told, "It's God's will, so accept it." We see the same connection between great suffering and God being made with respect to natural disasters that are sometimes called "acts of God." If I thought that the God of the three great Western religions intentionally caused massive destruction, horrible pain, and widespread suffering, then I would become an atheist.

> *I refuse to believe that you, God,*
> *desire your children suffer pain and sickness!*
> *If you get satisfaction from sufferings,*
> *I can't call you our Father, our Mother.*

August 4

No Stranger to Wonder

Albert Einstein believed that the most beautiful emotion we can experience is awe and wonder at the mysterious. He saw this fundamental emotion as the cradle of all art, science, and religion, and believed anyone who was a stranger to the mysterious, who could no longer wonder or stand rapt in awe, to be "like a snuffed out candle, dead." Einstein's image of a snuffed out candle should inspire us to insure that we invest some part of each day with wonder, seeking the mysterious amidst the commonplace. To be fully alive requires an attitude of reverencing the mysterious rather than trying to dissect it by seeking an explanation. Since by wondering you continuously rekindle your candle flame of life, a good resolution to begin each day would be, "I will not be a stranger to wonder."

> *Remind me that all of my emotions*
> *are children of Mother Wonder,*
> *so the more frequently I wonder,*
> *the richer will be my emotional life.*

August 5

What If?

Ponder how you would respond if you were challenged by your pastor to seriously think about what you say you believe. Instead of being admonished to believe dogmas, what if you were challenged to question them? What if, instead of supporting the conventional norms of social behavior, you were challenged by your pastor to question the religious validity of the government's decisions to wage war or to reduce payments to the poor? Religions and governments typically want their people to follow and not question. Any questioning of its authority, laws, or moral teachings is judged by church and state as a suspicious act of betrayal, treachery, and disloyalty. Our American freedom of speech involves the freedom to question out loud both the state and church. Seriously consider using this freedom.

> *Even if not challenged by my church,*
> *raise in my mind large question marks*
> *about dogmas and ancient moral laws,*
> *since by questioning I'll find your truth.*

August 6

Holy Communion of Tears

You are invited to go to holy communion whenever someone you know suffers the loss of a loved one. Holy compassionate communion is truly a sacrament of sympathy. Sympathy (from *sym,* "together in" and *pathos,* "pain or intense feeling") is a sharing in the pain of loss with others. Every expression of condolence—a card in the mail, attending a wake or funeral—is an act of the sacrament of sympathy. We find Jesus going to holy communion when he goes to Bethany to comfort the mourning Martha and Mary, and so elevates a common social action into a sacrament, a grace-infused deed. We often find ourselves tongue-tied when we attempt to express our sympathy to someone deeply mourning. Do not be concerned about what words you should say; instead strive as deeply as you can to share in the sorrow of another. The more you enter into a communion of sorrow, the more you will truly express your sympathy and compassion.

> *When I stumble in my sympathy*
> *tutor me to plunge into another's grief,*
> *to enter into a tearful communion*
> *and say that for which no words exist.*

August 7

Snakeskin Spirituality

Sins have sticky fingers! Some faults cling to us our entire lives, making the conquest of personal sins a major spiritual work. Because our thoughts, speech, and actions can easily be devoid of Godlike qualities, our failures can be many. As a result, people are often advised to select just one sin or failure and focus their attention on removing it. Once this sin is removed, move on to the next one. An old method of personal reform was to frequently review a checklist of sins for what failure next needed to be purged. In India, seven centuries before Christ, an important truth about sin was revealed by Divine Wisdom in the Hindu holy book, the *Prashna Upanishad*: "If anyone meditates on the supreme spirit . . . even as a snake sheds its skin, so they shall shed their sins." Spend time silently in God's presence, and your eyes will be opened to see your failings. Continue silently to be with God, and you will find your once acceptable failings now so unbearable that you will shed them as a snake sheds its old snakeskin.

> *Glue me to my prayer to sit silently*
> *with you, without words or scripture,*
> *so with enduring patience you will*
> *reform me from the inside out.*

August 8

The Power of Gravity

"Fire tends upward, stone downward," wrote the great St. Augustine in his famous *Confessions*. "It is by their weight they are moved and seek their proper place. . . . My love is my weight wherever I go, my love is what brings me there." These words, written over 1500 years ago, may help to explain where you are today and why. We tend to think of our major life choices as being based on fate or even random circumstances. Our lives often seem more the result of chance or fortune choices than of rational decision making. Consider reflecting on your life as Augustine did by reflecting on how love is the gravitational, magnetic agent that is the reason why you are where and who you are today. When next you must make some major decision, weight it down with a love heavier than a giant granite stone. Do that and be assured that after that decision has become reality, you will find yourself in the most auspicious of places.

> *In love that whirls the world around,*
> *may I find your secret that love*
> *also magnetizes good to me when I use it*
> *as my compass in making decisions.*

August 9

Don't Ask for Advice

When Louis B. Mayer was considering buying the motion picture rights to the book *Gone with the Wind*, he was given some rather unsound advice. Irving Thalberg, the MGM producer, advised his boss, "Fact is, Louis, Civil War pictures have never made a dime!" Of course, Thalberg's words did not prove helpful, as *Gone with the Wind* went on to become one of the most successful films of all time. Indeed, war movies of all types continue to be perennial favorites among cinema audiences everywhere. But if war makes good theater, why doesn't peace? If the lives of gangsters and violent action-heroes make great profits, why don't the lives of holy people? The answer to such questions is also the answer to the question of the whereabouts of prophets and holy heroes and heroines in our contemporary society. To be a prophet or holy person often requires going against the grain of what is considered popular and marketable in today's culture. Likewise, listening attentively to the Spirit's wisdom requires ignoring the conventional wisdom of the day. So, if you find yourself being called by God to become a prophet or a holy person, remember the advice given to Louis Mayer, and be wary of the words of the so-called experts.

Remind me that you never asked advice
from others whether to forgive sins,
heal the sick, or to eat with sinners,
heeding only the Spirit's guidance.

August 10

Pretending a Rich Life

Wonder and pretending are childhood companions that make life richly enjoyable, but sadly they fade away as we grow up to become serious adults. Wonder gives birth to playfulness, as when children wonder what it is like to be adults and then pretend to act like adults. Much of childhood play is pretending to be mothers, fathers, doctors, or other grown-up roles. Toys are pretending tools. Children use toys to wonder how it feels to act as a grown-up. True pretending requires being absorbed in make-believe that becomes the source of enjoyment and play. Since enjoyment is critical to the quality of a good life, why shouldn't we adults pretend more often? So, when next you must deal with some problem or difficult task, become like a child and pretend you have the solution. Then playfully pretend, using your imagination to live out that answer.

Encourage me to never grow up,
or discard the magic of childhood,
pretending and play-acting at life,
so I can find newer ways of living.

August 11

The Perfect Guru

The mind is marvelous beyond words, possessing the freedom to soar to the highest heights of imagination. The mind can travel backward into the past and visualize former delights that happened centuries ago. The mind can also leapfrog into the future to dream of what can be, and sadly this mind can also worry about what bad things may happen. The body, unlike the mind, cannot do any of these things; being firmly rooted in the present, your legs and body are grounded in a certain place and time. The body by necessity must do only one thing at a time, even if the mind is often off somewhere else. Yet, it is this lack of freedom that makes your body the perfect guru, spiritual guide, and teacher of how to experience God. The experience of God is found only in the present moment. So if you wish to advance spiritually, even to have mystic experiences, simply pay attention to your body. As unbelievable as it sounds, you will find God by asking questions of your body frequently throughout your day: Where are you? What are you doing? What are you feeling at this moment?

> *Thank you for my personal teacher,*
> *my body, who tells me to slow down*
> *when I'm tense from being too busy*
> *and grounds me in you in the present.*

August 12

Like Frying Little Fish

While it is wise to think carefully about decisions in life, don't think too much about them, else you become an "over-thinker." This advice is found in the ancient *Tao Te Ching* of China, "When frying little fish, don't flip them over too much." Over-thinkers often are perfectionists who must insure that whatever decision they make isn't a mistake. However, creative and adventuresome living is possible only when you don't over-think what you are going to do or not do. If you find yourself an over-thinker, flipping over and over some fishy problem, remember the wisdom of Mark Twain, who said, "Twenty years from now, you will be more disappointed by the things you didn't do than by the ones you did."

To enjoy life as an adventure
coach me to carefully think,
but not to fretfully over-think,
life's multitude of decisions.

August 13

The Absence of Pilgrimages

It is remarkable that for the first three hundred or so years after Christ's death, Christians showed no interest in making pilgrimages to the historic places of Jesus' birth, death, and resurrection. Apparently, to experience the power of his presence they felt no need to visit the historic sites of his life. Rather, they felt his presence in the breaking of the bread, in one another, in the poor and sick, and in visiting the imprisoned, just as he promised they would. As the centuries passed and Christianity aged, religious rituals and dogmatic beliefs replaced personal experiences of Jesus. It was at this historic point of decline in religious enthusiasm that believers, seeking to revive their zeal, went off on pilgrimages to visit Holy Land sites where Jesus had lived.

No need to pilgrimage from here where I live.
Wallop me with your electrifying energy,
you who are vibrantly present here today
as you were in the Holy Land for those awake.

August 14

The Paradox of Prayer

Forty-some years ago, as a young pastor, my custom was to drop in for a visit in the children's parish religion classes. Attending a kindergarten class one day, I was seated in the last row trying to be as invisible as possible. I listened as the teacher told the small children the following vivid story about the power of prayer: "Little Tommy and Jane were walking along the path one day when suddenly, right there in front of them, was a huge black dog! Tommy and Jane paused and prayed to Jesus," and then she paused briefly. "Can any of you children guess what happened next?" Instantly a young boy's hand shot up in the air, and when the teacher called on him, he said with great zest, "The dog disappeared! And in the middle of the path there was a big lion!" That innocent child's unexpected answer captures an important truth about prayer. God's response to our prayer often challenges us more than the situation that occasioned our petition. So if your next answer to a prayer is a more difficult situation than before, give thanks that God is inviting you to practice even greater faith.

> *I know no prayer goes unanswered,*
> *but if the answer isn't what I want,*
> *fortify me to embrace it with love,*
> *trusting you know better what I need.*

August 15

Surviving the Tsunami

The short reflections in this book are like small potted plants at the nursery, intended to be planted so they can grow roots and then flower. Now more than halfway into this book, ask yourself if any of these daily reflections have sunk roots into the soil of your life. If any have taken root, has one of them flowered? Are you any different now than you were before you began reading this book? Don't feel guilty if your answer to these questions is no. As an author I am aware that my readers are inundated with words. We all stand knee-deep in the surf as, one after another, towering waves of words from the media come crashing over us, only to race back out to sea for more. In this endless media tsunami, our survival instinct has taught us how to avoid drowning, or even getting wet! Instinctively we ignore what we read, hear, or see, and so the words leave us untouched. To be touched, and so to be changed, take one reflective thought from your daily reading, plant it in your heart-soil, water it by meditating on it, and I promise a beautiful flower will bloom in you.

> *Help, I am drowning in words*
> *in print, on radio, and television.*
> *Sharpen my discernment to know*
> *which are important, which are not.*

August 16

Each Day Is Your Birthday

A birthday can be either the day of your birth or the day of its anniversary. In the holy book of Hinduism, the *Bhagavad Gita,* the Lord Krishna says, "We are born into the world of nature; and our second birth is into the world of spirit." Your first birth required several hours or longer; your second birth is ongoing and lifelong, and like the first is also painful. Your first birth was painful for both your mother and you, but you cannot remember it. The labor pains of your second lifelong birth will be felt and remembered each day as you encounter the ordinary challenges of life. You will consciously feel those labor pains when you struggle to accept life's disappointments, broken dreams, and heartbreaks with serenity. You are being born more fully into the spirit each time you endure the pain of remaining nonviolent when the target of violent words, when you struggle to love the unlovable, and when you pardon others. So when next you feel the demanding pains of being loving and kind, forgiving and non-judgmental, rejoice since they mean today is your birthday.

> *When awakened, I am overjoyed that*
> *today isn't just another day, it's my birthday!*
> *So help me embrace, just as my mother did,*
> *the birth pains that help me grow more Godlike.*

August 17

You Must See the Rabbit

A young aspirant to holiness asked his teacher, "Why is it that some who seek God come to the desert and are zealous in prayer but leave after a year or so, while others, like you, remain faithful to the quest for a lifetime?" The old man smiled and answered, "One day I was sitting here quietly in the sun with my dog. Suddenly a large white rabbit ran across in front of us. Well, my dog jumped up, and barking loudly, took off after the rabbit with a passion. Soon other dogs joined him, attracted by his barking. The pack of dogs ran barking across the creeks, up stony embankments and through the thickets and thorns. Gradually, however, one by one, the other dogs dropped out of the pursuit, discouraged by the course and frustrated by the chase. Only my dog continued to hotly pursue the white rabbit." The young man sat in confused silence, and finally said, "I don't understand." The old man replied, "Unless you see the prey, the chase is just too difficult . . . you must see the rabbit!"

> *If I am not to lose heart*
> *and abandon my spiritual quest,*
> *you must teach me how to be an everyday mystic*
> *who finds you in life's holy humdrum.*

August 18

The Pyramid Conspiracy

Praiseworthy are those innumerable agencies striving to meet the needs of the world's poor, starving, and oppressed. Yet, does any group work to resolve the source of these worldwide injustices, namely, the Great Pyramid in which the fortunate few at the top enjoy the majority of the wealth while below them the vast majority of the powerless unfortunates suffer? This system also existed in Palestine at the time of Jesus. He laid siege to this evil tower with his Way of Life teaching: Share what you have with those in need, be loving and non-violent, and do not be intimidated by the Great Pyramid. The powerful at the peak of the pyramid strive to make us common people feel impotent, but we must resist their attempts. Rob Brezsny, in his book *Pronoia,* gives a call to resistance and to seriously ponder: "(Let us) collaborate, inspire each other to perpetuate healing mischief, friendly shocks, compassionate tricks, blasphemous reverence, holy pranks, and crazy wisdom."

> *Inspire me to mystical mischief*
> *and holy pranks, laughing off*
> *the edicts of the pyramid powerful*
> *who despise not being taken seriously.*

August 19

Starving With a Full Pantry

One of my favorite authors, G. K. Chesterton, in his preface to Dickens' *Pickwick Papers,* summed up my belief about wonders when he wrote, "The world will never starve for wonders, but only for want of wonder." Paradoxically, this insightful sentence was used as an inscription in 1933 on the General Motors Building at the Chicago Century of Progress Exposition. I say paradoxically, since it seems industrial progress not only has in the past but continues today to drain us of our sense of wonder.

> *Enkindle my childhood wilting wonder,*
> *exhausted by endless electronic gadgets*
> *that deplete my wonder at a singing bird,*
> *a cricket's charm, or a single star at night.*

August 20

Prematurely Freeze-dried

Clarence Birdseye, while working with the U.S. Government Fish and Wildlife Department in 1912, observed the natives of Labrador catching fish in fifty-below-zero weather. It was so cold that it froze the fish as soon as they were taken out of the water. Birdseye observed how months later the natives thawed and ate the fish. As you may have already guessed, these observations led to the first Birdseye frozen foods. Today, we not only have frozen foods, we can also have a freeze-dried funeral. In ecologically advanced Sweden, instead of using enormous amounts of energy to cremate the dead, the bodies of the deceased are dipped in liquid nitrogen, causing them to become brittle and then turn to dust. There is yet another type of freezing that these considerations prompt us to remember: spiritual freezing. The fourteenth-century Persian mystic Rumi said, "Spend not your time with cold faces in dead places or else your breath will freeze your breast and heart." Good advice if you don't want to have your heart prematurely freeze-dried!

> *When I discover I'm in a lifeless place—*
> *a party or in a church—show to me the exit!*
> *Encountering those with icy cold faces,*
> *alert me lest I suffer heart-soul frostbite.*

August 21

Be Not Afraid

Jumping in fright, as when mistaking an old twisted piece of rope in the grass for a snake, is a sign of the challenge of living today with a part of your brain that is still prehistoric. While we no longer live in a dangerous environment with giant killer predators such as our ancestors encountered, our central nervous system unconsciously reacts as if we did. Whenever we feel threatened, our primitive survival mechanism, the amygdala, reacts by pumping adrenaline and other hormones into our blood system, fueling the old fight or flight response. Nevertheless, it is possible to protect yourself from being imprisoned in fear, even when engulfed in daily reports of murder, terrorism, and mayhem. If you feel you're becoming a captive of fear, practice repeating frequently to yourself those reassuring words of the Teacher, "Fear not."

> *Since you love me, are constantly*
> *at my side, what do I have to fear?*
> *My bulletproof vest is your love,*
> *so even death I need not fear.*

August 22

The Magic of Singing

The Ainu Native Americans say that the salmon and the bear like our music and enjoy hearing us sing to them. Unlike we who walk only on asphalt and concrete and prefer the mall to being in nature, the Ainu live in close harmony with the animals of the forest and so understand them. It is unlikely today that you will encounter a bear, but should you encounter a barking dog, sing a pleasant song to it as a way to reassure the dog that you mean it no harm. Keep a favorite song in your back pocket or purse for snarling dogs—and also for menacing humans! Before you flip to the next page convinced that this idea of singing to dangerous dogs or humans is utter madness, pause and read on. The seventeenth-century English dramatist, William Congreve, in his play *The Mourning Bride*, says, "Music has charms to soothe a savage beast." His very next line, "to soften rocks, or bend a knotted oak," offers further useful implications. If today you must deal with some rock-hard-hearted person or someone notorious for being unbending, just hum to yourself a little soothing, softening, and oak-bending ditty.

> *When I'm frightened by dangers*
> *threatening me and want to run,*
> *may I sing so that magic music will*
> *encourage me and free my soul.*

August 23

Fear of Being Out of Control

When you feel you are in control, you feel reassured and comforted, even if it is an illusion. We see an example of this in the common fear of flying. In America, only a few hundred people at most die in airplane crashes each year, while over forty-four thousand die in motor vehicle accidents! Nevertheless, this overwhelming statistical difference doesn't cause a fear of driving because of the illusion that while in your car you feel in control. The goal of healthy living is to live in reality, not illusion. To achieve this goal, abandon trying to be in control, and strive to live happily despite all the dangers involved in being alive. Live, and also let others live, in reality. Refrain from manipulating and micromanaging others to maintain the illusion that you are in control of your life.

> *To enjoy life as an exciting adventure,*
> *more thrilling than any roller coaster,*
> *I strive not to be in control of anything,*
> *being safety-belted secure in your love.*

August 24

Are You Illiterate?

My Irish great-grandfather was illiterate, a result of imperial Britain's ban on the education of the Irish. He immigrated to America in 1840, and in the place on his immigration papers requiring his signature he made an "X." Today in the twenty-first century, the majority of adults can read and write. But even if you can, you may still be illiterate! According to Alvin Toffler, "the illiterate of the twenty-first century will be . . .

those who cannot learn, unlearn, and relearn." More painful than learning is unlearning; it is more difficult than teaching new tricks to an old dog. It requires kicking out from beneath you old structures that give you a secure sense of support. This century's new unfortunate illiterate ones will be those unable to unlearn what they were taught by schools, the state, and their church. For only those who are able to unlearn will in turn be able to learn new ways to live in a complex evolving age of change.

> *Force me to strenuously use an eraser*
> *to remove my mind's old knowledge*
> *that stymies my soul and stagnates me,*
> *so I'll be eager and ready to learn new ways.*

August 25

Stargazing Wonder

To simply sit as night falls and the sky gradually darkens can be an amazing experience. As the stars begin to appear, you can look out into the endless expanse of space and marvel. The night sky is filled with stars that sometimes seem so close that you could almost touch them. As the night progresses, we begin to sense that the earth is turning as the stars move across the sky. Not only is our planet rotating, it is also traveling at the speed of forty-three thousand miles an hour as it revolves around the sun. Truly awesome. The prayer of adoration and wonder may be the prayer of the twenty-first century. What fire, thunder, and the mystery of birth once invoked in the primitive person, the magnitude of space awakens in us.

> *Spur me not just to look at the stars,*
> *but with the Magi's astonishment gawk*
> *at how large, how far away they are,*
> *to be stunned with wonder beyond my mind.*

August 26

Back to Kindergarten

Kindergarten refresher courses should be mandatory for everyone. *Kindergarten* (from the Old High German *kinder*, the plural of *kind*, child) was originally designed as an orientation adjustment from home to school for children ages four to five. In this "children's garden" (such a delightful name for a place of learning) small children learn new skills of social awareness and how to interact with others. In a kindergarten refresher course we could play with the English word *kinder* and learn how to be kinder to each other and the stranger. Kindness is polite behavior that treats others courteously, respectfully, and acknowledges gratitude for simple services. Sadly, kindness can easily be neglected at home because of over-familiarity. Its neglect can result in curt exchanges and the absence of gratitude for small domestic acts. Tasks like shopping, preparing a meal, mowing the lawn, or taking out the trash are judged as shared domestic duties, and too often are insufficiently appreciated. On the street and at home, be kinder today than yesterday, and take nothing for granted. Everything in life is a gift.

> *Kindness and respect shown to others*
> *isn't just being polite, it is a loving act*
> *of reverence shown to the Holy One,*
> *since God invisibly dwells in everyone.*

August 27

Handle with Care

Native American Hopi children are taught never to pick any plant, not even a weed, if they are not going to use it. Likewise, Buddhist children in Tibet are taught that it is a sin to pick a wild flower and end its life. Unfortunately, the Christian tradition has often lacked this sense of spiritual interdependence with all of creation that is part of the Hopi Indian, Tibetan, and other religious traditions. The present ecological disaster is a moral failure of religion, especially Christianity, the dominant religious force in the industrial world. Native Hopi spirituality describes those out of harmony with creation as "two-hearted," meaning that they are selfish and deceitful. This teaching resonates with the Teacher's words, "Blessed are the single hearted." Those blessed with only one heart, the Hopi say, are those "concerned for the mutual welfare of all," including our fellow creatures in nature.

> *Broaden my boundaries of concern*
> *beyond myself, family and friends,*
> *to encompass humanity and creation,*
> *to be one-hearted in the Divine Heart.*

August 28

Jail Break

The unknown composer of the old hobo song, "The Big Rock Candy Mountain," created lyrics full of hope for those jobless men who had little hope and even less money. Even today its lyrical words speak of hope:

> In the Big Rock Candy Mountains,
> the jails are made of tin,

and you can bust right out again
as soon as they put you in.

As they passed through small towns, hoboes could be tossed in jail by the local sheriff for no greater offense than having no visible means of support. You and I can also be jailed behind icy-cold bars when a family member gives us the cold shoulder. Your pastor can jail you in guilt by sermonizing about how sinful some common social behavior is. Your boss can toss you in the clinker by embarrassing you in front of others over some minor mistake. When these unjust arrests occur, remember that such jails are made of tin and you can escape as soon as they put you in!

> *Remind me, all jails are made of tin.*
> *No jail can hold this child of God*
> *who lives believing in Paul of Tarsus's*
> *"Glorious freedom of God's children."*

August 29

Elder Wisdom

Elders in previous ages were storytellers and walking libraries of history and folklore. But we no longer sit around a crackling fire listening to wise old seniors tell us ancient myths and hair-raising legends. The majority of us didn't grow up with grandparents, great uncles or aunts who held us spellbound with vivid storytelling. Today elders are not the repositories of wisdom or legends—they're just "old" people! So I felt like I had been hit by a bolt of lightning when I read the following insight in Gary Snyder's *The Practice of the Wild*, "Books are our grandparents!" Look at your bookcase, and see those books on the shelves as your great uncles, grandmothers, and village elders. When most of our possessions grow old and worn they are discarded, but that's not true for old books. I have old tattered books shabby from over fifty years of use whose authors are now long dead, but which continue to be my wise elders. While treasuring the wealth of wisdom contained in our books let us also value those elders among us. They are living tabernacles of wisdom and we should have the humility to learn from their tales of yesteryear.

> *Listening to elders, may I become wise,*
> *for history is but a gigantic dusty wheel*
> *rolling around and around, ever-repeating*
> *the same mistakes and foolish blunders.*

August 30

Fire Escape

Long ago, clans desiring to get rid of undesirables without kill-
ing them would burn down their houses; hence the source,
some say, of the expression "to get fired." Paradoxically, that old
solution of fire remains the best way to deal with undesirable
relatives, fellow employees, or neighbors! It isn't your neighbor's house that is ignited, but that pile of tinder-dry planks
of beliefs stacked in your mind like, "Love your neighbor,"
"Always return good for evil," and "Pray for your enemies." Set
ablaze the dry timbers of "love your enemy" and the dancing
flames will spell out, "Be kind. Realize there are hidden reasons why they are disagreeable. Maybe they are emotionally
crippled." Be a pyromaniac. Light this fire, and you will be the
one "fired," set ablaze like that bush on Horeb. And listen for
what Moses heard, "Take off your shoes, you are standing on
holy ground."

> *Fire me when I live Jesus' teaching,*
> *torching me from head-to-toe,*
> *beyond faithful to become a devoured disciple*
> *engulfed in your fiery Holy Presence.*

August 31

Back to School

Summer is over. If students aren't back in school by now, they soon will be. Unfortunately, going off to school for most children means the slow death of their imaginations and creativity. For example, children are admonished not to play with different spellings of words; only one way is correct to spell every word. They are told that the sun must always be painted yellow, never purple. The great unspoken lesson is the necessity to separate work from play if you are to get ahead in life. Moreover, as electronics become more common in our homes, it seems small children suffer severe imagination impairment outside of school as well. With each additional year of schooling, we lose more of the important childhood tools for life. Good news: nothing is forever dead. So right now is a good time for a resurrection of your childhood imagination.

> *Tutor me to just play around,*
> *tinker-toying my problems,*
> *re-creating work like a game,*
> *living life as one long recess.*

Month of
September

September 1

O All-Nourishing Holy Abyss

Inside this visible world is another hidden world, the subatomic world. The term used to describe what happens inside this subatomic world is *quantum vacuum*. Amazingly, 90 percent of each atom is empty space, a vacuum. And the electrons and particles inside each atom appear to be whirling around as they come forth from "nothingness," only to again disappear back into it. Brian Swimme, a mathematical cosmologist, explains this action as "elementary particles crop up out of the vacuum itself—that is simply an awesome discovery . . . that the base of the universe seethes with creativity." He continues, "I use 'all-nourishing abyss' as a way of pointing to this mystery that is the base of being." Has Brian Swimme's "all-nourishing abyss" given to us a new wonder-soaked name for the Divine Mystery we so casually call God?

> *Hidden within everything*
> *is a second energetic cosmos,*
> *all-nourishing wonder*
> *at the heart of all life.*

September 2

Eden Language

The ancients believed that before his fall from grace, the language Adam spoke was poetry. This old belief is bewitchingly interesting since it asks what mysterious bandit has robbed us of our daily poetic speech. Once, not that long ago, ordinary conversation was more colorfully charming since it was sprinkled with bits of rhyme, poetry, and even snatches of Shakespeare. Does the contemporary demise of the poetic in daily life mean that Original Sin is intensifying since one effect of the garden fall was Adam losing his native tongue? Poems and poetic speech are magical. They possess the power to transport the far away to nearby and transform thinking into feeling. As has been said: "Long ago people could not only see but feel the stars because the sky was down where people could feel it." Poetry has beheading power, as Emily Dickinson said, "If I feel physically as if the top of my head were taken off, I know that is poetry! Is there any other way?"

> *When I am blown away by a song's lyrics*
> *or my heart flips at a colorful phrase,*
> *may I thank Poetry for arousing in me*
> *that naked touch of paradise, and you.*

September 3

A Speed Limit for Life

When I was a kid during the Great Depression, a popular and free entertainment for my family—except for the cost of gas which was only ten cents a gallon—was going for a drive in the Nebraska countryside. Driving out of the city we enjoyed looking at the corn, the other crops, and the colorful wildflowers along the highway. Today, driving isn't for going on a leisurely ride to look at the landscape, but for getting from one place to another as fast as the speed limit allows. At high speeds, even if we think we are seeing what we pass, we don't see much. As Mao Tse-Tung said: "If we look at flowers from a galloping horse, even though we may look daily, it is like not having seen them at all." I'm not promoting driving while gazing out your car windows, but rather to budget beforehand your driving time to allow a few minutes to stop and truly see whatever is along the street or road. The slower you move, the more you see, on foot or in an automobile. So move slower if you wish to see the wonders of life and creation around you.

> *When speeding through life, deputize me*
> *to arrest myself and sermonize me,*
> *"I caught you speeding. Slow down,"*
> *lest in that whizzing by I miss you.*

September 4

How to Be a Hero

Perhaps every youth aspires to be a hero, yet this aspiration is often stunted by having to make a living, caring for the needs of a family, and other social duties. To be a hero requires giving a gift, and if you are an average person then the gift you give is specified by your society. However, creative people must craft a particularly unique personal gift to give that usually isn't the one pre-determined by society. Creative people do not give the typical gift that society expects, and instead give the ultimate gift of themselves to the highest powers of life, to God. Yet, as Ernest Becker says, to renounce the world and oneself by placing the meaning of your life before the powers of creation is the hardest thing any person can achieve. It should not be surprising then, that history records only a few truly great heroes. Likewise, it isn't surprising that the average person, in his or her quest to be heroic, is content to only give those gifts specified by their society.

> *Inspire me to fulfill my heroic destiny*
> *by not giving society's specified gift,*
> *but by giving the indispensable gift of myself*
> *to the Amazing Mystery of the Cosmos.*

September 5

Don't Pray, Will Your Prayers

In the Native American Hopi language the word for prayer means "to pray-will," a word for which there is no equivalent in English. However, their pray-will is a cousin word to what Jesus taught about prayer. He taught that we are always to pray with faith—that is, to pray with the conviction and force of will that whatever is prayed for *will* happen! Praying for peace doesn't mean saying fuzzy pious words begging God to make the world more peaceful, but to involve oneself personally in bringing peace to the world. When I pray for peace with faith and in a pray-willing way as the Hopi do, I must will to be peace-filled in my own life. Only by ever-expanding circles of willed prayer will peace ever come to the world. In the first circle, I must will myself to be at peace in my thoughts, words, and deeds. In the second circle, I will myself to be at peace in my home and family. Then in the third circle, I will to be at peace in my neighborhood. Only then will peace continue expanding ever outward from me.

> *I desire to pray with will-power,*
> *praying with conviction that you*
> *also will what I pray will happen;*
> *so that what I ask will be your will.*

September 6

God at Your Fingertips

The Koran says that God is closer than the vein in your neck. What a beautiful invitation to pray. In fact, it suggests a new way to pray: Begin by placing your first and second fingers on your throat's jugular vein. Linger there as you feel the vigorous throbbing of life within you. Praying with your fingers on your jugular vein can be a sensual affirmation that God is not distant or remote, but is pulsating within you. God is life. What better way to be mindful of the nearness of the Presence than to actually feel it vibrating on your fingertips. To gain the attention of God, your intimate Beloved, does not require bellowing prayers, clanging bells, or thunderous pipe organ preludes. A silent sensual touch can profoundly awaken you to God's perpetual attention to you and your needs.

> *Needing to know you are near,*
> *let me touch my jugular vein*
> *feeling your throbbing presence within,*
> *all over, and around me.*

September 7

The Perils of Comfort

Worthy of pondering is an old Native American proverb: "Those who sit lazy by the fire will have a truncated life; it will be cut short by selfishness." While personal security and comfort is presented by contemporary society as the goal of a good life, for the Native Americans it was actually a recipe for a short life. Oh, you may continue to exist until a ripe age, but you will not be alive! Over and over again, folk tales—those storehouses of wisdom—tell of heroes and heroines who interrupt their quest to be compassionate to someone in need. In tales of the quest for the Holy Grail, the magical golden ring, or the elixir of life the heroes make seemingly foolish detours to help those in need, even if they are insignificant people. The best way to remain fully and vitally alive all the way up to the moment of your last and final breath is to constantly strive to be sensitive to other's needs and suffering, responding to their unspoken cries for help.

> *Remove my heart's hardened calluses*
> *dulling me to the suffering of others*
> *so to share bits and pieces of myself*
> *and, by so doing, find the secret of life.*

September 8

The Circle of Life

The first stunningly sacred image of earth taken from space showed that we live on a round planet. What makes that photo so shockingly sacred is that it is the first photograph of our round world revealing it as a single living organism, naked of national boundary lines and artificially created divisions. Sacred art should shock not soothe. The Divine Mystery contradicts our common beliefs about God, just as that image of a round earth contradicts the logic of our experience. Common sense tells us that we live on a flat surfaced planet, even if intellectually we know otherwise. A spiritual practice helpful for escaping from flat, straight-line thinking is to remind yourself frequently that you live on a round planet. The roundness of the earth declares that life follows the law of the circle, that whatever you do to others will infallibly circle around again back to you. This planetary lesson teaches that coming full circle of every good or bad deed may not be instantaneous, but your every action will eventually return to where it began.

> *Jam down on my head a dunce's cap*
> *if I think my deeds today are free*
> *of tomorrow's consequences,*
> *as they'll boomerang back to me.*

September 9

The Gigantic Fun House

A good mirror is like a photograph, unless it happens to be one of those mirrors in a carnival fun house. When you look in one of those curved beveled mirrors you see a laughable, distorted, unrecognizable image of yourself. The Moslem mystical Sufis have the saying, "You are the mirror in which God recognizes him or herself." If God looks into your divine mirror, does God recognize Godself? Or is the image in the mirror distorted and twisted by selfishness and petty interests? The distorted fun-house mirrors are intended to be comical, but does the Creator find what is reflected in the countless divine mirrors of humanity funny? In those millions upon millions of mirrors, some reflect a divinely beautiful image. These are of persons we call saints. The holy ones became beautiful divine reflections by endlessly polishing their mirror-selves. The next time you look into the mirror of your conscience and see an imperfection, regardless how slight, take immediate action. Polish your mirror until you have removed the disfigurement. And continue polishing your mirror as a frequent if not daily spiritual practice.

My personal reform would be improved
if I imagined every mirror was two-sided.
As I see myself, another is looking at me,
asking, "Who is that I see in my mirror?"

◆◆◆

September 10

A Puff of Jewish Wisdom

Ecclesiastes, the book of Jewish Wisdom, is famous for the line: "Vanity of vanities, all things are vanity." This scripture, written 2,250 years ago, reflects a contemporary view about the futility of the drudgery of life, "For what profit comes to a man from all the toil and anxiety of heart . . . all his days are sorrow and grief." The author claims that all life is vanity. In Hebrew, the word is *hebel*, which means "just a puff of breath." Since the toils and drudgery of life are but mere puffs of useless air, the author proposes to live in the moment; eat, drink, and provide yourself with good things for all too soon you will die! While sounding like cynical advice, this is really mystical, paradoxical wisdom. Only by living in the moment, enjoying each as much as possible, can you live in God! The Divine dwells in between the tick and the tock of the clock. Mystics have taught for centuries to live in the present. Few live there. Being busy, planning the future, they live in tomorrow and forget that life, as the Native Americans said, "Is as brief as the buffalo's breath in winter."

> *Inspire me to avoid killing today*
> *by thinking only about tomorrow.*
> *While prudently planning ahead,*
> *keep me busy enjoying life today.*

September 11

By Any Name

Religious people easily believe their religion has an exclusive divine copyright on salvation. The apostle Paul, writing to the first Christians in Rome, said: "Everyone who calls upon the name of the Lord will be saved." Notice he didn't say every Christian or every believer, but "everyone." This wide-ranging inclusiveness surely meant Jews as well as Christians, women and men, slaves as well as freeborn. The writer Patricia Sanchez encourages us to expand who is included in "everyone," saying we should never limit the loving generosity of God. Inexhaustible is the list of possibilities when calling upon the name of God: Allah, Yahweh, Krishna, Abba, Vishnu, Buddha, Lord, Father, Mother, the Divine Mystery, the Great Spirit. Space prevents continuing that list, but these are sufficient to grasp Paul's wondrous insight that God passionately desires everyone who lives to be gifted with salvation. And what is salvation? It is returning to the Sacred Womb from where all have come.

> *Let your unbounded generosity*
> *call me to love others as you do,*
> *desiring their good and happiness*
> *in this life and in the life to come.*

September 12

Eternally Valid Laws

In India, nine hundred years before the birth of Christ, an unknown Hindu saint realized that every thought, word, and action had its consequences. He named this reality the Law of Karma. Besides its short-term effect, each emotion or deed is a seed that gives shape to events in the future. The way we act and walk the path of life shapes who we become. Evil seeds produce evil plants; good seeds produce good plants. This law of life, which is reflected in Jewish Scriptures as well as in the parables of Jesus, is revealed again and again before our eyes. Yet some people are so careless with something as seemingly harmless as an angry thought or deed. It would seem that they do not take the existence of this cosmic law seriously.

> *Only a fool believes you can escape*
> *from your deeds when they come back to you.*
> *Alert me to watch my deeds carefully*
> *since I harvest the fruits of their seeds.*

September 13

Secret Prisons

America leads or is a close second among world nations for the largest number of people incarcerated in prisons. Besides inmates in state and federal prisons, there are tens of thousands more incarcerated in hidden, secret prisons. These are prisoners of emotional or psychological problems, and those held captive by extreme self-love, jealousy, envy, uncontrollable anger, greed, prejudice, alcohol, drugs, and other destructive behaviors. The recidivism rate of paroled prisoners is such that a large percent of them are soon returned to prison. Sadly, the same is often true for those paroled from their inner-prisons by religious conversion and psychological counseling. This raises three questions. First, when such staggering numbers of our population suffer imprisonment in public and private prisons, why is there so little compassion shown for them? Second, with personal prisons being hidden away, could you possibly be incarcerated in one of them? Third, if this is true, have you seriously considered escaping?

> *Am I in a prison invisible to others,*
> *where I am both guard and warden?*
> *If so, may I parole myself to attempt*
> *to live free outside my prison walls.*

September 14

An Alarm Clock Amen

Christians are admonished to attain the unachievable task of praying without ceasing. Addressing this literally impossible call to ceaseless prayer, the seventeenth-century Protestant mystic of the French Reformed Church, Pierre Poiret, wrote;

> God never asks the impossible of us. If one
> had always to be in church one would die for
> lack of the necessities of life; and were one
> obliged to be always on one's knees, who
> could bear the constant fatigue? But God
> asks only for a conversation to continue
> always between the two of us, and it can

continue when you are working, eating,
drinking, writing, and even while sleeping.

This ideal of having an ongoing conversation with God at our work or meals is fascinating. But most delightful is the idea of praying even while we are sleeping! Since earliest times spiritual guides have proposed praying at the bookends of the day, upon awakening and before falling asleep. But how do you pray while you are sleeping? One way could be to desire the One-Who-Never-Sleeps climb in bed with you, even if some of your dreams may be a bit erotic and strange. The best of all night prayers is a lover's invitation, "Come and share my bed."

> *Come Beloved, let us go to bed.*
> *Come and sleep right next to me,*
> *to share my wild and sweet dreams*
> *so I can awaken in your embrace.*

September 15

A Creed for Lips

In his 1957 book, *Viper's Tangle*, Francois Mauriac created a miserable character whose heart is a nest of vipers. Another character in this book speaks about this wretched man, about himself, and many of us when he says, "Our thoughts, our desires, our actions struck no roots in that faith in which we adhered with our lips. With all our strength we were devoted to material things." To sink roots of your belief in your thoughts and actions requires intention, passionate desire, and the constant work of connecting and reconnecting your beliefs to daily life. Rooted faith is evident everywhere in the world: everyone's life reflects what they believe. Faith isn't restricted to religious beliefs, for countless are the creeds in which we place our faith: success, popularity, money, power, war, sex, comfort, and security. To spend a few minutes examining the lives of others and your own reveals which beliefs are deeply rooted and those that only live on the lips.

> *Teach me to be a diligent,*
> *root inspector of my beliefs,*
> *so to keep them deeply planted*
> *and growing to shape my life.*

September 16

Alms from the Beggar

The Persian saint, Rumi, tells of a dream he had of a smiling beggar who offered him alms! Beyond that paradox, Rumi recalls how his heart leaped with joy at the radiating splendor of the beggar's tattered cloak. But then he sadly laments that he awoke since it was dawn. Beggars and panhandlers are pests whom we usually go out of our way to avoid. They tend to be disheveled and grimy so we are not inclined to be generous. We judge them to be alcoholics, drug addicts, or lazy bums. Grimy and disheveled could easily have described the beggar Rumi saw in his dream, only instead of asking for alms, he was giving alms and smiling! Reflect for a moment on Rumi's dream, it has prophetic implications for you. Does not every beggar, dressed in dirty rags or a three-piece suit, offer you alms?

> *Jesus promised that any alms*
> *we give to the needy, we give to him.*
> *So giving is really an exchange of alms*
> *and we are given the best portions.*

September 17

First Aid

A Buddhist parable tells of a man struck by an arrow shot by an unknown assailant. He refuses to allow the arrow to be removed or his wound treated until the archer is located and properly punished. Days grow into weeks and weeks into months as his

wound festers. Finally its poison kills him. The parable ends
with a question: who is responsible for this man's death—the
unknown assailant or the man himself who foolishly clung to
the arrow? When next your heart is pierced by an arrow of
angry words, you can cling to the arrow of injury like the dead
fool in this parable, or instead you can seek treatment. First
Aid for wounded hearts requires that you pull out the arrow of
injury yourself instead of clinging to it. Then clean the wound
by washing away desires that the offender be punished. Lastly,
day after day, repeatedly apply the miraculous all-healing salve
of forgiveness. This miracle drug can be found in your heart's
medicine cabinet; it's in everyone's heart. Rare are those who
use this salve. Use of this potent medicine requires faith in the
Galilean doctor who said it was the only cure!

> *Help me pull out the wounding arrow*
> *and disinfect the venom of victim-hood.*
> *Sterilize my poor-me attitude of self-pity.*
> *By my forgiving, heal me and the other..*

September 18

Cataloging Your Strengths

One day a disciple asked his spiritual teacher: "Master, please help me answer this application for a position I am seeking." The teacher responded: "Certainly, how can I be of assistance?" The disciple said: "I am asked on the application to list my strengths, and you being my spiritual guide and knowing me so well, I thought you could help me answer that question." The teacher smiled: "Of course. List your weaknesses!" This isn't as bizarre as it appears; recall the apostle Paul told Corinth's early Christians that in their weakness God's power reaches perfection. Typically we boast about our strengths and achievements; no one brags about their deficiencies and shortcomings. Yet Paul boasted of his weaknesses, and said he did so in order that God's power might dwell in him. So list your weaknesses and you will know the places in your life where God can be the most active. Expose your weaknesses, and be surprised how strong you really are.

> *Until you enhance my weaknesses,*
> *they're embarrassing shortcomings.*
> *So come fill them, transform them*
> *into surprising sources of great power.*

September 19

Children of God

In this book you have read parables and spiritual reflections taken from the world's great religious traditions, including our own American Native Indian religions. To find spiritual nourishment in religions other than your own is difficult for those who maintain that their religion is superior to others and contains all that is needed for union with God. However, the Teacher said that the Spirit of God is like the wind that blows wherever it wills. The Spirit Wind of God has and continues to blow over other religions and peoples leaving behind gifts of truth and wisdom in their teachings and spiritual practices. If you are one who believes the all-inclusive Spirit of the Holy descended in many planetary Pentecosts, the spiritual practices and wisdom of other religions won't be a threat to your faith. On the contrary they increase your faith in God, in that delightful, all-loving and inclusive God.

> *Jesus told us you were "Our Father."*
> *As a loving father you don't speak*
> *the truth to some of your children,*
> *leaving the rest in darkness, correct?*

September 20

Holy Memories

Without being invited, memories surprisingly drop by to visit. These unexpected visits of persons and events can be occasioned by a song, an old photograph, or for no known reason. In the Catholic Christian tradition, it is customary to pray for the dead, and praying for a deceased person triggers a memory of them that is itself a thought-prayer. When in the midst of our day a memory of someone dead or alive visits our mind, that recollection isn't some empty echo of the past, it is amazingly powerful. Too easily we underestimate the powers of a memory, unaware that thinking about someone is praying for them. A memory is the nuclear core of Christian worship that fulfills Jesus' request at his last meal before he died. Aware of the dynamic power of a lover's memory, he said to those at the table, "Each time you eat this meal, do it in memory of me." That sacred dinner-memory also radioactively energizes each of our memories of those we love with the miraculous power to make them present to us.

> *May every cemetery remind me,*
> *that while marble tombstones are nice,*
> *memories best honor our dead,*
> *resurrecting them to life again to us.*

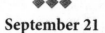

September 21

Autumn Equinox

O sacred season of autumn, be my teacher, for I wish to learn the virtue of contentment. As I gaze upon your full-colored beauty I sense about you an at-home-ness with your amber riches. You are the season of retirement, of full barns and harvested fields. The cycle of growth has ceased, the busy work of giving life is now completed. I sense in you no regrets; you've lived a full life. I live in a society ever restless, always eager for more mountains to climb, seeking happiness through more and more possessions. As a child of my culture, I am seldom truly at peace with what I have. Teach me to take stock of what I've been given and received; may I know that it is enough, that my striving can cease in the abundance of God's grace. I know the contentment that allows the totality of my energies to come to full flower. May I know that like you I am rich beyond measure. As you, O Autumn, take pleasure in great bounty, let me also take delight in the abundance of simple things in life that are the true source of joy. With the golden glow of peaceful contentment may I truly appreciate this autumn day.

In my imagination may I feel the earth
tilting 23 degrees to the sun today
in an equal balance of day and night;
to be in awe on this ancient sun feast.

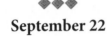

September 22

The Terrorized King

Once, long ago, a king astrologer nightly studied the stars for signs and messages. One night he decoded a strange pattern of stars and was terrified to read of a great calamity that would befall him on a certain day in the near future. Frightened, the next day he ordered a great stronghold to be built out of massive rock in which he would be safe from the predicted catastrophe. When the day of his calamity predicted by the stars arrived, he entered the stronghold and placed armed guards all around it. Once inside he was shocked to find an overlooked small hole through which he could see daylight. With leftover mortar he quickly filled the small hole so the disaster couldn't slip through. He sat down, relieved that he was finally safe. But he was quickly seized with panic as he realized that by blocking every possible opening through which disaster could enter, he had imprisoned himself without air or light. The king died that night. The stars had not lied. This old story teaches how easily we can surrender our freedom and imprison ourselves out of fear of being the victims of possible disasters.

> *Illusion, that there is any security*
> *from life's unexpected disasters—*
> *fire, disease, flood . . . heartbreak—*
> *so I walk hand-in-hand with you.*

September 23

The Cure

The desks and homes of perfectionists are extremely neat and orderly. They labor overtime to insure their work is fault-free and typically desire their life partners to be flawless as well. Their anxiety demands are often disastrous for them and others. But you don't need to be a perfectionist to be irritated by some flaw of your marriage partner. Such irritation is often the root cause of the most common of interpersonal problems. We know intellectually that no one is perfect, yet we still want those with whom we live to be flawless. A cure for this perfection obsession is to take whatever trait irritates you and greatly exaggerate it. Blow it up ten times larger than one of those balloons in a Macy's Thanksgiving Day Parade. You can successfully deflate what irritates you by exaggerating it to the point of ridiculousness since obsessive anxieties react to humor as vampires do to garlic . . . they flee from its presence.

> *Remind me, like all things in life,*
> *big problems begin as little ones,*
> *so while they are little, shrink them*
> *by humor and crazy playfulness.*

September 24

When Upset, What Do You Give?

Contemporary life is close to the boiling point with frustration and angry outbursts that are not the problem but the symptoms of the hectic pace of life. Many on the highways or in offices are like potential volcanoes whose hidden inner fires easily erupt into destructive violence. When this boiling over occurs, we give someone "a piece of our mind," be the person a store clerk or a fellow worker. That "piece of our mind" is as red hot as flowing lava. Living at the boiling point is dangerous, as the 1958 Nobel Peace Prize recipient, Dominique Pires, said: "If an atomic bomb falls on the world tomorrow, it is because I argued with my neighbor today." That insightful comment reveals how the chain of events you initiate can have a profound impact on the world. But the chain reaction can work for good as well. Instead of giving someone "a *piece* of your mind," you gave them "the *peace* of your mind." You can't give what you haven't got; to give the peace of your mind requires a mind full of peace. Becoming inwardly peaceful requires no secret knowledge. Just sit still, silently absorbing the calming presence of Divine Peace. A few minutes each day will work wonders of peacefulness.

> *With each breath fill my heart*
> *with peace and serenity;*
> *inflate me full so I can give*
> *away all day pieces of peace.*

September 25

Putting the Pieces Together

Anthony de Mello told a delightful story about the Devil and a friend who were out for a walk. Up ahead of them on the road was a man who suddenly stopped and picked up something bright and shining. After inspecting it, he put it in his pocket and continued walking. The Devil's friend asked him, "What did that man find in the road?" The Devil replied, "A shining piece of the truth." His friend said, "Doesn't that disturb you?" The Devil smiled broadly, "No, I'll see to it that he makes a religion out of it!" This charming mini-parable will be disturbing if you believe your religion has the fullness of the truth. Religion comes from the Latin word *religatio* meaning "to tie-together" or unite. Perhaps then the best religion is one of reconnecting all the various pieces of truth, wisdom, insights, and spiritual help God has scattered across the world. If as the story proposes each religion holds a piece of the truth, then wouldn't it be wise to respect other denominations and religions as treasure houses of wisdom? If so, perhaps a better name for a spiritual seeker is a treasure hunter of truth.

> *Clever of you, God, to scatter*
> *pieces of truth all over the earth.*
> *Make me a perpetual seeker*
> *in the sacred scavenger hunt.*

September 26

The In-Perpetuity, No Escape Law

A troubling problem is explaining the abundance of crime, violence, drug abuse, and the inescapable poverty in our affluent society. The answer might be a 1662 law made by the English settlement of Jamestown. Several years previously the English settlers had begun to import black African slaves from Angola which soon raised questions about the status of their descendants. They passed a law that decreed that all children born of slave women were henceforth stated to be slaves in perpetuity—time without end! That Jamestown law haunts us today in the twenty-first century. The descendants of those first slaves to this day continue to be born in perpetuity into a slavery of repressive poverty, poor education, broken homes, crime, and drugs. Only a fortunate few have escaped from these historical chains of legalized indenture. If tempted to indulge in judgmental prejudice toward the poor—whether black, brown, or white—or to wish they could be deported out of your city to another planet, remember the 1662 Jamestown law.

> *Make me curious about the histories*
> *of those whom I find disagreeable,*
> *so curiosity will lead to compassion,*
> *since they, like me, are home-made.*

September 27

Your Life Work—to Escape!

Albert Einstein said: "Human beings are a part of a whole called by us the 'universe.'" The common experience of seeing oneself as being something separated from others and the rest of humanity is an optical delusion of consciousness. This delusion imprisons one to a cramped restriction of desires and concerns that affect only oneself and a few others nearby. While it is normal for prisoners to dream of escaping, those incarcerated by their delusions don't. The Teacher Jesus was an escaped convict. Having himself escaped from the narrow confines of separateness, he went about urging others to escape from the constrictive prisons of themselves. The major work of a spiritual seeker is reuniting oneself with the whole, ending the ancient divorce of self from the universe, creation, and the rest of humanity. This primary task can be summarized as the dream of escaping. We can only escape if we work daily at it so as to become like the Teacher, an escaped convict.

> *Awaken me to my imprisonment,*
> *my lonely solitary confinement.*
> *Heal my old divorce from others,*
> *from creation, and all the universe.*

September 28

Falling in Love with Wrinkles

Echoing the words of John the Baptist in relation to Jesus, "I must decrease and he must increase," the French Jesuit,

Teilhard de Chardin, prayed, "God must grow greater in my life, in my Reality, and my interior world as I grow less . . . to accept, to love interior fragility and old age, with its long shadows, and the ever-shrinking days ahead . . . to love diminishments and decline." In this prayer Chardin speaks of loving the diminishments that come with old age. Though falling in love is usually considered a youthful adventure, he challenges us to fall in love with the ravages of old age by romancing our ever-dwindling days. The faces of those who are young and in love glow blissfully. The wrinkled faces of elders can also shine with a youthful inner radiance if, instead of only begrudgingly accepting deterioration, they fall in love with their aging.

> *In September's yellow days of decline,*
> *may I see an expectant pregnancy*
> *full of life soon to be born in green spring,*
> *and in my body's autumn see the same.*

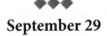

September 29

Musings of a Millionaire

Autumn is a sacramental reminder of death, if you wish to be reminded. So regardless of your age, let the feel of the chill in the fall wind, the sight of leaves turning yellow-brown, and the decreasing daylight hours be reminders of the brevity of life. While the average life expectancy today is seventy-eight, most desire to live even longer. Yet we are already millionaires in life compared to those of the Bronze Age (3200 to around 1100 BC) when life expectancy was seventeen! Autumn asks: have you, like some millionaires, squandered that enormous wealth of so many years of life? As September takes its last breaths, spend a few minutes reflecting on what you did with those extra bonus years since you were seventeen. If after reflecting you wish you could have used them to be a better, more generous person, consider performing an Ebenezer Scrooge somersault. Imitate that old miser in Dickens's *A Christmas Carol* who upon awakening one morning radically changed his life for the better!

> *Whatever my age, autumn awaken me*
> *To the fact that I teeter on the edge of*
> *   bankruptcy,*
> *soon my clocks will be broke—of time*
> *to invest my days in being better.*

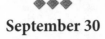

September 30

Renew Thyself

On this last dying day of September, instead of reflecting on the Greek wisdom of "Know thyself," ponder this old Chinese saying, "Renew thyself completely each day; do it again, and again, and forever again." Sounds easy, but it isn't. Being renewed in the age of maturity seems at best to happen only once or twice in a lifetime—falling in love later in life or finding some new challenging work. Nevertheless, like the morning routine of brushing your teeth, renewing your self each day will protect you from the worst of all diseases: growing old! September has grown very old and cannot be renewed, but you can if with enough passion you desire it each day. The only other option is regressing, the self-stagnating of your mind, heart, and spirit. You ask: stagnation of spirit? Yes, we are soul-body hybrids, what affects one affects the other. So, become addicted to daily seeking some innovative way to renew a different aspect of your life so you can die young.

Inspire me to become a holy addict
incurably hooked on being renewed.
Detoxify my apathy and lazy excuses
that sabotage my becoming younger.

Month of
October

October 1

Primeval Religious Wonder

Because the distance between us and our closest star, Proxima Centauri, is so vast, we measure it not in miles but in the speed of light. Proxima Centauri is only 4.2 light years away! A light year is the distance light travels in one year: 5,787 trillion miles! The vastness of the nighttime vista is heightened when we realize that traveling at the speed of light to the center of our galaxy, the Milky Way, would require a journey of thirty thousand light years. And if we wished to visit the galaxy M31, the closest neighboring spiral galaxy to ours, that journey would require two million light years! To reflect even momentarily on such facts has the power to bring every one of us to his or her knees in an act of adoration. The prayer of adoration and wonder may just be the prayer of the twenty-first century. What fire, thunder, and the mystery of birth once invoked in the primitive person, the magnitude of space awakens in us.

> *Star-gazing prayer staggers the mind,*
> *infinite is the space between us.*
> *O Stars, contemplating you humbles me*
> *and shrinks me down to my proper size.*

October 2

Chewing on the Past

"Chewing on the past," said Ernest Hemingway, "is a bum way to spend life." His observation is correct only for those who are starving in the present and must sadly survive on a diet of their past events. There is a difference between living on memories and occasionally savoring them as you would a fine wine. Our past experiences have often rushed by us very quickly with new ones demanding our attention right on their heels. So it can be a feast of great delight to reach into your memory bank and take out one memorable past occasion and slowly savor it. The recollection of past experiences in life enriches you today. Reviewing memories is better than reviewing your bank account. Memories reveal how wealthy you are! These beautiful recollections are far more valuable than stocks and bonds. The centerpiece of Christian worship is a memorial dinner, one with a mystical menu that recalls an ancient meal of friendship and love. Feasting on the past, rather than chewing on it, is an exceptional way to enjoy life.

> *"Eat and drink together in memory of me,"*
> *ritually blesses all our personal memories*
> *where those we remember become present,*
> *making all our remembrances into reunions.*

October 3

Healthy Sickness

Illness in Islam is viewed as a blessing and so should always be borne without complaint. When a Muslim inquires about another's health, the customary reply is, "All praise belongs to God," even if that person is sick. A devout Muslim believes that a sickness is a blessing as it is an occasion to cleanse oneself of past sins and because purification is the purpose of existence. Sickness as a blessing is balanced by seeing good health as an equal blessing, because it is a cause of joy and gratitude. We non-Muslims can adopt their response of praising God in sickness or health, in good times or bad, as a healthy habit. In our culture when trouble visits us in the form of a difficult problem or some mistake we have made, the frequent response isn't "God be praised," but "God damn!" The wisdom of Islam, the Hebrew psalms, and the writings of Christian mystics are in agreement that all aspects of life are occasions to praise God. So a healthy response to getting a raise, a flat tire, a good doctor's report, or the flu is: "All praise belongs to God."

> *If all of life is a chance to praise you,*
> *I'm gifted with an endless parade*
> *of mini-prayers and brief exclamations,*
> *proclaiming your abiding-presence.*

October 4

A Needed Broom We Dread

The cleansing power of sickness and suffering is found in Islam and Buddhism. In Buddhism as in Islam, suffering is generally not seen as a failure of health or as a punishment, but as purification. The followers of Buddha compare suffering with a mystical broom that sweeps away past mistakes and failings. Yet how does being sick with the flu (or worse, afflicted with cancer) act like a broom? One possibility is that illness can sweep away our favorite illusion of being invulnerable and in control. Health, being a precarious gift, should call forth miniprayers of gratitude every day. No amount of sanitizing hand washes can ever protect you from the swarms of viruses everywhere. So after recovering from a head cold or the flu, do you feel like you've been swept clean? And if you do, cleansed of what?

> *O headache or heart attack,*
> *sweep out the forgetfulness*
> *that good health is a fragile gift*
> *and expose the reality that I'm helpless.*

October 5

Nonconforms or Uniforms?

Uniforms have often been a source of controversy. In the middle of the fifth century, Pope Celestine I was greatly disturbed because his clergy began wearing uniforms—clerical dress. Celestine reprimanded them saying, "We should be set apart from others not by our dress, but by our conversation and the style of our lives." In 1844, the police of New York City staged a strike against the proposal that they wear identical blue uniforms. Railroad conductors and mailmen also refused to wear uniforms until after the Civil War. The reason for such strong opposition to uniforms is that they were viewed as symbols of servitude—only butlers and maids wore them in the old country. Today, youth are notorious for being rebels, yet they often dress themselves alike in the uniforms of rebellion. Being almost identical, their dress is not a sign of freedom but of conformity. If you wear a uniform, ask yourself what it symbolizes. Is it servitude to an institution, company, church, or the fashion of the day? Regardless of your age or the dress requirements of your work, how enslaved are you to style, to the opinions of others, or to the desire to be special?

Seeking to emulate your humility,
I conventionally dress like others,
lest a greater need says otherwise.
Guide me in what I should wear.

October 6

Guardian Dragons

Guardian dragons are not as well known as guardian angels. Do they exist? The poet Rainer Maria Rilke said that our deepest fears are like dragons guarding our deepest treasures. So, by being brave enough to not be frightened by your own dragons, you can discover your deepest treasures. Perhaps our greatest fear is the dread of impermanence, awakened by the fragility of those persons we love as well as our own. One of your guardian dragons may be the dread that nothing is permanent. By not running away but calmly looking this hideous beast in the eyes, you may discover that it is guarding a hidden treasure. That treasure, precious beyond all price, is that which is eternally unchangeable, that resides deeply within each of us and the cosmos. At this moment the cosmos, while being sustained by the deathless and changeless Permanent One, is perpetually changing and evolving, just as you are! In you and the cosmos, the fearful guardian dragon of Death stands watch over the most precious of all treasures—immortality.

> *Through the fearful, smoky flames*
> *of old guardian dragon Death,*
> *help me squint-see my treasure,*
> *life guaranteed without any end.*

October 7

An Obscene Word

Death is the greatest terrorist! So feared an enemy is death that we avoid thinking about it, unless forced to do so as when attending a funeral. We even find the word *death* unspeakable, and so replace died with "passed." In prayer, we refer to the dead as the "deceased" or "departed." When someone dies in parts of Africa they don't say they "have passed" or "departed," but rather that they "have arrived!" This beautiful expression is saturated with the belief that their beloved dead have finally arrived at the destination toward which they have been traveling all their lives. Upon hearing of someone's death, our Muslim brothers and sisters say, "We have come from God, and we return to God, and we are on this journey each day of our life." Regardless of our age or health, you and I are at this very moment on a journey back to God, and none of us knows if today is the day of our arrival. As you pass one milestone after another, live your homeward journey wisely and passionately.

> *Inspired, I squeeze the last drop of joy*
> *out of each day, not because I'll die,*
> *but because You have made life's joys*
> *appetizers of the delight of arriving.*

October 8

Stop the Devil From Dancing

The Teacher was firm in saying, "Do not offer resistance to the evildoer." This admonition not to defend yourself sounds unnatural and inhuman, which in fact it is! To abstain from returning injury for injury is a divine act intended to prevent the devil from dancing twice. It is believed the devil gleefully dances when someone sins against you, then dances again even more merrily when you react with vengeance against your attacker. The Teacher invites you to become a chain breaker, hoping the endless dance of evil in the world will cease. By refusing to offer resistance, you break the chain; you refuse to forge another evil link in hot anger. And so you do not add another link to the endlessly evil links extending back millennia. When a loved one has been murdered, it is not uncommon to hear the family claim that they will be unable to find peace until the guilty one has received the justice of capital punishment. This is not the peace that the Teacher offers. His peace comes only when the chain of hell is broken and we stop the devil from dancing.

> *Pondering revenge, I can hear him*
> *tap dancing, delighted the first evil*
> *will spawn an offspring of another.*
> *Come, eject my tendency to getting even.*

October 9

Forget About God

The Russian author Dostoevsky created a character named Father Zossima, a kind and wise monk, for one of his novels. One day an old woman comes to Father Zossima weeping because she has lost her faith. In a torrent of tears she tells the old priest how, after being devout her entire life, she now no longer believes in God and can no longer even pray. Father Zossima nods understandably and tells her to forget about God! Don't be anxious that you don't believe in God, he tells her, and that you can't pray. He sends her home, telling her not to even think about God, just go home and each day do one loving deed for someone. As she departs, bewildered, he promises her that in due time she will believe again in God; in fact, she would find it impossible not to believe in God! Wise Father Zossima knew that his strange spiritual advice was infallible, and had been so from the beginning. He realized every act of kindness or love performed for anyone is done to God who abides in every person. Every good deed performed for a neighbor or stranger, regardless of whether we believe in the existence of God or not, is done to God.

> *If I believe or not, deepen my faith,*
> *that all kindness is shown to you.*
> *The less I think I'm doing it to God,*
> *the more real God becomes to me.*

October 10

A Tale of Wonder Watching

The Chinese have a parable about a hunter who quietly moves with a spear in hand among the water reeds to kill an egret standing in front of him. As he is about to throw his spear, he notices the egret is attentively staring at something. Following the direction of his gaze, he sees the egret is totally focused on a frog he wishes to kill, resting on a lily pad. Then the hunter, looking more closely, sees that the frog is concentrated on a big, fat bug on the surface of the water only inches away. Leaning even closer, the hunter sees the big water bug is keenly watching a smaller bug nearby, about to spring upon it. The hunter imagines the little bug was no doubt totally focused on something even smaller that it was about to devour. The hunter was suddenly caught up in a moment of wonder that caused him to look over his right shoulder and up into the sky. His eyes filled with dread and awe, and then he dropped his spear and ran away.

> *Advise me how best to be*
> *part of nature's food chain,*
> *so to eat in awareness of all*
> *those below—and above—me.*

October 11

What Meets the Eye

In your yard there is a burning bush, so approach it with great awe and wonder. As you do, listen, and you may hear, as did Moses, a voice thunder out of the flames, "Take your shoes off; holy is the ground under your feet!" At this time of year all trees and bushes appear to be burning bushes as autumn paintbrushes them in shimmering yellows and blazing reds. "Bah, humbug," you say, "such talk of a burning bush in my yard is only an Irishman's poetic musings about the changing color of October's foliage!" To be able to see bushes engulfed in divine flames requires eager eyes, open to see more than what meets them. Thomas Merton, the Trappist monk and author, said that the spiritual life is a continual discovery in which God is found in new and unexpected places. Add your backyard to that list! What meets the eye is only the outer surface of people and things. If it were granted to our eyes to see what exists beneath those externals, we would instantly take off our shoes. Consider taking a walk in your yard or in a nearby park in your bare or stocking feet.

> *Open me to those wonders*
> *beyond what meets the eye.*
> *They are the meats the eye so*
> *dearly hungers to experience.*

October 12

The No Word Prayer

The god Harpokrates, whom the Greeks borrowed from the Egyptians, was known as the god of silence. He is usually depicted as a baby, nude and sitting on his mother's lap. She offers him her breast as he sucks his thumb. Perhaps this scene contains a sign or a hidden message for us. Part of the hidden message this myth holds lies in the fact that Harpokrates appears in the form of a child. The prayer of silence holds the power to renew us and to make us children again. Silence calls us to the domain of dreams and visions, to return to that pre-verbal period of our childhood. Silence also strips us of our defenses, makes us naked of those cardboard defenses we so often employ. If we allow it, silence slowly strips away our need to engage in arguments, to insist that we are right. Times of silence cut cleanly through the constant flow of words and rituals that so often keep God at a "safe" distance.

> *Aware you are Absolute Silence,*
> *why this ache to hear your voice?*
> *Open my ears to your holy silence*
> *soundlessly speaking directly to me.*

October 13

The Struggle Between Evil and . . .

Is the struggle between evil and good or between evil and hope? The Nazis diabolically employed hope in the Warsaw ghetto to manipulate the four hundred thousand Jews into refraining from armed resistance. Against the mounting evidence, most of the Jews clung to the faint hope they would not be among those taken away to the camps. Their hope that "others," not them, would be selected to be deported to camps made it possible for the Nazis to effortlessly deport massive numbers to "resettlement" camps. A Jewish deportee, Natan Selichower, wrote, "The Jews did not believe in their own extinction. At the very center of their 'spiritual refuge' sat God, who, having led them through the Red Sea, would surely knock down the walls of the ghetto." The Holocaust offers us a cautionary lesson: do not refrain from doing something about evil, hoping that God will intervene or that the evil will not come to our door. This struggle between hope and evil is a reality whenever evil appears, cleverly wearing the flag, waving a bible, robed in beautiful vestments or a corporate three-piece suit. Beware if evil comes dressed as any of these, or worse, disguised as hope.

To anchor all my hopes in reality,
remind me of the night the Titanic
struck that iceberg and everyone said,
"Don't worry, the ship's unsinkable."

October 14

The Power Tool of the Powerful

Propaganda is cleverly disguised misinformation or lies employed by presidents, politicians, and popes in the service of truth. Winston Churchill expressed this paradox of mistruth when he said, "In wartime, truth is so precious that she should always be attended by a bodyguard of lies." Hitler's minister of propaganda, Joseph Goebbels, added another important ingredient to the productive use of misinformation when he said, "Tell a lie often enough, and the people will believe it is the truth." If you're thinking today's reflection has no personal use for you, reconsider. Daily, you are being inundated by a flood of propaganda from your government, political parties, by thousands of television commercials, and from your religion. Holy propaganda isn't easily recognizable as misinformation. So carefully scrutinize and logically question proposed divine moral positions or statements attended by angel bodyguards.

Keep my tongue from the propaganda
of exaggerating my good works
and shrinking my mistakes to midgets.
Inspire me to be honest or be silent.

October 15

The Dream of Being Famous

Heroes and the famous are often presented as role models. Outstanding women or men can be athletic, musical, entertainment, and even religious role models. Whatever your age, you can secretly aspire to be like some movie star or famous athlete. While their professional excellence is truly admirable and inspiring, should anyone really desire to imitate them? A Yiddish proverb says, "If I try to be like him, who will be like me?" Read that proverb again slowly. Let it be a bugle sounding the call for you to be as fully as possible who you are, a one-and-only person, unique in all of human history. Even if you lack the gifts of the famous or the holiness and good works of the great saints, strive to be only you. A learned and holy rabbi once told his disciples, "When I get to heaven God isn't going to ask me, 'Rabbi Yosef, why weren't you more like Moses?' No, God will ask me, 'Rabbi Yosef, why weren't you more like the Yosef whom I created?'"

I am unique, but I feel inadequate,
unimportantly small, so common.
Come, encourage me just to be me
and believe in what can't be seen.

October 16

Never Lost

The road of the spiritual quest has many forks and side paths on it. At each of them is a sign with a large question mark. Lacking a map, the seeker continuously wonders, "Am I on the right road, or should I take this other path?" Naturally insecure, some seekers go off in search of a spiritual guide, but this logical choice is fraught with dangers. The Teacher warned, "Be cautious of the blind leading the blind." In the twelfth century, a community of Jewish scholars and mystics gathered the wisdom of ages together in a collection called the *Kabbalah*. In that compilation of Jewish mysticism is a wondrously reassuring gem of wisdom, "The Blessed One will guide us on the path." So don't be worried whether you have taken the right road or made the right choice in your spiritual journey. Trust that the Divine Guide has led you to do wherever you are at this moment. Trust, when the time comes for you to make a change and travel a different path, the Guide of Guides will point out the new way for you to travel the path to home.

> *Blessed are those who feel inadequate,*
> *for they must constantly lean on God.*
> *So I trust my deficient prayers are full,*
> *as I pray leaning on your big shoulder.*

October 17

The City of Temples

The daily prayer of Islam proclaims, "There is no God but God." Believers of all religions could wisely include it as part of their daily prayers. In a city nearby to me, a group of Buddhists recently erected a temple for their worship, causing certain fundamentalist Christians to object loudly to it as pagan worship of "strange gods" in their city. I found this a most unusual response since the city is already crowded with temples to strange gods: banks, corporate and government offices, casinos, ballparks, and churches. Yes, churches, where the Bible, ancient traditions, or the hierarchy are paid homage to equally with God. The city also has a vast multitude of private household and office temples. These smaller temples include shrines to the pagan gods of efficiency, perfection, cleanliness, glamour, and youth. So pray several times a day with whole-hearted devotion, "There is no God but God." This would be a very revolutionary prayer in every community.

> *Raise the embarrassing question in me:*
> *Which god or gods do I really worship?*
> *Which one do I serve with all my heart,*
> *you, the Almighty One, or lesser ones?*

October 18

Use It or Lose It

Every muscle, organ, and faculty of our mind-body-spirit can be developed by exercise. Each of us has numerous daily opportunities to exercise our willpower by freely choosing to respond generously to life situations that require sacrifice, such as being asked to wait for something or having to stand in line at a checkout counter. Use such accidental and unplanned occasions as an exercise of your willpower by freely choosing to wait with patience and graciousness. You can choose not to react with anger when you are cut off in a traffic jam or to respond with flexibility in adjusting your schedule when your child gets sick or some unexpected work comes up at the office. While small and seemingly insignificant, each of these

accidental exercises can strengthen your will toward greatness
of heart.

> *"Use or lose it" explains my hot anger,*
> *my willpower weak from no exercise.*
> *Every rudeness and unkind word shouts*
> *at me, "Weakling, you're not exercising!"*

October 19

Kill Your Imagination

If you are looking for God, first listen to that faintest of whispers in your inner ear, "Before you come looking for me, kill
your imagination!" No one has ever seen God, so throughout the centuries artists have created their own images of
the Unimaginable One. These God pictures are impressed in
our imagination in childhood and then reinforced by others
in stained glass windows or biblical illustrations. As a result,
whenever we hear or see the word "God," our imagination
spontaneously creates an image based on the one inscribed
in our childhood mind. All those false artistic images of God
lodged in our imagination are the reason we never encounter the Divine One! Kill your imagination to kick-start your
faith. Once your belief in the enfleshment of the Creator in all

creation is firmly established, then go looking for God. Look for the Invisible One in your morning cup of coffee, in the small black fly on the window, in the tragedies in the evening news, in the faces of those you love, and in the face of someone you dislike.

> *How wise of Judaism and Islam*
> *in forbidding any images of you!*
> *Blind me to all your false images,*
> *so to see you vividly in everyone.*

October 20

Forgotten Treasure

The seventeenth-century author, Sir Thomas Browne, wrote this about the wonders of Africa: "We carry with us the wonders we seek without us." His words remind me of an old Portuguese saying from the days of the sixteenth-century explorers: "Those who bring back gold from the Indies, take it with them." When searching for the Divine Mystery, remember you carry within you what you seek in scriptures, in worship services, and in spiritual books. Each of these can be of great assistance in the quest to become more godlike, more holy. But they are invaluable resources only if, as the Portuguese said, you take with you the gold you seek in church, in the Bible, or any spiritual book. A critical exercise for all spiritual explorers is to begin not by going outside but inside, to search for the wonders they carry within themselves. Be it the wonders of Africa or the gold of God, rejoice that you can find what you seek without ever leaving home!

> *Expunge the thought that I do not*
> *hold buried gold of you within me.*
> *Be my miner's lamp*
> *as I go exploring deep within.*

October 21

Sacred Striptease

Long, long ago in pre-bible days, before there were priests, theologians, pastors, or churches, how did people know that there was a God? And millennia before there were temple sanctuaries, ritual days of worship, and sacraments, how did people experience the sacred? The answers to these questions require a striptease of the layers of your religious practices so as to return to a primitive pre-church spiritual awareness. Being naked of all beliefs and religious practices, go exploring in your common daily activities and encounters for the presence of God. Gently peel back the thin-skinned surface of love, friendship, meals, sickness, and fears of what awaits you after you die. You'll be surprised by what you find. When next a dark thunderstorm rumbles overhead or you watch the giant full moon slowly rise, forget what you learned in your high school science class and engage in the primitive prayer of wonder. All of these awesome experiences are how people experienced God before religion arrived here on earth.

> *Teach me the acrobatic skill of being*
> *a church and a churchless worshipper,*
> *so my prayers to you, Awesome One,*
> *can be infinitely more encompassing.*

October 22

Idol Factories

Once, long ago, the manufacture of idols was very profitable. While today making idols of silver or gold could be compared to the making of buggy whips, it hasn't completely disappeared. Whenever confronted by the unexplainable, something that defies logic and understanding, our temptation is to create an idol. These counterfeit gods comfort us when we face a sense-less tragedy like the death of a child or a giant tsunami. The most popular idol today, paradoxically, is a deformed god! This idol is made by stripping away all the mystery from the Divine One to create a small, understandable God in order to explain whatever we find unexplainable. The Protestant reformer John Calvin asserted that our hearts are "factories of idol-making." Among these false gods there is a sometimes beneficial, sometimes harmful inconsistent God; a sin-punishing God; or a you-had-it-coming, retaliating God. Institutions easily make idols out of themselves that require unquestioned loyalty, obedience, and sacrifice. There's an old adage that is still worth pondering: "All idols require human sacrifices."

> *A fake god, institutional or social,*
> *is counterfeit and unreliable*
> *when compared to you; so I choose*
> *never to be a human sacrifice to any idol.*

October 23

The Fish Fight

The newly married coyote lived with his bride near a river. One day his bride asked him if he would catch a fish she could prepare for their supper. The bridegroom coyote eagerly pledged to bring her a fish, hiding the fact he didn't know how to swim.

As he neared the river, through the trees he saw two otters fighting over a large fish they had just caught. "I saw it first, so I should have the largest portion," said one otter. The other otter tugging at the fish said, "But I saved you from almost drowning while you were catching that fish." As their argument grew more heated, coyote strolled out of the trees and offered to settle their argument, if the two otters agreed to his decision. They both agreed to that, so coyote cut the fish into three pieces. He gave the first otter the head and the second otter the tail. "The middle," he said as he walked away, "belongs to the judge." This old Native American parable is very contemporary: lawyers mediating between two arguing parties usually walk off with a large portion of the money. When tempted to argue, ponder this from ancient China's *Tao Te Ching*: "A good person does not argue, and one who argues is not a good person."

> *Arguing is always toxic,*
> *creating angry feelings.*
> *So forever remind me*
> *to discuss, but never to argue!*

October 24

Stepping-stones

Prayers are but stepping-stones to silence, so don't linger too long on their words. We prefer never to move off them since stepping into the void of silence is as frightening as stepping off a cliff and falling into pitch black darkness. Do not be frightened of this holy canyon of wordless emptiness for it is the Holy of Holies hole in which dwells the Mystery of All Mysteries. Regardless how high your IQ is, that Awesome Divine Mystery which is beyond the reach of your mind reaches out to you from the dark silence. To plunge into prayerful silence requires great faith since we equate silence with nothingness. To think of seeking God—the absolute fullness of life, love, and power—in nothingness seems insanity. Ah, the playful paradox of prayer! We only enter into the sanity of sanctity by what seems to be insanity.

> *Push me off the pages of my prayers*
> *to fall into the ebony pool of silence,*
> *there to swim side by side with you*
> *in the dark, passionate abyss of your love.*

October 25

O Hallowed Hunger

Our prehistoric parents lived hungry because food was scarce. It had to be either trapped, speared, or killed by hand. When their hunt was successful, their hunger was satisfied, only to quickly return. Living hungry is the secret to holiness! Our prayers should make us hungrier, and not satisfy our cravings. Every departure from church and every reception of Holy Communion should make us more, rather than less, hungry. Unfortunate are those who feel satisfied after a once-a-week church worship, a daily Bible reading, or saying a handful of prayers. Our clever Creator gave each of us an insatiable, ravenous appetite that constantly signals our brain when it needs to be fed. Like our prehistoric parents, we also should live hungry while not trying to satisfy our hunger by nibbling on the berries and roots of the fleeing pleasures of wealth, status, or fame. Finally, rejoice in your hunger. It is the infallible sign of the existence of that which you can easily doubt exists.

> *Give me the wise insight to see*
> *in my perpetually unsatisfied hungers,*
> *that cavernous, bottomless craving*
> *of a hungry heart that you alone satisfy.*

October 26

The Silent Killer

The Russian author Leo Tolstoy wrote a short story about a greedy man who was offered as much land as he could walk around from sunrise to sunset. He was given only one condition: he had to be back at the starting point by sunset or he would lose his life. At sunrise the man began eagerly walking northward through rich grain fields until about noon, then, turning westward, he walked across vast green fertile lands until late afternoon. When the sun was in the western sky, he turned south and began to walk faster. Late in the afternoon, he turned eastward and began running so he could reach the place where he had begun before sunset. Denying his great weariness by thinking of all the land that soon would belong to him, he began dashing wildly toward his destination. Just as the sun was beginning to set, he staggered toward the starting point. In one last burst of strength, with all his might he leaped to cross it, only for his heart to explode. He dropped dead. Tolstoy ends the story, "He now had all the land he needed, a plot six feet by two." Indeed, greed—not cholesterol—is the silent killer.

Warn me: If I chase after money,
it will catch me and I will be its slave.
Inspire me to only chase after love,
since what I chase will catch me.

October 27

A Good Looker

"She's a good looker" is a slang compliment that first appeared in print in the early part of 1890. That over-a-hundred-year-old flattering remark for someone of stunning beauty is also the best description of a would-be saint. Unfortunately, most consider becoming a saint to be an achievement of a few select monks and nuns, selfless missionaries, or a handful of wise scholars of the Bible, the Torah, or the Koran. In reality, holiness—becoming God-like—is the divine assignment implanted when each of us was in the womb. Looking to find God is the first requirement for becoming God-like in your actions, thoughts, and speech. But where to look for God? The logical answer is in a synagogue, church, or mosque. Look instead in the least likely places. A saint in every religion is a "good looker!" Be on the lookout day and night; keep watch. Saintly sages of all religions say, "Whoever you go looking for will eventually be who you look like."

Counsel me, that by looking for you,
I then will begin to look like you!
No halo will appear, yet all those
encountering me will behold you.

October 28

The Apocalyptic End of the World

Some Islamic imams, seeing how temptingly fat the local magistrate's favorite sheep was, went to him wailing, "Oh, a terrible disaster! The ancient predictions say tomorrow is Judgment Day, the end of the world!" Wringing their hands, the weeping clerics said, "Your Excellency, the fattened sheep you raised with such care mustn't be wasted, so we've come to help you eat it." The magistrate was grievously saddened by the prophecy, but he replied, "If the end of the world is indeed upon us, then you are right, what point is there in keeping my favorite sheep? But allow me, reverend sirs, to prepare the feast. Take off your cloaks and go into my lush garden where it is cool and rest." After the imams left, the magistrate built a wood fire and placed the sheep in a large pan to cook. Then he threw the clerics' fine cloaks into the roaring fire. When the meal was ready, he called the imams to dinner. Upon their return they wailed loudly at the sight of their beautiful cloaks reduced to ashes, "Excellency, what have you done to our cloaks?" The magistrate only shrugged his shoulders, "Since tomorrow is the end of world, what possible need will you have for your cloaks?"

> *Since prophecies and prayers*
> *have logical and personal consequences,*
> *remind me that if prayers for peace*
> *are answered, millions will be jobless!*

October 29

Wondering Your Way to Wisdom

"Without wisdom there is no wonder," said Rabbi Eleazar ben Azariah, "and without wonder there is no wisdom." Wonder and amazement are how a child reacts to what adults see as commonplace. The loss of being amazed is understandable, since with age wonder wanes, and sadly, according to Rabbi Azariah, so does wisdom. Children, like cats, are born explorers, which is another innate talent lost upon leaving childhood. Other than outer space, few if any unexplored places remain on earth. Another name for wonder is amazement, and that is a clue to finding an unexplored place that is close to home. Life itself is a maze, a mysterious labyrinth itching to be explored.

With the eyes of a child hungry for wonder, consider exploring the complicated maze of your life's history; travel through old dried-up disappointments and unexpected small victories, stop to sleep with shrunken or lost loves, and you will discover not a new land, but something far more important—wisdom.

> *Confirm me as a unique being,*
> *with a life history equally so.*
> *Be my companion as I explore*
> *the miracles of my amazing life.*

October 30

Fear of the Fever-Van

Automobiles quickly get out of the way of ambulances with flashing lights and wailing sirens, but these medical vans transporting the sick do not invoke fear in us. In England, a hundred or more years ago, upon seeing an ambulance, children would turn up their coat collars and recite this incantation: "Grab your collar, don't swaller, never catch the fever." Or: "There goes the fever-van, never touch the mealy-man." These incantations included the ritual of holding your breath until the fever-van was out of sight. In these last days of October, images of skulls, skeletons, tombstones, and death fill store windows and decorate our homes and yards. But in Europe of previous centuries, when pestilence and plague killed half the population, the sick were greatly feared. Today ambulances do not incite fear or prayers to ward off evil. Yet praying as they pass can still be appropriate. Upon seeing an ambulance, consider saying a brief prayer for the sick or injured person that they are transporting to a hospital.

> *May red flashing lights and sirens*
> *call me like church bells to pray*
> *for the diverse needs of the person*
> *carried in that passing ambulance.*

October 31

Crocodile Bait

On this All Saints Eve, let us marry together two folk proverbs from different parts of the world. The bride is Malaysian: "I'd rather be swallowed whole by a crocodile, than be nibbled to death by tiny fishes." And the groom is Romanian: "Before you find God, you are eaten by the saints." This marriage of folk proverbs contains the wisdom that God is a crocodile who swallows us hook, line, and sinker. Or as the Teacher would say, ". . . with all your heart, mind, soul, and body." To

be eaten by the saints, those pious do-gooders with their artificial smiles and cardboard halos, is like being nibbled to death
by a swarm of small piranhas. Maybe this was the reason why
the Teacher always preferred to be in the company of sinners
and prostitutes instead of the saints of his day. Ask yourself the
unasked question: Why did prostitutes and sinners seek the
companionship of such an obviously deeply religious man as
Jesus? Did those un-churched and religious and social rejects
of his day seek out his company because they perceived him to
be a large and hungry crocodile?

> *Swallow me, as you devoured Jesus,*
> *not by nibbling at him now and then,*
> *but in one big bite of body and soul,*
> *so that like he I can be totally yours.*

Month of
November

November 1

Ancient-Beyond-Belief Star Light

Astronomers estimate that the universe began about 13.7 billion years ago. Recently the giant telescope atop Mauna Kea in Hawaii recorded starlight from the most distant galaxy yet seen by humans. Astronomers calculated that this starlight began traveling toward earth over twelve billion years ago! The stars provide an awesome opportunity for wonder, yet star watching today has been eclipsed by light pollution and smog. However, if you go out in the country far from the glare of illumination, perhaps you still might be able to have a mystical experience. Don't dismiss the possibility of being a mystic by thinking that it is only for the super-saints. Everyone who has experienced being totally absorbed in music, art, a sexual experience, or nature has had a mystical experience. Non-mystics, if any exist, would have to be those exclusively living on the surface of life and whose spirits are immune to wonders and the awesome nature of our existence.

> *Remake me as an awe-fascinated primitive,*
> *de-adult me so as to wonder like a child*
> *at our nuclear-blast furnace star, the sun,*
> *even if I can't see the other billion stars.*

November 2

I Wonder

November is the traditional Christian month to remember the dead. A possible activity this month could be visiting a cemetery and reading the tombstones as a reflection on your own death. Years ago, grave markers were inscribed with reflective thoughts intended for the living, such as the following epitaph found on a child's grave.

> It is so soon that I am done for,
> I wonder what I was begun for.

At what age is it too soon to die? Like that dead child, reflect on what purpose you were "begun for" when you were born. Questioning one's life-purpose usually happens in one's late teens or early twenties. From an early age some seem to be blessed to know what life work they want to pursue, while others are still wondering about it even in their fifties or later. If you are now firmly settled into your life's work and no longer question "what I was begun for," consider wondering about it, since some find their real life purpose only later in life.

*Guide me to ponder, other than
my present work, what mission
of yours was I also begun for
that I've yet to find and begin?*

November 3

Adopt a Guide

Bookstores are adoption agencies, bringing together not parents and children, but rather readers and authors. Good booksellers can tell simply by the glint in a reader's eyes if that person is hungry for spiritual wisdom and will take good care of the author they adopt. Bookstore adoption counselors over the years have learned how to recognize those best suited for this or that author adoptee. A good bookstore is a virtual nursery of spiritual directors and inspirational guides of all religions for those seeking the holy in their daily lives. No need to go to India or some monastery; in a bookstore, prayer guides and wise gurus will come to you, instead of you having to go to them. While one would expect to find spiritual guidance in prayer, meditation, and holiness at your local church, this product is not typically offered. So, if you have an anemic spiritual life, a lackluster prayer life, or a bland love of

God, seriously consider visiting a local adoption agency—
your bookstore.

> *Thank you for the gift of book guides,*
> *some a thousand years old, some new.*
> *They are my compass companions today*
> *as I zigzag along the Way to you.*

November 4

Eulenspiegelism

Early November is election time, and many candidates run
for office on a platform of "No New Taxes!" Beware of their
tempting political bait lest you suffer from Eulenspiegelism.
Duke Eulenspiegel of Brunswick was a fourteenth century
German duke famous for his cruel jokes and pranks. Legend
tells how one night twelve blind men begging alms came to
Duke Eulenspiegel's castle. He graciously welcomed them and
compassionately listened to their woeful tale of hunger. Then
he said, "My good men, go to the inn in the village square.
Eat, drink, and be merry. Here are twelve gold florins to pay
the innkeeper for your dinner." After enjoying a large delicious
meal, the innkeeper presented the blind men with an equally
large bill. Whereupon each said, "Let he who received the gold

florins pay the bill." Actually none of them had been given a single florin! Being blind, each supposed that another one of them had been given the duke's generous gift! Today many people are like those blind beggars, expecting someone else to pay the bill. Who pays the bill for your sewers, highways, bridges, schools, and police protection? Don't be hoodwinked by politicians or blinded by greed; do your duty and pay your share of the services you use and enjoy as a citizen!

> *Unbend the crooked thought that,*
> *"My money belongs to me!"*
> *My duty is to pay my share,*
> *and not be a public parasite.*

November 5

Beautiful Old Age and Death

In Japan, the viewing of cherry and plum trees in full blossom in the spring is both a pleasant and spiritually fruitful activity. The blossoms of these trees are treasured because their fragile, delicate flowers are so short-lived. Moreover, for the Japanese, viewing these blossoms is a religious experience, as the flower shows forth the beauty of death. Because of our extended life expectancy, death usually does not come in the full bloom of youth, but at an advanced age when we are old and wrinkled like a dead flower. In the West, we throw old wilting flowers in the trash. The Japanese, however see beauty in faded, dying flowers. In this month of remembering the dead, consider having your own religious icon of life and death. Purchase a single blooming flower and appreciate its beauty in full bloom. Then prayerfully watch it slowly die, but don't dispose of it! See beauty in its stages of dying. Let its wrinkled, curling leaves and wilted petals be a silent meditation for you of how to die naturally and beautifully.

> *Instead of seeing old age as unattractive,*
> *help me see in my wrinkled, fading youth,*
> *the beauty of cherry blossoms on the wind,*
> *so to make my dying slowly a work of art.*

November 6

Bed, Wonderful Bed

Before reading this reflection take a minute to ask, "What do I most look forward to doing?" Having answered that question, now continue reading. In a recent study by the Barna Group, adults were asked what activities they looked forward to. Seventy-one percent answered extra time in bed. Spending time with friends ranked second at 55 percent, and slightly below that, at 54 percent, time to listen to music. Only 40 percent of those surveyed answered that they looked forward to attending church. We should, however, be careful about how we interpret that latter figure. Looking forward to going to church and to encountering God are not the same thing, unless you are of the belief that God is found only in church buildings. Blessed are those who believe that sleeping-in, music, and being with friends are also ways to encounter God.

> *Explode my narrow notion of church,*
> *to include time resting in bed, reading,*
> *being with friends, and listening to music*
> *as worship times with you, my God.*

November 7

Dying Gracefully

Reflecting on death this month shouldn't make it a somber time, since death should be approached with a good sense of humor. To the degree that you are able to laugh at death, you are free of the fear of death, since humor is an aspect of freedom. Being overly serious about death, especially your own, implies you are held in bondage by fear of it. Being able to laugh about your death is an expression of acceptance, a joyful "yes" to the joys of existence and how transitory life is. A number of great spiritual teachers have said that you must die a little each day if you are to live spontaneously and joyfully in the present. Once a holy spiritual master was on his deathbed and his closest disciple decided to bring him his favorite pastry treat before the master died. The disciple went to the village and returned with a little cake that the old master accepted with a weak but broad smile. As he slowly nibbled on the little cake, his other disciples crowded around his bed and pleaded, "Master, do you have any departing words?" Wiping a crumb from his lips he replied, "Ah, yes!" As the disciples quickly gathered closer around his bed, he said, "My, but this cake is delicious."

> *Since human life is a Divine Comedy,*
> *insure the best humor for your last act,*
> *so daily practice dying a happy death*
> *by greeting with a grin each little death.*

November 8

The Great Escape Artist

Harry Houdini was known as the world's greatest escape artist. This Hungarian immigrant was famous in the early twentieth century for being able to escape from any type of confinement—even being handcuffed, strapped in a straightjacket, and padlocked in a steamer trunk encircled in countless iron chains that was thrown into a river. An even greater escape artist is described for us by the seventeenth-century Polish mystical writer Angelus Silesius, who wrote, "God is the purest naught, untouched by time or space; the more we reach for him, the more he will escape." Silesius was correct, for when we believe we have comprehended the Divine Mystery, as easily as Houdini slipping out of his padlocked chain-encircled trunk, God escapes our grasp. The Divine Mystery defies being handcuffed by theologians and delights escaping from their dogmatic straightjackets: "Words can't hold me, dogmas can't define me, so come then my beloved ones and chase after me." Since this is reality, let us find our joy not in trying to contain God but rather in endlessly chasing after this truly greatest escape artist.

May I keep elastic all my beliefs,
since you can out-escape Houdini,
slipping from ironclad definitions
that comfort us, but can't hold you.

November 9

Changing Your Mind

As you deal with having to make difficult decisions, realize that "I've changed my mind" is a declaration of repentance, an act that Jesus said is essential to entering the Kingdom of God. While this expression is commonly used for changing from one choice to another, it can also mean exchanging your present state of mind for a different one. Paul spoke of the necessity of changing one's mind when he wrote, "Put on the mind of Christ." The result of this mind exchange is that you begin to think like, fantasize like, dream like, and judge like Christ. Yet the mind "has a mind of its own" and doesn't cherish being evicted. So even as you "change your mind," your old mind will continuously attempt to return to its former domicile. By daily prayerful reflections on your thoughts, your judgments, and even your dreams, you will come to know whose mind you have in mind.

Am I a freak with one head and two brains,
each wrestling, trying to control the other?
When my Christ's mind wins most times,
then that contest is over before it begins.

November 10

The Empty Boxcar

One of the most familiar of all prayers and wishes is for peace. Yet that prayer for peace too often races past us like an empty boxcar in a long train of prayer petitions. Too often peace is an intellectual concept that none can object to but is empty of concrete meaning. When praying for peace, are we praying for a personal tranquility of mind or that our lives be devoid of conflicts and discord? Are we praying for a financial security that banishes worries and restless anxieties or for the end of all wars? For the ancients, peace was none of these, but rather the name for the Divine Mystery. To dwell in peace is to inhabit any place so saturated with the Divine that there is no room left for anything ungodly, unjust, or evil. In some countries and cultures, *peace* is the commonly exchanged greeting: *shalom, shanti, salam.* This ageless greeting is not a wish that the other be freed of conflict or discord, but rather that they enjoy residing in the great intimacy of a personal friendship with

God that includes security, contentment, prosperity, and tranquility of heart and mind.

> *May I back up prayers for peace*
> *by the work of being nonviolent*
> *in my thoughts, words, and deeds,*
> *as a walking holy dwelling of God.*

November 11

Continuous Communion

Life is perpetual communion. First, you are constantly in communion with your feelings, thoughts, and yourself. Further, you are endlessly in communion with others in conscious and unconscious ways. You are also in living communion with the created world in which you are immersed, even if you, like most of us, view creation simply as stage scenery for our little human dramas. Finally, you are in unrelenting communion, even if you are unaware of it, with God and the Spirit of God. Life is constant Holy Communion because the world was created to be Cosmic Communion between God and every creature and entity in the world. This communion flows from life as a seamless unity of every person, creature, plant, animal, and star. Holy Communion is more than simply another religious ritual; it is the model for and the definition of all life. So ask yourself, "Am I self-excommunicated?"

> *Mend my malfunctioning mind,*
> *addicted to isolated alienation viewed*
> *as different, separate from others,*
> *so I can live in Holy Communion.*

November 12

How to Make a Feast

To have a feast doesn't require spending all day laboring in the kitchen over a hot stove, or spending lots of money on a variety of food and drink! These are often part of the memories of feasts like Thanksgiving, Christmas, Passover, or any festival. If you desire to have a feast for any one of the approaching holidays, be encouraged by the words of the nineteenth-century German philosopher Friedrich Nietzsche, "The trick is not to arrange a festival, but to find people who can enjoy it." He gives a wonderful recipe for a feast: a few people who love one another and enjoy each other's company (the guest list can be as small as two or three), along with some food and drink. To that recipe add the most important ingredient, a touch of magic. Don't worry if you don't know the secret words to conjure up magic. You already possess magic! It sleeps in everyone as love and simply needs to be gently awakened. You need only a pinch of the magic of love to enchantingly transform the ordinary and common into the magnificent.

> *Stir up my childhood wish to be magician,*
> *not to pull white rabbits out of a black hat,*
> *but to be a wizard who by love magically pulls*
> *a delicious feast out of a black stew pot.*

November 13

Hollow Congratulations

Gratitude is at the heart of all prayers. The medieval mystic Meister Eckhart recognized this truth when he said, "If the only prayer I ever say is, 'thank you,' that would be enough." Gratitude comes naturally when good things happen to us. It isn't natural to be grateful and rejoice in the successes and achievements of others—that's supernatural! To congratulate others on their good fortune is simply good manners, yet these expressions, while polite, often easily lack authentic joy. Congratulations and joyfulness are interlinked since "congratulations" comes from the Latin for "to come together in joyfulness or gratitude." This also implies going to communion. In our highly competitive American culture, the aggressive drive to win is reinforced by school, sports, and cut-throat business practices. Rejoicing over the achievements of another is difficult because we are sick, we are competitively infected. The best antidote for the poison of envy is honest congratulations. To be honest is easy if you wisely know that we all are interconnected. The wise rejoice in another's success as if it were their own, since in reality it is.

> *Cure me of my icy ego-blindness*
> *making me separate from others.*
> *In a Holy Communion of applause*
> *I see that in other's gifts I'm enriched.*

November 14

The Forgotten Companion

The eighteenth century German Protestant mystic, Gerhard Tersteegen, wrote, "God is essentially present with us in a manner that is incomprehensive to us. He fills heaven and earth; in him we live, move and have our being. He is also near our most secret thoughts, inclinations, desires and in-tentions." While today Tersteegen's reference to God as "he" seems awkwardly masculine to us, it does personalize the companionship of God's presence in our personal dream factory and our secret desire laboratory. Tersteegen's reflection on God's complete involvement even in our most secret thoughts opens the door for some interesting reflections. The next time you are thinking some thought so secret that you would never reveal it to anyone, pause and ask yourself, "What does my Easily Forgotten Companion think of that thought?" Is God a Peeping Tom who violates our most private inner world by knowing our most secret unknown inclinations? Or is this Divine Intimacy of intimacies lying next to us in the darkest recesses of our mind rather a sign that God is truly our Beloved of Beloveds?

> *Anchor my hope in your love of me*
> *that treasures me, even the naked me,*
> *with my secret faults and dark desires,*
> *along with all my loving, graced deeds.*

November 15

Household Ecstasy

The earnest student came to the teacher asking about mystical experiences: "Are they only for the spiritual elite? What must I do so that I can know ecstasy?" "Your answer is right here on the front page of the newspaper," the teacher said as he folded the newspaper inside out. "It's a news article about Dr. Jean Claude Kaufmann, a sociologist at the Sorbonne University in Paris. He reports that more than half of the one thousand women he surveyed said they found housework pleasurable. Nearly all who worked in their homes said that their housework heightened their emotions in some way. One woman in his survey said that she ironed immediately after breakfast to experience 'explosions of joy.' Another became 'inflamed with passion' by touching the 'meanest dishcloth.' Now you know," continued the teacher, "why Jesus, like a slave, washed his disciples' feet at the Last Supper and said to them, 'That my joy may be yours and your joy may be complete.'"

> *Open my soul to dishcloth ecstasy,*
> *so my daily chores will be exotically*
> *delightful since they'll be rendezvous*
> *trysts with you, my secret beloved.*

November 16

Piggybacking Doubts

Once we become adults, our childhood certitude is gone forever. Doubts about God, the existence of angels, the unquestioned holiness of saints, or the truth of the dogmas of religion inevitably arise. But adult belief isn't about certitude. Rather it is about living with impenetrable mysteries and the itchiness of doubt. To believe as an adult is to be confronted with ambiguity and to allow your childhood beliefs to wrestle with adult questions and be haunted by misgivings. To the extent that we have been conditioned to equate religious doubts with a deadly disease, it isn't easy to live with the anxieties caused by the loss of childhood certitude. If you have doubts riding piggyback on your faith, don't be anxious. Doubt doesn't imply a failure of love, but rather the opposite. To question and doubt implies a loving trust in the unconditional love of God. Remember, the first and greatest commandment isn't "Thou shall believe in me!" The first and greatest is "Thou shall love me." Jesus extolled the power of faith (perhaps a better term would be trust!). To trust God is a greater expression of love than the certitude of childhood faith.

> *I believe in many things.*
> *Creed beliefs are valuable,*
> *yet more precious and critical,*
> *is my faith that you love me.*

November 17

God Honking

Poets and spiritual authors frequently write about how they hear God speaking in the grandeur of a great forest, in a cascading river, or in the golden splendor of a sunset at sea. Yet the majority of us live in noisy urban areas. As someone said, we spend our days living and working in boxes (houses and offices) looking at boxes (computers and television sets). So God is mute, or so it seems, to those living in the noisy racket of traffic and the hubbub of city life. But perhaps not! The insightful Trappist monk and author, Thomas Merton, wrote, "It is God's love that speaks to me in the birds and the streams but also behind the clamor of the city." These words of Merton are superbly encouraging for us city dwellers. They tell us that it isn't necessary to retreat deep into a forest to hear God speak to us. God can be heard speaking in the accelerating roar of a diesel bus, the honking horn of a car, or the ear-shattering howl of a motorcycle if our ears are wax-free. Earwax causes hearing loss. If God is silent in the clamor of the city, check to see if your ears are free of wax—church candle wax. If you restrict God's voice only to candle-lighted worship services, you won't hear your Beloved's voice in rush hour traffic.

When you speak in church language,
I delight, easily hearing your voice.
Help me to be bilingual; to hear you
in the holy hullabaloo of urban life.

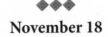

November 18

The Earthquake

Not surprisingly, the common person is shrewd enough to keep God at a safe distance by limiting close encounters to only once a week for an hour or so in church. You don't have to be a genius to know that getting any closer than that to the Divine Mystery is extremely dangerous to your lifestyle. We know from the lives of the saints what happens to those who get too chummy with God. Instinctively, in our gut, we know the wisdom of the old Jewish saying, "God is not a kindly old man with a long white beard; God is an earthquake!" When measuring close encounters with God on the Richter scale, the needle skyrockets way off the chart as the Holy Earthquake shatters lives and expectations. So the next time you play around with the idea of becoming a saint, think about it for a couple of months before putting your name on the dotted line.

I'm embarrassed to say, I don't desire
that you, God, come very close to me.
I prefer middle-class suburban holiness
to Mount Sinai or stigmata encounters.

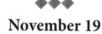

November 19

Patron Saint of Feasting

Christian saints depicted in statues as thin and gaunt made excellent patrons for fasting, but we need a patron saint of feasting. One possible patron saint for the feasting of the coming holidays would be the Zen monk Pu-Tai. This tenth-century wandering Zen monk is now well known. He is the laughing Buddha with a bulging belly found in the lobbies of Chinese restaurants. Pu-Tai was a fat, Zen Francis of Assisi who chose not to live in the comfortable security of any monastery, but to become a penniless wandering holy man. Children were delighted when they saw this jolly, roly-poly man come merrily dancing into their village. The main spiritual practice of Pu-Tai was playing games with the village children, a practice he did so naturally it appeared that he had come full circle back to his childhood. So let us pray: Saint Pu-Tai inspire us as we celebrate the holidays to enter again into the freedom of children. Liberate us from being obsessed with what our bodies look like, so as to be more concerned about the fatness of the joy and love in our hearts.

> *Let me fast from sophistication,*
> *the lust to be suave and educated.*
> *So freed from an artificial facade,*
> *I can be playful, simple, and holy.*

November 20

The Thanksgiving Problem

Being hungry was an almost daily experience for our ancestors, not only in primitive times but well into the beginning of the twentieth century. Crop failures and famines were common, most types of food couldn't be preserved since refrigeration was unknown, and there was little national and international transportation of fresh foods and vegetables. While the nobility and the wealthy enjoyed lavish meals on a regular basis, the majority of people feasted only at Christmas and other holy days. So they became known as "feast days." The majority of Americans today eat as only kings and queens once did. This presents the problem: how do we truly enjoy feasting on Thanksgiving? Feasting requires more than an abundance of food. Authentic feasting requires companionship with those we love in our family, friends, and neighbors. The main course at every real feast is the loving affection, laughter, and telling of stories with those we share the meal. At any feast, the food, whether meager or magnificent, is only secondary.

Tutor me in this paradox of life:
the rich starve while the poor feast
on love and friendship that makes
them richer than kings or queens of old.

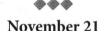

November 21

A New Name for the Faithful

Religious people are typically called "believers," a defining word implying that faith is primarily expressed by believing in certain doctrines or dogmas. Believers place great importance on knowing the Bible, memorizing sections of it, correctly reciting all of the Ten Commandments, and knowing by heart their church's catechism. While these can be religiously beneficial, would our world look any different if those of all faiths were called "doers?" One doesn't need to believe a single doctrine to be a "doer" of charity to the downtrodden or a "doer" of volunteer work in a soup kitchen. One doesn't have to be a believer, even in God, to be a doer of nonviolence by publicly taking a stand against war and this country's scandalous billions of dollars spent on military weapons. How different would be our homes and our world if we were faithful to authentically being doers of all the teachings of Jesus of Nazareth, instead of only being a believer in certain doctrines about him?

> *Stir me to use my dogmatic beliefs*
> *as Kingdom tools to remove war*
> *from this conflict-wounded world,*
> *and renovate, remodel my church.*

November 22

A Kitchen Rule for All of Life

A good saying to post on your refrigerator door is the African Swahili proverb, "A bad craftsman quarrels with his tools." Whenever a cooking mistake is made, the search for a convenient scapegoat then begins. The usual first choice is whatever tool was used: the oven didn't heat correctly, the recipe was wrong, the yeast was too old, and on and on. Good chefs know many culinary mistakes were creatively turned upside down to become some new dish. Kitchen legends abound of cooks working with a time deadline transforming a blunder into a new taste delight. A kitchen rule useable in all of life is: Before beginning any task, wash not only your hands but also your heart! Scrub your heart clean of memories of childhood mistakes that made you feel guilty or ashamed. Your heart cleansed of embarrassing memories, a mistake today won't then be the cause of shame but of creative reinvention.

> *Wipe away my past mistakes*
> *that tattooed me with shame,*
> *so to make my next mistake*
> *a creation of something new.*

November 23

Good-bye

In England, Charles Davies, at the age of sixty-seven, had just concluded a solo of "Good-bye" at the annual dinner of the Cotswold Male Voice Choir with the words, "I wish you all a last good-bye." He bowed, and as the audience applauded, he immediately collapsed and died. In northern latitudes, these last days of November are stark and gray. In late autumn, trees slumber, having surrendered up their leaves. This is the season for letting go and taking leave. Nature, while only sleeping, appears to be dead, and scribbled upon each of these days in invisible ink is that ugliest of graffiti—Death. Here's a practice for those who are awake to the presence of death in the mystery of life: Before retiring at night, say, "good-bye" instead of, "good night." Whether spoken to your children, spouse, or a companion, "good-bye" has the awesome power to remind us how tenuous is the tissue-paper-thin gift of life. A conscious, love-filled "good-bye" spoken at bedtime or at the door when a loved one departs is both a blessing in secular disguise and a sign that you are indeed awake.

> *I'm asleep, even when not in bed.*
> *Awaken me from my zombie state*
> *to the constant nearness of death,*
> *so to live fully alive and grateful.*

November 24

Listening to and Challenging God

In the days when everyone read aloud rather than silently, reading was sometimes called "listening to the voices of the pages." This old definition of reading is wonderful because it reminds us that in every book the author is actually speaking directly to us, even if we hear his voice with our eyes and not our ears. This "listening to the voices of the pages" when reading scripture was especially important for early spiritual masters who saw it as an activity of the whole person—body, mind, soul, and imagination. Today, when reading any sacred text, strive to hear the voice of God speaking personally to you. Listen to the voices of the pages of scripture as in any conversation by entering into a dialogue with the author. The author may be divine, but don't listen to the words like a sermon from on high. Rather engage them as in a lively dialogue as did old Abraham who haggled with an avenging God over destroying Sodom.

> *May Saint Abraham inspire me to haggle with*
>   *you God*
> *when something in the Bible is not applicable*
>   *today,*
> *so that in a prayer debate we can find*
> *what is and what is not your will.*

November 25

Holy Consumerism

Karen Armstrong, the author of several excellent books on religion, makes an intriguing observation when she says that for many people religion has become just another consumer item or service. How many people use their religion to undergo a transformation, and how many expect attending church or synagogue will provide them with a little moral uplift? Understandably, religion couldn't escape from being swept up into the magnetic whirlpool of consumerism that so dominates our culture. Envision an intersection with a Wal-Mart store on one corner, a Taco Bell on another, a Home Depot on the third, and on the fourth your parish church. Each of the four places provides some service and is eager to attract customers. While to refer to worshippers as customers is disturbing, isn't that how many approach the "service" they attend? If the service at the Taco Bell isn't good, customers go elsewhere, which is usually what happens with religious customers too.

> *May I never come to pray*
> *like a dissatisfied customer*
> *but rather as your beloved, grateful and accepting*
> *of whatever happens in our holy rendezvous.*

November 26

Boot Camp for Prayer

Boot camp is notorious for its demanding, rigorous exercises that force some to drop out before finishing. Prayer requires the same rigorous and disciplined formation to conquer the prehistoric trait to physically defend oneself, especially one's ego. When one's pride is injured, the ego strikes back even if only with the silent aggression of sulking. Bookstores offer books on how to practice meditation, yoga, and prayer, and over the section holding these books should be a large sign in bold black letters, "These Books Are Not for Those Who Haven't Gone to Boot Camp." In some ancient spiritual traditions, if you desired to learn prayer, yoga, or how to meditate, you were first required to undergo difficult, emotionally painful exercises in order to become completely nonviolent. It was an inclusive nonviolence; you were forbidden to kill or injure another, even to swat a mosquito, say an angry word, or make an impatient gesture of disgust. Only when you had satisfied your drill sergeant guru that nonviolence had become second nature to you were you allowed to begin to learn spiritual exercises like meditation and prayer. If your prayer fails to transform you and your life, consider attending boot camp.

Help me make my home a boot camp
where I can rigorously drill myself
in nonviolent words, deeds, and thoughts
so my prayers can be rich and beautiful.

November 27

Be Careful, Not Careless

Thanksgiving, like the frenzied mad dash of the Oklahoma Land Rush, ushers in the holiday shopping season. Contagious is the hectic velocity of the marketplace that so infects the home and the workplace. A brown cardboard box is marked "Handle with Care" when there is a set of fine china or a delicate computer inside. Perhaps we all should wear signs saying "Handle with Care!" Unseen within us, beneath the surface, we are all fragile in some way—ill health, a hurting relationship, or some financial worry. We all need extra gentleness. A cardinal rule in life is to treat others with loving care, striving to avoid any behavior or words that could jar or offend them. And if we comprehended fully the implications of the Sacred Mystery that resides within others, we would see with spiritual eyesight these words are written on their foreheads in invisible letters: "Handle with Reverence."

> *Like a stockroom worker,*
> *caution me to always avoid*
> *handling others carelessly,*
> *lest I do damage to you.*

November 28

Unerring

Many believe that the Bible is God's unerring word. But practicing what the Bible teaches can present serious problems. In Leviticus 23:22, God says, "When you reap the harvest of your land *(read: cash your paycheck)* you shall not be so thorough that you reap the field to its very edge *(read: spend it all on yourself)* nor shall you glean the stray ears of grain *(read: and spend any leftover money).* These things you must leave for the poor and the alien." To be compassionate to aliens strikes a raw nerve today because so much prejudice is felt toward immigrants, documented or not. God, it seems, has a special love of aliens. If you trust the Bible, that is the infallible word of God. In Leviticus 19:34, God says, "You shall treat the alien who resides with you no differently than the natives born among you; have the same love for them as for yourself; for you were once aliens. . . ." Those last five words thunder at us Americans—each and every one of us is descended from immigrant aliens, many of whom suffered vile prejudice. So convert your prejudice about alien immigrants to love, or thumb your nose at God.

When the Bible makes life difficult,
can I rip out what I find distasteful?
Why do you ask impossible things?
Why must I love others, as do you?

November 29

Heaven and Hell

"Once upon a time," began the dragon, "a great samurai warrior with two great swords hanging from his belt approached a monk and said, 'Tell me, holy monk, about heaven and hell.' The orange-robed monk looked up at the warrior from where he sat and replied in a quiet voice, 'I cannot tell you about heaven and hell because you are much too stupid.' The samurai warrior was filled with rage. He clenched his fists and gave a fierce shout as he reached for one of his swords. 'Besides that, you are very ugly,' added the monk. The samurai's eyes flamed and his heart was incensed as he drew his sword. 'That,' said the small monk, 'is hell!' Struck by the power of his teaching, the warrior dropped his sword, bowed his head and sank to his knees. 'And that,' said the monk, 'is heaven.' You see," continued the dragon, "the words of the monk touched old wounds, perhaps wounds that were made when the warrior was a child and was called stupid, dumb, or ugly. All of us have wounds—old ones and new ones—and whenever the monster appears, when hell breaks loose, we know that our old wounds are talking to and guiding us."

> *Why question if hell really exists*
> *when hot in anger I've been there?*
> *So heal my old sore, angry wounds*
> *so they won't send me to jail in hell.*

November 30

Handicapped Only

On the gates of heaven, besides the sign reading "Welcome, one and all," there is another sign, "Handicapped and Disabled Entrance." Saint Therese of Lisieux said, "Think of yourself as a little child just learning to stand on her feet." Learning how to stand up is a vulnerable, unstable stage in life that few if any would actually desire to revisit. Therese's spiritual instruction could be rephrased, "Think of yourself as disadvantaged, disabled, and crippled when it comes to participating in life's rat race." In our competitive society that prizes being self-sufficient and independent, dependent small children are truly disabled persons. Therese of Lisieux, the cloistered nineteenth-century saint, was only rephrasing Jesus' words on the necessity of becoming again like children. This does not mean being cute, but rather becoming as dependent as a small child learning to walk while holding a parent's hand. This image gives us a good, livable definition of faith: walking hand in hand with someone you love and trust.

> *Let me reach out my hand to yours,*
> *not just when I'm troubled or fearful,*
> *but every day, so I can learn to walk*
> *with your hand holding mine.*

Month of
December

December 1

What to Do With Wonder?

"The root of religion," said Rabbi Abraham Heschel, "is what to do with awe, wonder and amazement." Wonderful insight since from the root of wonder and awe grows religion, even if you are not religious. From that same root of wonder grows the flowering plant of prayer and adoration of God. Without wonder and amazement God becomes something we imagine we can manipulate by tricks of piety, fasting, lighting candles, or sprinkling of holy water. To approach the Divine Mystery without a sense of wonder easily turns God into a philosophical concept or definable theological principle. Yet it is impossible to define the Wondrous One other than as a baffling mystery. December is a sacred time of wonder, of the holy lights of Hanukkah and Christmas glowing in the pitch-black darkness of winter: "'Tis the season to be jolly," or more accurately, "'Tis the season to be wonder-filled," in the eyes as well as the heart.

> *As I enjoy luminous strings of lights*
> *and flame-topped flickering candles,*
> *remind me they are not just decorations,*
> *they are sacraments of wonder of you.*

December 2

The Boogeyman in the Dark

The incalculable colored lights of this yuletide season aren't turned on until night since during the day they would be invisible. Darkness is essential to this holy season, even if our ancient ancestors feared the darkness, or rather what lurked in it. At this time of year as the hours of darkness grow longer and longer, our ancestors gathered to celebrate around great bonfires and filled their shelters with lamps and candles to ward off the feared evil lurking in the darkness. Who of us cannot understand this primitive fear of darkness, since childhood fears of the dark linger faintly even into our adulthood. This fear of night led to viewing darkness as the kingdom of evil and light as the kingdom of the good. However, Gregory of Nyssa, a saintly monk of the early centuries, gave us a rare insight saying, "The vision of God for Moses began with light. Afterward God spoke to him in a cloud. But when Moses rose higher and became more perfect, he saw God in the darkness."

> *Darkness disarms us, steals our vision,*
> *disables us, so we find it frightening.*
> *If God is darkness, while terrifying,*
> *fear not, for in the dark hides a lover.*

December 3

Welcome Wonders

December could be called the month of hospitality, as it is a festive time to entertain friends and family amidst the gleaming lights of Christmas candles and Hanukah lamps. The seventeenth-century poet Richard Crashaw lyrically gave us a hospitality assignment, "Welcome, all wonders in one sight! Eternity shut in a span. More than magical are the lights of this season; they and the other wonders are eternity encapsulated in a period or span of celebration." Indeed, "more than magical" as Crashaw said of all the flickering lights. Their magic is unquestionable. The sight of barren trees decorated in strings of lights is almost like a fairyland, as if the stars had descended to decorate their leafless branches. These luminous wonders, in which eternity is encapsulated, stir the soul! More than pretty, even the beautiful Christmas lights in your home and city summarize eternity. What a stunningly wondrous image for heaven is Christmas: the blizzard of lights, the love-gifting, and the festive gatherings of family and friends.

> *Indescribable eternity is hidden*
> *"in a nutshell," in plain sight.*
> *"Keep Jesus in Christmas." Yes, but more*
> *importantly, see and keep heaven in it.*

December 4

Playing as You Pray

A story is told of the distinguished rabbi Levi Yitzhak of Berdichev. Standing in the synagogue on the eve of the most solemn feast of Yom Kippur, he prayed, "O Holy One, in a few hours the Jews are coming to ask you for forgiveness for all their sins and many wrongdoings. But I want to give you, the All Holy One, a chance to be forgiven for all the terrible wrongs that you have done." Rabbi Yitzhak then proceeded to rattle off a long litany of divine visitations of evil: the deaths of innocent children, crippling illnesses, plagues, and vicious anti-Semitic attacks on Jewish homes and shops. On and on he went until he reached the end of his long list of God's wrong-doings. Then he concluded, "Are you not God, responsible for all that happens?" Rabbi Yitzhak then paused, looked heavenward and said, "So God, let's make deal, we'll let you off the hook if you will let us off." The daring familiarity of this prayer reveals Rabbi Yitzhak's deeply personal, intimate friendship with God. So boldly and blessedly energize your prayers with a little kosher humor of profound joy.

When next it's time to pray,
remind me that you enjoy humor
and being challenged by me,
we two being bosom buddies.

December 5

Outlaw Christmas!

From the way our cities and homes are decorated today you would never guess that displays of Christmas were once outlawed, denounced as signs of a pagan festival. When the Puritans came to power in England, they immediately outlawed "Papist Christmas." They made any type of religious service on December 25 illegal under pain of punishment, decreeing it be a day of fast and penance. This prohibition against decorations or outward signs of Christmas continued in America in the New England states. Until 1856, December 25 was a common workday in Boston, and anyone failing to come to work was fired. Public schools were in session on Christmas day as late as 1870, and any students who failed to attend were gravely punished. The arrival of Irish, German, and Italian immigrants with their great enthusiasm for celebrating Christmas began to change this intolerance, but slowly. Ministers sternly warned their congregations against this "new" and morally dangerous custom of celebrating Christmas. Finally, those "dangerous" immigrant customs defeated the anti-Christmas religious prejudice. This tidbit of history leads us to ask: what wondrous new gifts will today's maligned immigrants bring to our American society?

> *Interrogate me to see if I'm a closet bigot,*
> *prejudiced about the cost of Christmas,*
> *disguising my dislike of buying gifts or*
> *sending cards, and so glad when it's over.*

December 6

Midwife Imagination

Young children of today can suffer from a dire poverty of imagination! Children of affluent families have an overabundance of toys, the majority of which require little, if any, use of their imagination. Electronic games and fairy tale videos are so realistic that they require no imagination, thus stunting this natural ability even into adulthood. A grade-school teacher who has poor Mexican immigrant children in her class told me that they have active imaginations. If you have only a wooden stick, imagination is required to pretend it's a toy gun. Childhood pretending is an excellent way to prepare

for Christmas, a time to be reborn, not in the fundamentalist sense, but to be rebirthed by the Spirit. Stir awake your
slumbering imagination to create a vivid image of a kinder,
gentler, and less nit-picky you, and pretend to be that person.
There are only nineteen days left till Christmas. Ask the Spirit
of generosity, kindnesses, compassion, and prayer to be your
midwife, and to assist you in giving birth to the best gift you
can give your family and the world—a new you!

> *Heal my handicapped imagination,*
> *so I can dream a new picture of me,*
> *then use it as a blueprint to pretend*
> *that I am today, already that person.*

December 7

The Trapdoor

It is not uncommon to come face to face with the mystery of
not knowing what to do and worrying about making the right
decision. Instead of seeing such encounters as times of uncertainty, see them as occasions to wonder. Instead of worrying,
wonder about which is the best decision. You may be surprised
by how spontaneously you find yourself praying since wonder
is a doorway to prayer, or better yet, a trapdoor. Uncertainties

in life are not the only occasions to trip the trapdoor of wonder. Creation abounds with such trapdoors, from a majestic snowcapped mountain range, to the lifting ability of a tiny ant, to the acrobatic elm tree sprout growing up through a crack in a concrete slab. These trapdoors aren't magical. Each of us holds the power to trip them if we are wonder-seekers. Upon awakening after a night's silent snowfall, those who enjoy surprises like hidden trapdoors look out their bedroom window and say, "Look at the white, blanketed, sparkling crystal wonderland," and zap goes the trapdoor to prayer. While those who don't like to be surprised look out their window and say, "Looks like it snowed last night."

> *May I practice tripping the trapdoor*
> *by looking in drab, dirty, gutter water*
> *to see reflected a glorious setting sun,*
> *and drop instantly into a prayer of awe.*

December 8

A Bolt Out of the Blue

A recent news item told of a door-to-door salesman selling bibles who had been struck by a bolt of lightning—on a cloudless blue-sky day! Impossible! Not really—these highly extraordinary lightning bolts striking down from a cloudless blue sky were first reported in the 1800s, and are actually believed to be much older than that. Folk expressions such as, "Like a bolt out of the blue," come not from fantasy but fact. So be prepared if God should visit you "like a bolt out of the blue!" The Kabbalah of Judaism warns that we must live prepared to be surprised by the All Holy One. Good advice! The Bible abounds in bombshell visits by God, appearing as an angel, a burning bush, a cloud, or a blinding-like-the-sun light. Bolts out of the blue, then and now, are considered impossible, especially when they are invisible. So a lightning-like strike of inspiration was more acceptable if it was said to come from an angel, a burning bush, or a puffy white cloud. Don't expect an angel to visit you or to come upon a burning bush, but tattoo on your heart the Kabbalah's warning, "Be prepared to be surprised."

> *Come, inspire me, even if I do my best*
> *to avoid any direct contact with you*
> *who resemble ten thousand lightning bolts.*
> *So please come, gently, and inspire me.*

December 9

Failure or Gift?

The Master continuously admonished his disciples not to worry about what they would wear, eat, or any of their daily needs. To worry then is a failure of discipleship. Yet not to worry about your health, financial security in your retirement years, or losing your job seems unnatural! Parents worry about their children even after they have become adults. They worry about their grandchildren, so regardless of the pleas of Jesus not to worry, we do! So when next you find yourself worrying about something, rejoice since it is a surprise double gift. Worrying first of all is a type of Holy Communion, of being united with God! When you are anxious over your own or another's needs, your loving God is as much, if not more, concerned. The second gift is that when you are worrying about others, you are not absorbed with your own needs, and so are liberated from constantly being focused on yourself. Indeed, Jesus repeatedly told us not to worry about our needs, but to trust God! Worrying about another's welfare, however, is a type of loving concern, and we were told to love others as we love ourselves. For those who have problems with praying, worrying can be their prayer.

Encourage me to worry with faith
in your great loving concern for me.
In that Holy Communion of trust,
I can draw the strength not to worry.

December 10

Barefoot Reverence

Hindus and Muslims show reverence for the Sacred by removing their shoes before entering their temples and mosques.
Moses, in the presence of the Holy One in the fiery burning
bush, was told to remove his sandals. If God is truly abiding
in all things and places, perhaps we should all go barefoot perpetually. That holy ritual isn't such a good idea in the winter
unless you wish your feet to suffer the martyrdom of frost-
bite. A practical sign of reverence in winter (or summer) and
that doesn't draw attention or ridicule, is to make a ritual bow
of reverence. This slight bowing of the head is an ageless acknowledgment of being in the presence of someone superior
or something holy. Our humdrum world is crowded with
burning bush tabernacles of the Invisible Divine Presence—
meals of friendship and love, expressions of affection, acts of
kindness, or someone's sacrifice of time and energy to meet
a need of yours. You can bow before the wonder of your

lightning-fast computer, the miracle of softly falling snow, the marvel of a small child's smile of recognition, or the holiness of hospitality invested in a hot cup of coffee.

> *May I reverently nod my way to heaven*
> *when it appears right at my fingertips*
> *in manifested love and in simple kindnesses:*
> *earth being overpopulated with heaven.*

December 11

CPR on Wonder

In 1840 Thomas Carlyle announced the amazing good news, "The age of miracles is forever here." Notice, he didn't say here *now* in this inventive age of the steam engine locomotive, the photographic camera, and other new miraculous wonders, but "*forever* here!" While miracles may continue to be forever, miracle-wonder has a short life span. Like clothing exposed too long in the strong light of the sun, wonder fades. Amazement's diminishment begins with familiarity and shrinks further by repetition, until astonishment loses its voice, and there is only silence. When the wonderful loses its voice, it no longer thunders. *Astonish*, coming from the Latin, *extonare*, means "to thunder." A good way to restore wonder's voice is to select some common mute marvel like the electric light and do without it. Fumble and stumble around in the dark, then when properly prepared, flick the switch. Hear the soundless thunder of awe when pitch-black midnight suddenly becomes bright as high noon. Wow! While not as earthshaking as a thunderclap, it is an earthbound rumble of wonder. Use it frequently to revive the sense of astonishment.

> *Expand my soul to see that "Wow!"*
> *is a prayer of adoration and wonder.*
> *May I restore my brain-dead wonder*
> *by holy wowing my way through life.*

December 12

Beware of Being Ambushed

This reflection's title sounds like military advice not to be caught off guard by a surprise attack from an enemy hiding in a concealed position. The majority of us are comfortable with our lives as they are; we don't want to be ambushed by God. While finding the stories of Mary of Nazareth, Israel's prophets, and the saints inspiring, we personally don't desire a visit from the Divine Surpriser! Ambush comes to us from the old French, *embuschier*, "to hide in the bushes." So be on your guard in these days full of holiday evergreens! Those evergreen branches that are saturated with the memories of childhood and Yuletide carols can easily hide a most undesired visitor— God! Christmas awakens in us a spiritual hunger for some personal religious experience of God. While we prefer a non-threatening church with its expected experience of God, we should not be afraid of what surprises may be hiding in the bushes or evergreens.

> *Half of the pleasure, it is said,*
> *of any gift is surprise; may we*
> *then be unexpectedly surprised by*
> *the best of all gifts, you.*

December 13

The Holy Itch

"Teacher," pleaded the student, "help me satisfy the great hunger I feel for God." The teacher asked, "Is what you feel truly a hunger, or only a spiritual itch?" The student replied, "I'm confused, Teacher. You say a spiritual itch? What did you mean?" "A hunger is a deep longing that is not easy to satisfy. An itch, on the other hand, is irritating and wants to be scratched. But it doesn't last long. Moreover, there are many who are eager to make money by selling you their special brand of itching oil. And if your irritation can be met by their wares, you aren't dealing with a real hunger." Jesus called those who are hungry for holiness blessed. Indeed, blessed are they, for their hunger shall grow more intense the more they try to feed it. And an old desert manuscript records Jesus as saying, "Give us this day our daily bread, and lead us not to nibble on fortune cookies."

> *Catalogs and stores make me itch*
> *for many things I don't really need.*
> *Make me starving, ravenously hungry,*
> *for that which only you can satisfy.*

December 14

Steep Me in Christmas

As the sounds and sights of Christmas fill our cities, we can be tempted to divest ourselves of material interests and concentrate on the spiritual so as to better celebrate the approaching feast of the Nativity. This is understandable, but unhealthy. What is truly needed is to follow the advice of Pierre Teilhard de Chardin who said, "Steep yourself in the sea of matter." This Jesuit priest and paleontologist who died in 1955 comprehended the implications of the incarnation as God becoming flesh not only in Jesus, but also in the world. If one believes in the incarnation, the enfleshing of God, then like a teabag we must steep ourselves in the material world; in things, people, events, and everything in that sea of matter that is this life. We usually think of material things as particular items, but Teilhard's perspective is different. He uses the attention-grabbing word "steep," meaning to slowly soak so as to absorb. The best way to celebrate Christmas is to steep yourself in material, creative things in order to soak up and absorb all of the earthiness that is saturated with the enfleshment of the Divine.

> *Instead of handling a pencil or any particular*
>   *thing,*
> *may I take the time to slowly steep myself*
> *in the object so to be absorbed in you, God,*
> *who are imbedded in all earthy things.*

December 15

Blind to God

"My God, I left behind the whole world to search for you. But you were the whole world, and I could not see it," said the eleventh century Islamic mystic Kwaja Abdullah Ansari. These and his other words of wisdom were collected by his followers and published after his death. Why published only after his death? The mystical insights of this Islamic holy man are the fruit of prayerful intimacy with God, and over the centuries those who express such insights have become the targets of vicious attacks by fundamentalists of every religion. God speaks to all those who come close in intimacy, regardless of their creed. Those who are not afraid to draw near to the divine fire find their age-less doctrines incinerated, yet in the ashes they find the gold of truth. So we need not be surprised that the more precious than gold words of Ansari finding God in the whole world echo yes-terday's insight of the Christian mystic Teilhard about the need to steep ourselves in the sea of the world, of matter.

> *Not by fasting or the penance of denial*
> *will I find the Divine Lover I seek,*
> *but in plunging hungrily deep in the sea*
> *of the God-in-flesh of this world.*

December 16

Do More Than Housecleaning

Maria Montessori, the famous educator, said, "The first idea the child must acquire in order to be actively disciplined is that of the difference between good and evil, and the task of the educator lies in seeing that the child doesn't confuse good with immobility and evil with activity." Often children are told to "sit still and be good," as if nonactivity were the same as goodness. Simply removing evil isn't sufficient; active performance of good is required. Traditionally, Christmas is time for housecleaning, both of your house and your soul. The Master told a parable about a householder who swept the house clean of an evil spirit. Then the homeless evil spirit wandered about but found no place to dwell, and so returned to its old home. Finding it all clean and tidy, the spirit invited seven other spirits more evil than it to come and live there with him. After cleaning your home, decorate for Christmas. Then do the same with your life: once swept clean of evil, decorate it with good and charitable deeds.

> *Be my broom to sweep my heart*
> *clean of evil thoughts and deeds,*
> *then point out to me seven new*
> *good spirits to come share my life.*

December 17

Homogenized Good and Bad

The fourteenth-century Christian mystic Julian of Norwich had an insight about the mixture of greed and kindness in this Christmas season when she said, "Our life in this world consists of a wondrous mixture of good and bad." Like Jesus' words, "The poor you will always have with you," Julian says, "good and bad you will always have among you." She could be an Advent patron since she lived a life of solitude in a small hermitage cell connected to the church of St. Edmund. To retreat into a hermitage as a solitary is the calling of only a very limited few, yet we are all called to times of solitude, regardless of how busy our lives. What better way to prepare for the approaching feast of Christmas than by spending an hour or more in silent solitude. But who has time for an hour of solitude with gifts to wrap, decorations to complete, and all the other chores of this holiday? While intent upon decorating our homes and churches for Christmas, shouldn't we also take time to decorate our inner selves with graceful silence? If you could steal out of the hustle and bustle an hour of solitude, you might be more accepting of the mixture of good and bad in the world, and in yourself.

May I accept all of who I am,
for by embracing my dark side
along with my good side, I'll be
more tolerant of the darkness in others.

December 18

The Infant in the Crib

Nativity scenes abound in these Christmas days. The crèche is a crude stable, with images of Joseph, Mary, and an infant in a manger in between them. Christians proclaim in carol and creed that this infant was the Love of God in human flesh. The entire celebration of Christmas pivots on this one belief, too wondrous to be true, that the love of God was enfleshed in a brother human. The brilliant German theologian of the twentieth century, Karl Rahner, said, "Each individual man or woman is a unique and unrepeatable term of God's creative love." Rahner's "term" means an expression that should awaken us to the greatest of all possible Christmas gifts: you and I are each unique and "unrepeatable" expressions of God. Do not underestimate the awesome implications of that. Ask yourself, if I am a human enfleshment of God's love, how should I act? To reinforce this life work each time you see a Nativity crèche, stop and use your imagination to place your face on the infant's face in the manger!

> *I shudder to think of myself as a savior,*
> *an embodiment of you, All Giving Love.*
> *So come help me save, that is, liberate,*
> *others from sadness and being unloved.*

December 19

The Absolutely Worst of All Sins

Of all the vices, sexual sins are the worst in the Christian moral code. Some of these are judged so grievous that Christians have insisted they also be civil crimes with heavy penalties. Yet among preliterate hunting and gathering cultures, like the Native Americans, children were taught that the worst of vices was stinginess. Not sex, but greed in all forms, was abhorred. Their moral code upheld the importance of gift giving and had the rule: "The gift must always be on the move." The Teacher of Galilee, whose birth we are about to celebrate, knew how lethal greed was. He taught: "Avoid greed in all forms." Like Baskin-Robbins ice cream, greed comes in many flavors: lover's greed hoards affection jealously; religious greed is stingy with its sacraments; intellectual greed is avaricious of its ideas; clock greed is tightfisted with time . . . and so on. Today examine your life for greed in any form.

> *Open handed, not tightfisted,*
> *I keep my gifts on the move.*
> *When I feel my fingers curling,*
> *come and bend them outward.*

December 20

Holidaying

"Happy Holidays" is the inclusive greetings for Hanukah, Christmas, Kwanza, and New Year's. While appearing harmless, it can be a dangerously delightful invitation. Americans are hard workers, and they are worked hard. Of all the countries in the industrialized world, Americans have the least vacation time! Workers rise up: take serious your Christmas cards that wish you "Happy Holidays!" If your boss offers you that wish, go holidaying. A holiday is a British expression for a time free of work, and so the British speak of "holidaying in Florida this year." Overworked and stressed, how do you extend the life of a one-day holiday to the length of an annual vacation without losing your job? Is there some secret way to spend the holidays holidaying, and still report each morning for work?

> *Work is Eden's curse for sin,*
> *so goes the old paradise myth.*
> *Yet humans are made for work;*
> *so from drudgery may I holiday.*

December 21

The Winter Solstice

It takes approximately 365¼ days for the planet Earth to complete its annual orbit around the sun that determines the solstices and equinoxes. That's why these events may vary by a day or so. Regardless, in these nights of the longest darkness we celebrate the ancient festival of the Winter Solstice. As the dark shadow of space leans over us, we are mindful that the darkness of greed, exploitation, and hate also lengthens its shadow over our small planet Earth. As our ancestors feared death and evil and all the dark powers of winter, we fear that the darkness of war, discrimination, and selfishness may doom our planet and us to an eternal winter. May we find hope in the lights we have kindled on these sacred nights, hope in one another and in all who form the web-work of peace and justice that spans the world. In the heart of every person on this earth burns the spark of luminous goodness; in no heart is there total darkness. May we on this winter solstice, by our lives and service, by our prayers and love, call forth from one another the light and the love that is hidden in every heart.

> *Wisdom me with sun astuteness*
> *to see that life, like the seasons, cycles.*
> *Then when all is chilly and bleak,*
> *I'll know spring will spiral 'round.*

December 22

Mazel Tov

Stars are one of the many symbols of this holiday season. Stars atop Christmas trees and over nativity sets represent the star that guided the Magi. A star is part of the familiar Jewish greeting *mazel tov* as well. In Hebrew *tov* means "good" and *mazel* means "star." To wish "good star" or "may a good star shine on you," is to wish good luck, congratulations, and even "thank God." *Mazel tov* seems to have been borrowed by the Hebrews from their neighbor Persia. The ancient religion of Persia, today's Iran, was Zoroastrianism. Its god was Ahura Mazda who created 486,000 good or lucky stars under which fortunate people were born. Ahura Mazda, an equal opportunity creator, also created the same number of unlucky stars under which unfortunate people were born. These stars were called *disasters*, from *dis-astro*, for "bad stars." The Star of Bethlehem signaling the birth of the revolutionary reformer Jesus was a bad star, a disaster, for religion lovers. While for others that star was a *mazel tov*.

> *In all seasons, to any Jew or Christian*
> *"mazel tov" is a beautiful holy wish,*
> *asking that you be blessed and fortunate*
> *to live in a cosmos of a billion good stars.*

December 23

Tell Time with Two Clocks

In our news-saturated age we are fed daily media meals of cheerless stories: war atrocities, ghastly horrors of torture, murders on urban streets. At the same time in these days, we are inundated by the old Christmas carols, calling us to rejoice and be merry regardless of the news or our personal struggles and disappointments. Being joyful was easier prior to 24/7 news on television and the Internet when the majority of people lived more contentedly in small villages or on farms and without all the conveniences and comforts of modern life. Even when the daily news spreads an ominous cloud over our global village in this merry season, go out of your way to live in joy. That is how you are supposed to live! Some twenty-five years after the death of Jesus, Paul of Tarsus said: "Rejoice always!" This disciple and itinerant preacher urged the Christians of Thessalonica to live in joy by living in Christ, even while they were living in very difficult and trying times. The joyful carols of this Yuletide season call us to return to living by two clocks: one set in today's time, and the other set in Christ time.

In spite of the news of today, may I live in joy.
In spite of health problems, may I live in joy.
In spite of Christmas stress, may I live in joy,
since it is the infallible way to live in God.

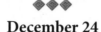

December 24

Once Again an Enchanted Time

Centuries ago it was believed that after sunset tonight and
into tomorrow, the powers of malignant spirits, ghosts, and
witches were suspended for the rest of the Christmas season.
The presence of the Christ Child, mysteriously born again
each Christmas, rendered powerless all evil spirits. Aware of
this belief, Shakespeare referred to it in the first act of his play
Hamlet, "Wherein our Savior's birth is celebrated, no spirit
dare stir abroad . . . no planets strike . . . no witch has power to
charm. So hallow'd and so gracious is the time." But household
disagreements, excessive drinking, and the tensions caused by
conflicting family schedules shatter this night's enchanted spell
that holds evil spirits captive. The witches whom Shakespeare
said had lost their charm are rejuvenated by physical fatigue
and weariness of festive preparation. Christmas, having grown
aged and unexciting by almost two months of commercial
overexposure, and Christmas carols having lost their magic by

months of hearing them, all contribute to a possible plague of evil spirits. To spin again the web of enchantment of this holy night, take some quiet time to focus on the real purpose of Christmas so as to make it truly a holy night.

> *While I've madly rushed to Christmas,*
> *help me not be too weary to enjoy it.*
> *Save my Christmas from evil spirits,*
> *who nibble it to death with details.*

December 25

Too Wondrously Incredible

That God so loved creation to become incarnated, embedded in the flesh of one of us and in all created things, is too joyously wonderful to comprehend. This significant decision of the Creator to enter into this earth by plunging into all that it means to be fully human has profound implications. Typically, religion is an escape from the world. The moment you enter a stained-glassed Gothic cathedral you profoundly experience having escaped from the nitty-gritty and grime of this world into another heavenly world. The majestic organ music and ageless rituals of worship reinforce the serene heaven-come-down-to-earth architecture. The marvel of Christmas is that

God preferred to become flesh not in a sanitized, beautiful artificially divine world or temple, but in the grime and crime of our grubby world. True Christmas should not comfort us but challenge us to find God in the roar of whirling gears and rumbling engines of work, as well as in the organ music of cathedrals. All lighted Christmas trees should illuminate every tree and bush as being aflame with the Divine Mystery.

> *The core of Christmas is too naughty*
> *to go to church, too daily to be divine.*
> *Peek behind Christmas' religious veil*
> *and be awed by its raw earthy reality.*

December 26

Christmas Eyesight

Our normal eyesight is conditioned by powerful prejudices that create endless vision distortions of ugly or beautiful, enemy or friend, good or evil. Jesus loved to say, "Let those with eyes see!" On this day after Christmas, that challenge asks, "What are we supposed to see?" The answer to that is found by asking another question, one implying a surgical eye implant, "With whose eyes are we supposed to see?" And the answer is with the eyes of Jesus. To see the world with the eyes of Jesus is to see it and everything in it as he did. The Christian belief that Jesus was God in human flesh means that God was absorbed in his body—his eyes. A surgical implant of Jesus' eyes is impossible, but what is possible is to have Christmas eyes like those of the shepherds and the Magi who were able to see the Divine Presence in a crying newborn baby in a dirty stable. The enchantment of these days is still with us, so pretend you have Magi eyes. See others as lovable and uniquely precious. Look beyond the color of their skin, their youthful or decrepit bodies, their poverty or wealth, their religion or the absence of it.

> *Give me a tardy Christmas gift of eyes,*
> *like those of poor shepherds and Magi kings,*
> *whose x-ray vision dissolved the outward*
> *and revealed the inward to them as Divine.*

December 27

The Gift of Magi Wisdom

The wise men or Magi from the East brought gifts of gold, frankincense, and myrrh. However, being wise men, I wonder if along with these gifts they also gave to the young couple in Bethlehem gifts of wisdom to share with their son. Did they gift them with the secret knowledge of how they were able to find their way to the manger and kneel before their infant son, the Divine One? Did they gift them with the source of their inscrutable insight by which they were able to accept the infant in the crude animal feed-trough as the Divine One they sought? As Magi scholars, had they discovered that source of wisdom in the scrolls of the *Dhammapada* of the teachings of Magi Buddha? This wise sage of India, while not mentioning a star, had indeed written the secret of finding the Divine One: "With gentleness overcome anger. With generosity overcome meanness. With truth overcome deceit. Speak the truth. Give whatever you can. Never be angry. These three steps will lead you into the presence of the Divine!"

> *If I seek what the Magi sought,*
> *remind me that anger and deceit*
> *eclipse the star, but generosity,*
> *truth, and peace lead me to him.*

December 28

Ah, Ah, Ah

Words are magnificent tools for handling all kinds of situations, but they unfortunately have their limits as some situations or experiences can leave us nakedly tongue-tied. To be left speechless can be as embarrassing as being left clothes-less. Be prepared to be naked before God, for Rabbi Abraham Heschel says, "To become aware of the ineffable is to part company with words." To experience God, the Infinitely Indescribable One, is to say *adios* to words since divine encounters pickpocket our prayers leaving us wordlessly openmouthed. The real issue, however, isn't words, but rather the kind of words one uses in prayer. Even speculating about changing prayer words may bring the prayer police to your door to check the dogmatic correctness of your words. Is there no option to being tongue-tied? Yes, and it may be found in T.S. Eliot's description of poetry as "a raid on the inarticulate." Instead of the usual prose prayers, untie your prayer tongue by praying poetically. The language of the heart and soul is poetry since it has the liquid magic to speak to—and of—the inexpressible, which describes perfectly being in the presence of the Divine Mystery.

> *Calm my fears of being flabbergasted,*
> *so stunned wordless by wonders am I,*
> *left openmouthed, stuttering "Ah,"*
> *the holy cousin of "Amen."*

December 29

Wobblers

As this old year quickly is ebbing away, it is possible to worry that its disasters, wars, and calamities will inflict the New Year with even greater woes. Aware of the old folk saying, "The devil you know is better than the devil you don't," some would like to simply recycle this present old year now on its last legs. The scholar of mythology Joseph Campbell offers some good advice for those longing for a return to former times. "Trying to hang on to youth, trying to hang on to what was really great twenty years ago, throws you totally off. You've got to go with it and seek the abundance that's in the new thing. If you hang on to the old thing, you will not experience the new." A good end-of-the-year vow is to pledge not to join that large crowd of wobblers thrown off-balance by trying to look like and act like they did twenty years ago. Unless you throw away your hair dyes and hairpieces, you'll never know the adventure and fun of becoming someone new. Not only people, but institutions, especially religious ones, also can be off-balanced wobblers by trying to hang on to what they were and how they acted long ago, instead of seeking the abundance found in being new.

Give me the third degree to see if I'm
thinking, praying, and acting just as I did
ten or twenty years ago, and if so, prod me
to experiment with new ways to live.

December 30

Getting Ready for New Year's

Midnight tomorrow begins a most significant day, so respect
the old superstitions about what might bring you bad luck.
Don't anticipate January by putting up a new calendar today.
Don't have any unpaid bills on New Year's Day or you'll have
the bad luck of owing money all year long. Pardon any unfor-
given personal offenses. Open all your doors at midnight on
New Year's Eve so the spirit of the old year can depart, and at
the same time get rid of any old spirits of regret or revenge. On
the first day of the new year, don't work by doing the laundry
or washing the dishes, lest misfortune befall you. Treat yourself to a leisurely holiday. Make a new year's resolution to have
more leisure in the coming year. Woe to those on New Year's
Day who aren't wearing anything new. So today go and purchase some new piece of clothing, and, if that's not possible,
wear a new attitude. For good luck, purchase some red underwear. Red is the color of good luck for the Chinese, and

wearing red underwear on New Year's Day guarantees a year of good fortune and happiness. If red underwear isn't your style, give away some of your good clothing to the poor. Then have a fortuitous and blessed new year.

> *Even if I am a bad luck agnostic,*
> *may I be free of debts by pardoning others,*
> *and make my New Year's work-free*
> *so I can enjoy a new year of good luck.*

December 31

"Happy New Year" to Me

Typically we wish "Happy New Year" to others, but extend that wish to yourself in the spirit of Sir Henry Bate Dudley. In a letter written in 1776, he said, "Wonders will never cease!" Tattoo those four reassuring words on your heart as you come to the end of this book since the quest of wonders delightfully never ends. Rejoice that you will never run out of wonders to nourish the roots of your inner life. Without a sense of wonder, a healthy religious life soon withers and turns into a pious habit, wondering being the root of a dynamic religion. Some of the wonders you have considered in the previous days of this year were evident, while others were springboards to bounce you into a lively wondering. To live with the delight of one won-der after another requires constant vigilance. Guard yourself against creeping sophistication, that "know-it-all" superior-ity that is incapable of surprise and childish awe. The mystic fruit of being surprised by the amazing and the wondrous is a happiness not found in wealth or fame. So, at the magical midnight hour make this wish, "May I have a happy New Year filled with wonders."

> *O jangle awake my snoozing eyes,*
> *sleepy from seeing the same old thing*
> *when, like motion pictures, wonders*
> *continually flash by on life's screen.*

Author's Postscript

Completing a book for publication gives one the sense of a great liberation, a fact that may come as a surprise to many readers. Regarding this irony I found an explanation in these words of Winston Churchill, "Writing a book is an adventure: it begins as an amusement, then it becomes a mistress, then a master, and finally a tyrant."

In a few descriptive lines, Churchill captured the demanding art of writing any book. It begins with a love affair with an idea that could be called a mistress of creativity, but when that imaginative work is completed, then there appears the oppressive taskmaster who demands what you've written be refined over and over again. Since no author is faultless in communication, even after having done three or more edits of the manuscript, the taskmaster requires that you edit it just one more time. Just when you're tired and ready to throw in the towel, a tyrannical dictator appears who commands, "You must finish this book since you have already spent so much time on it. You can't just put it aside to be completed later. Now—this minute—finish it!"

This book of daily reflections is now completed. I'm liberated and also bemused, but not in the sense of being meditative. Rather I feel amused—inspired by my muse—to depart on to another adventure of amusement and find there a new imaginative mistress. Before plunging into that creative crucible, I wish to thank the person responsible for this book:

With Gratitude
I dedicate this book to
Thomas Grady
my publisher at Ave Maria Press
who conceived the idea of this book,
and when I stubbornly resisted
encouraged me to write.

⬦⬦⬦⬦⬦⬦⬦⬦⬦ Acknowledgments

The meditations indicated below are reprinted in this book, often with some adaptation, from the following works by Edward Hays. These and all Forest of Peace books by Edward Hays are available from Ave Maria Press, P.O. Box 428, Notre Dame, IN 46556, www.avemariapress.com. In all cases the reflective prayers were created to be included in this book.

Chasing Joy: June 26, July 11, December 4.

The Great Escape Manual: February 16, February 19, March 8, April 12, May 17, September 28.

Holy Fools & Mad Hatters: January 25.

In Pursuit of the Great White Rabbit: August 17.

The Ladder: January 17, April 28, May 5, June 4, November 15, December 13.

The Old Hermit's Almanac: January 30, May 27, August 9, October 5.

A Pilgrim's Almanac: September 12, October 12.

Pray All Ways: March 27.

Prayer Notes to a Friend: February 29, April 23, June 18, July 18, September 6, November 9.

Prayers for a Planetary Pilgrim: March 21, August 25, September 21, October 1, October 18, December 21.

St. George and the Dragon and the Quest for the Holy Grail: February 4.

St. George and the Quest for the Holy Grail: November 29.